Small Feet on the Run

Small Feet on the Run

Childhood during World War II Remembered and
Arguments against War

Sieglinde Martin

Foreword by Peggy Faw Gish
With a Contribution by Anita Schorn

RESOURCE *Publications* · Eugene, Oregon

SMALL FEET ON THE RUN
Childhood during World War II Remembered and Arguments against War

Resource Publications
An Imprint of Wipf and Stock Publishers
199 W. 8th Ave., Suite 3
Eugene, OR 97401

www.wipfandstock.com

PAPERBACK ISBN: 978-1-4982-9613-7
HARDCOVER ISBN: 978-1-4982-9615-1
EBOOK ISBN: 978-1-4982-9614-4

Manufactured in the U.S.A.   OCTOBER 3, 2016

To Bela, Max, Leif, and Annika

Table of Contents

Illustrations

Map

Germany and its Neighboring Countries on the Eve of World War II

Figures

Foreword

"Never again!" so many of us have said concerning the "holocaust" against Jews during the Second World War. It was truly a horrendous and tragic chapter in history. Jews, as well as other minorities and dissidents in European society were systematically killed, tortured, and treated as less than human. It is right that these atrocities have been well documented and people around the world continue to mourn and pass down these stories to the next generations.

Other stories of that war are not as well known—those of soldiers on either side of the battles, of the general populations living where the fighting and bombings took place. What hardships and horrors did they experience? What did they have to do to survive? And what about the children caught in war's jaws? What would they say to us today about war?

In *Small Feet on the Run*, Sieglinde Martin focuses on the children in this war. The stories she shares capture their inner voice, their dreams and aspirations, as well as their feelings of terror, desperation, and helplessness. These are children who had to run into bomb shelters, wear gas masks, and watch buildings collapse. Many had to move from place to place as the war came to them, or were separated from their families. As resources became scarce, they felt compelled to steal coal from train cars to heat their homes and scavenge for food. In spite of the danger and chaos around them, these children also demonstrated resilience, resourcefulness, and playful spirits. The reader is drawn into the reality of their lives and struggle, without losing hope or feeling overwhelmed.

↜

We are challenged with the question of whether what these children endured "to some extent parallel what children in the Middle East, in Iraq, Syria, and Yemen, and other war-torn areas experience right now?" From my thirteen years of peace work in Iraq, before, during, and after the 2003 U.S. invasion and from following reports of other war-torn areas, I answer, "yes."

↜

The most indelible reality of war has been its destructiveness—the "hell of war"—as I term it. In Iraq, as elsewhere, war broke apart a whole society, its physical infrastructure, and the lives of all those who were killed and maimed, as well as the moral and social cohesion that has held it together. The resulting chaos, pain, anger, fear, and trauma have spawned more violence and revenge that will plague future generations. To regain that social trust and cohesion is something like putting "Humpty Dumpty together again." I am convinced that war does not address our current international problems, but only creates more pain and suffering. The resulting chaos and anger, in turn, has become the breeding ground for the creation and spread of terrorist groups and activity.

In the midst of war in Iraq, I met parents who were unable to care for their family's physical needs and families living in fear of hunger and homelessness. Even now, most Iraqis experience daily threats from ongoing bombings, kidnappings, or the need to flee their homes out of fear of violence. Children are traumatized with little understanding of the forces that shattered what security their family had.

Ibrahim* has a panic attack whenever he hears loud noises or explosions. Jamila sits lethargically in her chair, severely depressed. Yusef is permanently handicapped by bombs that hit his home. Along with her family, Miriam has to hide in underground root-cellars when planes fly over her village, bombing her home. She doesn't know if their house will still be there when they come out. Sa'id wanders around a tent camp for those displaced by violence, not knowing if he will ever have a normal home again. Even though these children also exhibit resilience, resourcefulness, and playfulness, I believe that these are things that no child should have to endure.

It's not surprising, then, that the wisdom this author has gained from recording these Second World War stories, as well as her own personal childhood experience during that time, have led her to work for peace as an adult living in mid-Ohio. She has seen how war affected her family, friends, and others that she has interviewed. She applies what she has learned in the two thought-provoking closing chapters, "Arguments Against War," and Never Again War."

My experiences, too, have compelled *me* to speak out and work to prevent future war. With her and increasing numbers of people around the world, I want to echo the iconic words, "Never Again!" but also work to make that become the reality for every woman, man, and child. To do that, it's helpful to understand the historical and political events leading up to that war's genocide, so that we might recognize current fascist political forces and do what we can to resist and prevent them from taking power.

By Peggy Faw Gish

All mentioned here are real children, but their names here have been changed.

Peggy Faw Gish, long-time peace and justice activist and author of *Iraq: A Journey of Hope and Peace* (Herald Press: 2004) and *Walking Through Fire: Iraqis' Struggle for Justice and Reconciliation*, (Cascade Books: 2013).

Acknowledgements

So many people encouraged and supported me over the four years I worked on this project, yet it was an easy decision whom to acknowledge first. I am most thankful to you who shared your childhood experiences with me. You inspired me to write your stories and made this book possible. It belongs to you.

While I stayed in Germany: Marianne, Annemarie, Brigitte, Ingrid, Erika, Irmgard, Hannelore, Manfred, and my brother Wolfgang shared with me what they remembered from World War II and its aftermath. So did: Frances, Annelies, Nadia, Christa, Heinz, and Ildiko in the US; and Almut's contribution comes from Canada.

All of you spent hours narrating what had occurred in your distant past and patiently responded to my questions. Some of you provided your own writing and supporting documents. It is not easy to recall childhood stress and to relive long buried anxieties. I thank you for doing so regardless. If I caused you sleepless nights, please forgive me and know that you caused the same to me.

It is difficult to remember dates, names, and the sequence of events from bygone years. Debbie Perantoni helped to fill in details of her mother's story by providing old hospital and refugee documents, as well as photos. I thank you for them and for your account of the trip to the Ukraine.

I thank Mrs. Fuldner for her recollections of important events in Ingrid's early childhood. These and the memoirs of Almut's mother and of my grandfather added depth, fullness, and accuracy to the corresponding stories.

I thank Anita Schorn for including her fascinating saga. I am sure that readers will enjoy the story of the extraordinarily brave Anna.

My three brothers Wolfgang, Helgi, and Reinhold consistently encouraged and supported me. I will always be thankful to you. You provided background material, helped with the research of specific topics, listened, gave advice, and of course shared your recollections. I especially enjoyed Wolfgang's adventures, which became the first part of our combined story.

Most true-life stories are fun to tell and listen to for the immediate participants, but how do you write them so that an unfamiliar reader will enjoy them too? Reinhold took several days out of his busy schedule to discuss, critique, rearrange, and propose changes that would make the text clearer, sharper, and easier to read. His advise and suggestions lead to the overall format of the book.

My German grammar and spelling were in need of correction. Ingeborg and Franz Janssen dedicated many hours to this project. I thank you both very much.

My talented stepdaughter Elena Ezeani later edited each story and improved them in many ways. I am very grateful to you.

This is how the German book for German speakers emerged. It took much time and work, but the encouragement of my extended German family made it a rewarding endeavor. Besides my brothers, my dear sisters-in-laws Annemarie, Brigitte, and Dagmar, good friends and relatives, Marianne, Irmchen, Erika, Antje, Ingrid, Beate und Dieter cheered me on. Thank you.

I had written Frances and Nadia's story first in English. Now it was time to write all chapters in English for English speakers. I wanted to share them with my family and friends in the US and the storytellers living here wanted to do the same.

Of course rewriting the book in English was more work and took more time. When this phase was completed, corrections by native English speakers were needed. Fortunately, my American family was ready to help. My son Frank, my daughters Kristine and Ulrike, and even my grandson Leif and granddaughter Annika corrected stories. I thank you very much.

Next my classmates and friends of the German language study group at the Worthington Senior Center: Sylvia Teaque, Sarah Ferrar, Ann Kangas, and Don Ker spent uncountable hours poring over the stories. I am so very thankful to your corrections, help, and encouragement. Additional help came from the new members Jim Giesike, Karen Thimmes, and Bertina Provenmire. Thank you.

After so much help, did my writing still need editing? Yes, it did. With skill and enthusiasm, Donna Williams plunged into the task of correcting and rewording. She did so not just once, but read and corrected each chapter three times! It was an exhausting effort. Never tired, she also decided to replace my crude handwritten map showing towns and villages mentioned with a perfectly clear computer generated version. Donna, I do thank you so very much. You made it possible that the manuscript found a home with Wipf and Stock Publishers.

My friends at Central Ohioans for Peace: Christa Gharbo, Bob Holmes, Ken Johnson, Rose Stevens, Bob Hart, Dorothy Barnes and Janet

McLaughlin have been cheering me on over the years. Thank you. And thank you Melonie Buller for having me do my first book presentation before it was published.

Last, but not least, I thank Peggy Gish for her eloquent, insightful foreword.

Frequently used Foreign Terms

German Terms:

Mutter, Mutti, Mama	Mother, Mom or Mommy
Vater, Vati, Papa	Father, Dad, Daddy
Großvater, Opa	Grandfather, Grandpa
Großmutter, Oma, Omi	Grandmother, Grandma
Tante	Aunt
Onkle	Uncle
Schätzchen	my dear one
danke or danke schön	thank you
gefährlich	dangerous
Straße	street
Wasser	water

Terms used by Russians soldiers

Babushka	grandma
Frau	woman, particular for young desirable woman
Nix	none
Soldat	soldier
Uri	wristwatch

Hungarian Term

Édesanyám	dear mother in Hungarian

Some of the names appearing in the stories have been changed.

Introduction

World War II began September 1, 1939; it ended May 8, 1945 in Europe and September 2, 1945 in Japan. During that time fifty-five million perished, approximately twenty-six million soldiers and twenty-nine million civilians. Millions more died in the following years, due to the devastation and upheavals in the aftermath of the war. These are staggering numbers. What do they mean to us today?

Here in the US, my home for over fifty years, the time of the Second World War is remembered for its patriotic spirit and its brave fighting force of courageous soldiers. It is the story of a war that brought the people of the nation together. While the young men fought bravely overseas, the civilians at home worked hard to supply them with the weapons, gear, and food needed to persevere. Everyone contributed to the war effort and celebrated its hard-won victory. The US freed the world from tyranny.

In Europe, World War II is remembered differently, especially in Germany, the country of my birth and upbringing, where the civilians were exposed to all the dangers of war just like the soldiers. Frequently they suffered even more, and as the statistics tell us, died in even greater numbers than the fighting forces.

It is over seventy years ago that WWII ended. Most of its participants have since passed away. But the children, who lived through it or were born during the war, are mostly still alive. What do they remember? How did the war affect their lives? How did they survive? Eighteen witnesses of the war share their childhood experiences in this book and provide us an insight into what war meant to them.

I was born in 1940 in the Rhineland and remember the last nine months of the war as a four-year-old. What do people several years older than I remember? I should have known. After all, I have two older brothers and many older relatives and friends. But I didn't. I never knew of the adventures of my brother Wolfgang, who is six years older, until I asked him. The same is true of the other childhood remembrances recounted in this book.

In 2013 I returned to my hometown Langenfeld in Germany for an extended stay to care for my ailing 102-year-old mother. While there, I became interested in the events and experiences that had shaped my generation. Do they to some extent parallel what children in the Middle East, Iraq, Syria, and Yemen, experience right now? What does it mean to a child if his or her society is engulfed in war?

I approached relatives and friends who were about five to eight years older than I and was astonished that everyone had a story to tell. Everyone's life had been impacted in various ways by the war. Back in Ohio, I interviewed friends or friends of friends, who had lived through the war in different parts of Europe. Again I was surprised when they related events I had never heard about, even though they are part of readily available World War II history. Hearing their stories deepened my understanding of the ramification of war and its effect on children.

Often it took many sessions for the full story to emerge. I would write what I had heard after each interview. In doing so, I quickly noticed inconsistencies or gaps in a narrative that had initially escaped notice. Follow-up questions yielded additional answers. Often the person interviewed would talk to relatives, who might remember additional details. In the meantime I researched the location, town, landscape, and war events as well as anything general and objective that related to the story.

After an initial rough draft, each narrator reviewed his or her story. More additions or corrections followed. It was essential that each story be internally consistent, and the historical facts were correct. In short, I looked for the true experiences the children had lived through.

The intent was to faithfully recount each child's experiences during wartime and immediately thereafter. A remembered event might not seem especially exciting or extraordinary. Yet small details, which appear to be of marginal importance, may later turn out to be significant for a given situation. For instance, Marianne tells us about being happy that her pee warmed her legs. How much must she — a normal-eleven-year old — have suffered from the cold to perceive it this way!

Most stories are followed by a summary of salient facts related to the personal experience of the child. These short reports may underline the dangers that surrounded the child, or they may inform the reader about facts of interest.

Some events reoccurred in various forms in many stories. Foremost among them were the bombings. Everyone who remembered the war remembered bombing.

Bombs meant fear, anguish, desperation.

"The heavens were trembling," is how Ildiko described it.

"I cried in terror," remembered Anna.

"I heard the sound of bombs exploding and started running . . . Bombs! We are being bombed! I screamed," recalled Heinz.

"But the bombing was bad," Annelies said, paused, and looked at me with pain in her eyes.

Francis stated: "Sometimes at night I remember the sound of air-raid sirens and the heavy drone of bombers, which you could feel as well as hear. To this day if I hear bombers on TV, I still have the feeling I should be going down and hiding somewhere."

I was surprised that most narrators told me that at least once during the war they had been fleeing with their families from war events or had been refugees. The fear of getting lost or losing their mother was the anguish they still remember.

Another fundamental fear children most often experienced was centered around food.

"I was always hungry," states Ingrid.

"I shouldered my knapsack and scoured the neighborhood for edibles," Christa said.

How many children died during WWII? The children of these stories survived, but a small twist of fate could have turned deadly for each of them. Yet, even as adults, they don't dwell on this. They remember funny things and good times between misery.

None of the stories talked about heroism in war. Even Wolfgang, who desperately tried to cling to his belief in battle glory, was bitterly disappointed by the harsh reality of war and defeat. He became an anti-war activist.

I share my brother's sentiments. To me, war means death and sorrow. The conversations I listened to as a small child convinced me of this forever. Accordingly, I share anti-war arguments in the last two chapters.

And yes, bombs are extremely scary. I am sure the children in Syria, Iraq, Afghanistan, and Yemen agree.

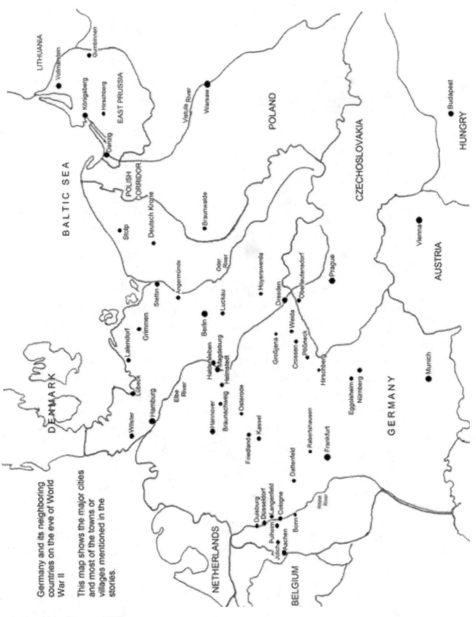

Germany and its neighboring countries on the eve of World War II

This map shows the major cities and most of the towns or villages mentioned in the stories.

designed by Donna Williams

Francis "helping" to cut the grass

Chapter 1

"Will Father Christmas
Know Where I Am?"

*Frances, born October 1937 in Quinton, a suburb of
Birmingham, England.*

FRANCES'S PARENTS HAD BEEN married for just three years and she was
only two years old when the war started. The war affected her family early
because they lived on the outskirts of Birmingham, a major industrial center with large manufacturing plants for trucks, planes, and other techni-
cal goods necessary for defense. Consequently, German bombers targeted
Birmingham frequently during World War II.

Frances recalls:

My father was carrying me outside in the middle of the night. Looking
up into the darkness, I saw the stars for the first time. I also saw something
else—huge searchlights crisscrossing the sky. Startled and wide-awake, I

1

shivered in the cold. My father had snatched me out of my warm bed because of the air raid alarm and took me to our air raid shelter under the garage.

Outfitted just for us, the shelter had two folding cots for my parents, and a wooden bunk bed with a brown wool tartan blanket as a curtain for me. My mother placed me in my bed, gave me another good night kiss, closed the curtain, and expected me to fall asleep again. Of course, I was not sleepy anymore. Through a gap in the curtain, I saw my parents sitting on their cots. They played cards and drank hot cocoa by the light of an oil lamp that stood on a small table between them. I felt left out of the fun.

There must have been many repetitions of this event. One time, we had an air raid warning on Christmas Eve and my father carried me on his shoulders to the shelter. I worried, "Will Father Christmas know where I am." Well, he knew. In the morning I found my long, brown, knitted Christmas stocking. Father Christmas had filled it for me with an apple, nuts, some coins, and a small toy.

Another time I sat on my father's knees listening to the radio. "Sweets will be rationed," the announcer intoned. "Fran, did you hear that?" my father asked. Yes, I had; and little precocious me jumped off his lap in protest and ran to my mum to share the bad news.

Of course not just sweets, but almost all food was rationed during the war. Everyone had a rationing book and had to register with a local grocer who was provided with enough food for registered customers. The rations curtailed my mother's cooking, although I did not notice it at the time. For instance, at Christmas we had no cookies. How can you bake for the holidays if all you have is one egg, 4 oz. of butter, and 12 oz. of sugar per person/ per week for all of your meals? Imported fruit and some deserts were never available. I did not know oranges, lemons, bananas, pineapples or ice cream until I was seven years old or older.

To supplement the limited diet, everyone had a garden or an allotment to grow as much food as possible. They were called Victory Gardens. Ours was not far away from our house. Sometimes when we went there, I was allowed to ride in the wheelbarrow. My parents spent a lot of spare time working in the garden growing vegetables, potatoes, and some berry bushes. I was their "helper" and had a little plot of my own, where I grew radishes. As they became plump and red, I was eager to eat them, but disappointingly, I did not like their taste at all.

We were fortunate that my father was not drafted into the military, because he worked for CAV Lucas, a company that made auto accessories and other mechanical items needed by the army. Two of my uncles and an older cousin were drafted and served several years without being wounded, imprisoned or killed. I heard that our family was very relieved, when the war ended, and they had survived without harm. Many British soldiers were less fortunate. My parents talked about men that never returned from the war.

The men at home had to work harder during the war. My father left early for work and returned late. I only saw him on weekends. In addition, he was a volunteer fireman. While our house and neighborhood were not destroyed, other sections of Birmingham were. The German Luftwaffe bombers would attack at night, and usually the explosions caused destruction and fires. Then my father was called to duty.

My father's fire-fighting suit hung by the front door. It was yellow and black, and I knew it was 'fireproof', so it probably contained asbestos. Next to the suit hung his fireman's hat, a loop of rope, and some length of hosepipe. On the floor sat a stirrup pump and a large menacing ax, which I was not allowed to touch and never did.

A gasmask was issued to everyone in Britain, including children. My mask was very special. It had black ears, a Mickey Mouse face and when I was breathing through it, the black ears wiggled. My friends thought it was very funny. I looked forward to our war drills in school when we had to wear our masks. But there was a frightening reason for them: to protect us from poisonous gas used by the Germans. Fortunately, this never happened.

When I was three years old, I entered pre-school and when I was five I was already riding the public bus to school on my own, which astonishes me today. Maybe this was normal at the time because everyone used public transportation during the war years.

My father had a car but never got to use it. Petrol was rationed. With his monthly allowance of petrol he had the luxury of driving around our block once. The rest of the time the car sat in our garage.

The war made it almost impossible to import cloth. Most of the material available was used by the military for uniforms and parachutes. We had sixty-six clothing coupons per year, which was equivalent to one complete outfit. Growing children were allowed ten extra coupons. Second-hand and privately sold clothing was not rationed. Evening classes were set up to teach housewives how to make new clothes from old ones.

In addition, my mother studied numerous magazines to learn how to re-trim an old dress, turn a dress or shirt inside out by undoing the seams and re-sewing it, as well as other useful skills.

We had to save water in case the reservoirs were bombed, which fortunately never happened. A line was drawn on the bathtub and you were only to fill the bath to the line.

The British war slogan was: "reduce, repair, restore, reuse, and recycle." Nothing was ever wasted.

My sister is five years younger than I. Before my mother's due date, Auntie Pat came to take me by train to my grandparents in Cheshire. All the trains were steam driven and the inside of the stations were black with soot and smoke. Most interesting for me was the black St. Bernard dog that came through the long train corridor with a collection box on his back, collecting money for the St. Bernard orphanage for children.

I stayed with my grandparents for a month, and one day I was called to the telephone and told that my new baby sister had been born. Apparently I said: "Call her Susan." And that became her name.

During the war, all houses had to have solid black curtains at every window. They had to be fully drawn at night so that no light could escape, as this would show German bombers where houses and towns were located.

My baby sister Susan was sick quite often. One night when my father was out on the fire engine, my mother was especially worried, because Susan had whooping cough. She coughed and coughed, and stopped breathing. Just then the air raid warden knocked at the door and began to ream my mother out, because she had not fully drawn the curtain, and light was shining through the window. When the warden saw little Sue turning blue, he immediately helped my mother and soon Susan was breathing again.

During air raids, we were not allowed to turn on any light. In order to get around in the dark, we had little disks, about two inches across, affixed to the stairs, doorways, and edges of furniture. They glowed in the dark, so we could make our way out of the house without using light.

All trains and buses had blackout on the windows with the exception of a small diamond shaped opening, so people could see the names of the stations. Later, riding by myself on trains in London, I found it rather difficult to know where I was by looking through these small open spaces. After missing my end point and having to return to it with a train in the opposite direction, I resorted to counting the stations I needed to travel.

Huge blimp-like balloons, called barrage balloons, were suspended at strategic places. They deterred enemy airplanes by making it harder for them to bomb their targets. The cables that anchored the balloon were a hazard to low flying planes and their pilots. Once, a barrage balloon floated down onto Ridgeacre Road, not far from our house, and we all went to see it being towed back down the hill to its mooring.

Because of my sister's sickness, I was always told to play very gently with her. So I was pleased when we had a child living with us, with whom I could interact without extra restrictions. Her name was Doreen. She was twelve years old and sent to us by the Ministry of Defense.

A letter arrived and rather than expressing: "Thank you for offering . . .," it simply stated: "I hereby require you to receive Doreen . . . " Doreen's house in Carshalton, a suburb of London, had been destroyed. As she was homeless and her father was a soldier at war, we provided a temporary refuge for her. Doreen stayed with us for several months and then returned to her family again.

I was seven when we moved to a suburb of London. As we walked by the bombed-out buildings, the terrible destruction caused by the war became real to me. At the roped-off sites we could look down into basements with caved-in walls and room divisions.

Nature softened the image, giving hope for a better future. Wherever a little dirt had accumulated, delicate rosebay willow weeds bloomed between the stark ruins.

In 1944, at the time when we had high hopes for the end of the war, the Germans launched deadly flying bombs[1] towards the city. Often they fell short of their target. One bomb landed on the sports field in our neighborhood. The explosion shattered the windows of nearby houses and dug a deep crater into the field.

Aftereffects

Sometimes at night I remember the sound of the air raid sirens and the heavy drone of the bombers, which you could feel as well as hear. To this day if I hear bombers on the TV, I still have the feeling I should be going down and hiding under something.

My teeth and bones show signs of calcium deficiency, which is most likely caused by my insufficient diet when I was young.

Growing up I learned not to waste or throw away anything or attach too much importance to material things. So it is only fitting that today I volunteer at a second-hand shop of the American Cancer Society.

The Blitz

The Blitz refers to the bombing of Great Britain's cities by the German air force during the Second World War between September 1940 and May 1941. It started in the afternoon of September seventh when about 300 German bombers attacked London for two hours and again during the night, causing the death of 436 Londoners, and injuries to 1,500 more people.

From this day on, London had to endure bombing raids each night for fifty-six consecutive nights. The worst attack on London occurred on the

---

1. A pulsejet-powered cruise missile.

night of December 29th, when German bombers dropped firebombs on the Old City of London. The heat from all the burning buildings started a firestorm with super heated gale force winds drawing in torrents of air to fan walls of flames. They ravished the area between St. Paul's Cathedral and Guildhall, and several old churches were destroyed.

London, View from St Paul's Cathedral after the Blitz

Each night, air-raid sirens would wake the people of London from their sleep. They took shelter wherever they could find it—in the underground tube stations or in basements of warehouses or schools. Often the shelters were inadequate, crowded, and lacked sanitation or privacy. As many as 170,000 Londoners would flee to the underground on any given night.

During the Blitz, 20,000 Londoners died and over one million houses were flattened or damaged. All together London was attacked seventy-one times. Poor areas of the city, particular the East End, suffered badly during the onslaught.

Not only London, but also ports or industrial centers like Birmingham, Belfast, Glasgow, Manchester, Liverpool, Plymouth, Middleborough, and Sheffield were attacked. The North Sea port of Hull, an easy target for in- or outbound German bombers, was subjected to eighty-six air raids. The Spitfire and tank factories were heavily targeted in Birmingham.

Coventry, with its ammunition, automobile, and airplane factories, was devastated. On November 14, 1940, Coventry experienced a massive air raid. The attack destroyed not just three quarters of the industry but also 4,000 dwellings, the city water system, two hospitals, two churches, and the beautiful St. Michael's Cathedral built in the fourteenth century. A journalist described it as follows:

"Coventry is now like a city that has been wrecked by an earthquake and swept by fire."[2]

During the eight-months-long air war, a total of about 34,500 people were killed. Hitler had intended to significantly weaken Great Britain's military capability and force the government to negotiate an end to hostilities. Neither goal was achieved, nor did the Blitz undermine the morale of the British people.

Rationing of Food in Great Britain

Prior to the Second World War, England imported 70 percent of its food. After the start of the war and the German occupation of European countries like France and Belgium, the import of commodities became limited to Allied Nations like the USA and Canada. Ocean liners that carried grain and durable goods from these countries to England were endangered by enemy submarines.

In order for the country to sustain itself during the long siege and to build up its military capacity, it was essential that each British citizen had enough to eat. Only then would everyone have the ability to contribute to the war effort.

To prevent wealthy people from eating scarce and therefore expensive groceries, the British government started a food-rationing program. By January 1940, butter, sugar, and bacon were rationed. Shortly thereafter, meat, cheese, eggs, margarine, oatmeal, crackers, and canned or dried fruit were rationed.

The amounts of milk and eggs were adjusted to need. Small children and pregnant women were entitled to more milk than the rest of the population. Children and some invalids received three eggs per week and pregnant women two, whereas other people got only one egg per week.

Frances provided the following sample of weekly rations for the average consumer:

Butter 4 oz., Bacon 4 oz., Sugar 12 oz., Cheese 2 oz., Meat 10 oz., Sweets 2 oz., Chocolate 2 oz., Tea 2 oz., Milk 2 pints, Egg 1

In addition, the government subsidized essential foods, like bread, flour, milk, and eggs, so even the poorest person could afford them.

Restaurant menus were curtailed; no dinner costing more than 5 shillings could be served. Two hundred public restaurants opened their doors in schools or churches, where people could eat simple meals costing nine pence.

2. Daniell, "Revenge by Nazis."

To assure that the food rationing had no harmful effects on hard working laborers, the University of Cambridge tested the restricted diet. The results confirmed the government policy. An article in Medical News Today,
June 21 2004[3] describes that the wartime diet improved the health of the
British people; infant mortality declined, and life expectancy rose, discount-
ing death caused by hostilities.

3. Medical News Today, "Wartime Rationing Helped the British Get Healthier than
they had ever been."

Annemarie, standing, with her friend

Chapter 2

My Father Built an Air Raid Shelter for Us

Annemarie, born October 1935 in Pulheim, close to Cologne, Germany

ANNEMARIE WAS THE SECOND oldest of six siblings, who grew up in a farming village on the west side of the Rhine River, about eleven miles northwest of Cologne. Her father farmed and grew young fruit trees on their land while her mother cared for the children and ran the large household. Together with their grandmother (called Oma) and an unmarried aunt Gertrud, the family lived in an old rambling farmhouse surrounded by other farm buildings and a large barn. Their farmhouse was located in the village as was common in many parts of Germany. For children in search of playmates, adventure, and fun, the village was a nice place to grow up.

Asked about her childhood Annemarie responded:

"I had a happy childhood. We had a lot of fun."

"Didn't you notice the war?"

"Oh, sure. I will tell you about it."

9

The door at the rear of our barn led to our vegetable garden. That's where I was when a terrible earth-shaking roar approached from the sky. At the same time I heard Joseph, yell out in panic, "ground, ground!"

Instead of looking up to find the cause of the roar, I followed his urgent command and dropped instantly to the ground. Joseph ran out of the barn and threw himself over me. We lay there frozen in fear while the enormous boom thundered over us. When we got up, we saw several low-flying planes vanish into the distance. They could have shot at us, and if they had done so, Joseph would have died protecting me with his body!

Joseph was from Poland. He had volunteered to come and work in Germany. For several years he had been working and living on our farm. My father (we called him Papa) was glad to have Joseph's help but he needed more workers. His German workers had been drafted into the army. Every morning, Papa drove with his wagon to the foreign labor camp housed in our old schoolhouse and got some of the workers. They had not volunteered, but had been forced to work in Pulheim or elsewhere in Germany.

~

Papa did not have to serve in the army because he had six children and was a farmer. Many farmers were excused from service to ensure sufficient food production. The same was true for uncle Ferdinand, the husband of my grandaunt Lena, who farmed nearby. Sunday afternoons, my grandmother would visit her sister Lena and usually my aunt Gertrud and I would come along. We would sit at aunt Lena's big table with her family and have the cake she had baked and coffee; I had a cup of fresh milk. Uncle Christian, Aunt Lena's oldest son studied music at the university. He was a tall, quiet young man. With his dark, curly hair and glasses, he looked very much like the serious student he was. I was in awe of him and his accomplishments. I knew of no one else in our village doing something so special as my uncle Christian.

My uncle Hans, Christian's younger brother had a very different disposition. Outgoing and fun-loving, he was still a big kid who might join my pranks. While the adults were sitting around the table talking, I would slip away and play with Fritzi, the shorthair dachshund. I loved Fritzi. He was the most patient creature on earth. I tied a scarf around his head and made him look so cute. Then I put my dolls dress on him and made him look hilarious. It was the highlight of my afternoon when uncle Hans thought of fun activities for Fritzi to do all dressed up.

I vividly remember my young uncles, even though I was barely five years old. It was at this age that I saw uncle Christian for the last time. He was drafted into the war very early and soon thereafter died in combat. He was perhaps the first man from our village who died in this senseless war. I don't know how and when the sad news filtered down to us small children that uncle Christian was no more. It was incomprehensible to me. From then on my sixteen-year-old Uncle Hans was my elderly granduncle's only helper on the farm.

⌒

After the war had started, my Papa's work had increased during the day and at night. Like all his neighbors, who had not been drafted, he had nightly duty at the anti-aircraft cannon, stationed outside of the village. Beginning in 1940, the British air force flew bombing missions over Cologne, and since Pulheim was in close vicinity, it was endangered as well. Papa heard that air raid shelters were being built in Cologne, yet none were planned for Pulheim.

Papa was concerned about our safety and decided to take it upon himself to build an air raid bunker for us. I watched as he and his men excavated a deep pit in our yard. They covered it with wooden beams and straw. It was just big enough for all of us.

When the air raid sirens wailed at night, Mama would wake us up, and we would run out of the house into the bunker in our garden. Sleepily we would sit on benches and listen to Mama, Oma, and Aunt Gertrud murmur prayers. We wished to lie down, but the bunker had no room for cots.

When the danger had passed, Papa would return from his anti-aircraft duty and tell us the good news. One time he called out to us: "Come and see!" pointing in the direction of Cologne. I saw a fiery red sky in the distance. In the middle of the glow, tall and black, the two spires of the cathedral of Cologne stood defiantly. Cologne was burning. As the war dragged on, I saw Cologne burning several more times.

I am not sure if it was in the summer of 1942 or 43, when I traveled by train with my aunt Gertrud to Cologne. Holding her hand, I walked past huge mountains of rubble and ruined houses. The facade of a house was gone and in the exposed room on the second floor stood an easy chair; a torn curtain spookily fluttered out of a dark window without glass; a broken cabinet sat tipped to the side against a cement block. We did not walk along the Hohe Straße, the prominent, old shopping street close to the cathedral. Where was it? Instead we walked on a footpath—a trail made by people picking their way through the rubble—to the Neumarkt, one of Cologne's busy squares. Here some shops were open for business. After aunt Gertrud had completed her errands, we visited a small movie theater by the train station. I don't remember what film we watched, but I do remember the weekly newsreels before the movie started. A huge formation of airplanes flew across the screen.

～

The war was in its third year and getting worse. More frequently, men from our village died in battle and were returned home in a casket for burial. Oma would attend the funeral and I would accompany her, even though none of my sisters or brothers did. Oma would wear her black dress and dark coat and I wore my Sunday church outfit. We would join the solemn procession to the graveyard behind our church. Quietly the people would gather around the gravesite. The honor guard would lift the trumpet to his lips and slowly the notes and the voices of the mourners would rise up into the sky. "I once had a comrade . . . " The melody and the words would deeply touch my heart, a great sadness filled me as tears rolled down my cheeks. I cried even though I had not known the fallen soldier, and I would always go with Oma to the funerals even though it made me sad. Perhaps it was the early experience of loosing my uncle Christian that touched me. None of my siblings had known him as well as I.

By this time my uncle Hans had turned eighteen, he too was drafted into the war. Of course, Aunt Lena was very worried about him, yet everyone assured her that Hans had always been lucky and God would spare him the fate of his brother. I missed Uncle Hans. Without him, Sunday afternoons at Aunt Lena's became pale and boring.

For some unknown reason, more people from our village disappeared. A retarded boy had lived at the end of our street. He walked awkwardly, with his shoulders hunched and regarded us with a puzzled stare when we called out to him and teased him for fun. At least we thought it was a fun thing to do even though it was not nice at all. One day the boy was gone. He was just not there anymore. We asked our mother. "I think they took him to a hospital," was all Mama knew. He never returned home. Today I assume he was most likely a victim of the Hitler's criminal program of "Elimination of unworthy Lives."

～

Papa was more and more worried about us. He too had seen the destruction in Cologne and knew about similar devastating bombardments in other cities not far from us. Of course our earthen bunker would never withstand a direct bomb hit. Papa realized that we needed better air raid protection. He and his helpers broke through a wall of our basement and added another room with a thick concrete-reinforced ceiling. Now we had a real air raid shelter. It was bigger than our bunker outside. Papa invited two neighboring families to join us there during air raids. A row of benches provided seating for everyone. Here we waited while more voices joined the prayers.

Our new sturdy shelter did not protect us from the new menace in the sky. In 1944, Germany's air defenses were no longer effective and low-flying Allied fighter planes swooped over the countryside at daytime strafing soldiers or civilians. These planes were terrifying. It was dangerous to be outside. I constantly relived the day Joseph had protected me with his body. We were more exposed to the enemy warplanes than other parts of Germany because Pulheim was close to the outskirts of Cologne as well as the other industrial centers along the northern Rhine valley.

Rabertshausen

Papa was looking for a place for us to live in the countryside away from any urban centers. He found it in the village of Rabertshausen, in the German state of Hesse, located southeast of us. After selling some trees there, he had noticed a big empty farmhouse. The owner, a bachelor, had killed himself a few months ago. "Could my family live here for a while? I want them to get away from all the bombardments," Papa asked neighbors. "Well, it would be all right with us, but the house is in very bad shape inside," was their response.

Papa talked with a neighborhood friend about his plan. Together they drove to Rabertshausen in the friend's car, an old truck that was converted to run on gas produced by an attached wood-burner. People called cars like this "Rotzkocher," "snotcooker" in English. Papa and his friend made the house livable for us—removing trash as well as cleaning and painting it. They decided that the friend's family would live upstairs and we downstairs.

In the summer of 1944, the old snotcooker was loaded with our mattresses, bedding, clothes, cookware, and all ten of us. Off we went to our temporary safe haven. Slowly the truck crawled along bumpy roads damaged by four years of war. I was 9 years old, sitting next to my aunt Gertrud, squished between our possessions. We worried about low-flying planes spotting us and believing we were a military transport.

Luckily we traveled without incident, but towards the end of our journey the old truck died. Here we were at night, in a dark, strange village with a truck that did not run anymore. Papa could not see what had caused the problem. Since the beginning of the war, strict rules prohibited any outside lighting at night, as it would show British bombers where houses and towns were located. To go against this rule would endanger the village and its inhabitants. What to do?

"Let's split into groups of two or three, go in different directions, and knock on doors," Papa decided. "Just tell them what happened and ask for an overnight stay." We were all taken in by kind strangers. Aunt Gertrud and I slept in one of the farmhouses that night. In the morning Papa and his friend repaired the truck. We continued our journey and reached Rabertshausen in good time.

We had enough room in the empty farmhouse but no furniture, not even or a table, because there had been no room on the truck for these items. Papa had sent the furniture and two hundred pounds of potatoes by rail. We waited for weeks and then months for their arrival. Friendly neighbors helped us out by lending us some benches and a few other furnishings.

When we heard in the fall that the railroad station of the nearby town of Giessen had been bombed, we believed that our things had been destroyed. How surprised we were, when in November, we received the news that our shipment had been found in an unscathed railroad car sitting outside the main station. One of the farmers went with Papa to Giessen; chugging along on a farm tractor, they retrieved our things.

Papa had been visiting us that week. He had brought us produce from the farm and enjoyed seeing us. He also was the bearer of very sad news from home— Uncle Hans had been killed in action. How tragic, poor Aunt Lena had lost both of her sons!

⌒

Papa did not stay long with us, but returned to Pulheim, ran our farm, and did his anti-aircraft duty. During late 1944 and early 1945, intense battles were fought along the western border of Germany. If the battles were lost, the American troops would quickly advance to the Rhine, conquering part of Cologne and the low lands on the west side of the Rhine, including Pulheim. When the possibility of such an event seemed imminent, all civilian men between the age of sixteen and sixty were ordered to join the Volkssturm, the civilian defense corps, to assist our soldiers in a last ditch effort to keep foreign troops out of Germany.

In February 1945, the US Army had passed the border and was advancing within Germany. At that time, the party boss of Pulheim came to our farm and asked Papa to lead a Volkssturm group of twenty men. They gathered in our yard; each got some gear, a gun and some provisions. The military order was: march to the West Wall, a defensive wall along the western border of Germany, contact the officer in charge, and do as ordered.

Papa and his small band walked about half of the way. The news from the front was going from bad to worse. Before he left Pulheim, Papa had made plans for such a situation. He didn't believe it made sense for them to be the last soldiers to die at the West Wall. He got his men together and talked to them without the permission of his superior. He later recalled his words for us: "Let's face it, the war is lost. It makes no sense for us to march on. I say, let's disperse. Everyone tries to find his own hiding place. If you can't think of one, come back with me to my farm."

We had an old root cellar beneath our pigpen. To get in, you had to open a trap door in the floor. Crooked stone steps went down into it. That's where Papa and his band hid out. It was a secure place, which was essential, because military rules applied to them. Even in the last days of the war, deserters would be shot. The men spent two days in their hideout before the American troops arrived. For Pulheim and the surrounding area, the war was over. On March 6, 1945, Cologne was conquered by Allied Forces.

⌐

Over two months later, the war ended in Rabertshausen. On April 17, 1945, intense nervousness gripped the villagers. Everyone was advised to put white sheets in their windows. I thought it made the village look funny. Even we children knew what the sheets implied: "We surrender." The war was lost and it was finally over.

Huge American tanks and trucks rumbled down the narrow cobblestone village street in front of the house we stayed in. The people were hiding inside their houses and worried: "What will happen to us?"

I saw my five-year-old brother Franz in the street in front of the house. He had slipped out unnoticed. Red-cheeked and wide-eyed, he looked excitedly at the parade of enormous trucks and tanks. His fearlessness encouraged me to join him. Soon several children and even some adults stood at the side of the street. And then I witnessed something I will never forget. A tall black soldier, standing in an open vehicle, leaned all the way down to Franz and gave him a chocolate bar.

The loud, massive, respect-commanding American troops rolled through the village and never returned. Later, I saw sad groups of German soldiers in tattered uniforms shuffling along our street. Where were they going? I did not know.

Return

In the fall of 1945, Papa believed that things had settled down, and it was safe for us to return home. Papa borrowed the same truck we had used before. This time we did not have to worry about low-flying planes, but other obstacles made our trip even longer.

All the bridges over the Rhine had been destroyed during the last months of fighting. We had to go to Remagen, south of Bonn, where the Americans had constructed a temporary wooden bridge. American soldiers guarded it. Only a few vehicles or pedestrian could cross safely at a time. We waited in a long line of cars for hours. Our passports were checked and we were treated for lice, which we did not have. I remember the white powder on my arms that had a strange smell. I later learned that it was DDT, which is now banned for its harmful, cancer-causing effects.

Our house in Pulheim appeared undisturbed from the outside, but many things were missing inside. The Polish maids, who had taken care of our house while we were away, might have taken some of our things home with them, when they left after the war. While understandable, it was upsetting for Mama because nothing could be easily replaced. German stores were empty.

We were, nevertheless, far luckier than the people of Cologne. Our house was neither damaged nor destroyed, and we had water and electricity. Our farm produced all the food we needed and even more. With the surplus we bartered for items we did not have like coal for heating or shoes for us children to wear in winter. We also gave away food. Mama later told us that up to five people would come to our door each day and ask for food. Everyone received some.

Once we too experienced a food shortage. During the night before the planned butchering of our pig, it was stolen. In the morning when Papa went to its pen, only a few pig entrails were left. What had happened? Our good watchdog had not barked to warn us of an intruder. My father suspected one of our workers, but had no proof. It was a big loss for us. Winter was approaching. We had counted on the bacon fat to barter for coal for our cooking stove.

That year, my sister Theresa, who was two years older, my one and a-half year younger brother Gert, and I stole coal from a freight train. Trains loaded with coal regularly passed Pulheim without stopping. Everyone in our village needed coal and wished for a chance to get some. Once several of the men in our village managed to have the coal train stop in the open field outside of Pulheim by illegally changing a railroad signal to *stop*.

The good news spread like a wild fire. We three children rushed with a wheelbarrow and a handcart to the train. Theresa and Gert climbed onto a coal wagon and threw the coal down as fast as they could. I gathered and loaded it. Around us other people were doing the same. Everybody was watching the signal, ready to jump off as soon as it changed. We also had to avoid being too close to the parallel train track in case a train approached from the opposite direction. No accident happened. Happy we returned home with our "fringste"[1] load of coal.

In 1946, Theresa and I were enrolled in the Ursulinen Schule, a school for girls in Cologne. For some bacon, my mother bartered a very nice leather school bag for me. It relieved a bit of my anxiety as I carried it proudly on my first day to the school. My parents had to pay tuition for us, which they also did with goods.

To get to school, Theresa and I had to travel by train to Cologne, get off at the main railroad station, and walk about ten minutes to our school. Only a small part of the prestigious school, founded in 1639, had survived the war. Consequently, too few rooms were available for the scheduled classes. To get the best use of the available space, one set of classes would use a room in the morning and another class would use it in the afternoon. The schedule was switched weekly to be fair to all students.

The changing schedule didn't make our commute to school any easier. Theresa and I frequently had very long waits, because few trains were running. Often the station platform was packed with people, who would push into the doors of the arriving trains or climb in through the windows. Men would stand on the outside steps of the train holding onto the bar by the door or sit on the roof of train cars during travel.

How had it been possible that we two ten and twelve year old schoolgirls got on the train? Regardless of the general distress, some of the adults would let us board the train before they fought their way on. It even happened that people lifted us in through a window.

At school we learned the required subjects, but optional lessons, such as art, music or gym, were frequently cancelled. Whenever the weather allowed it, we gathered in the schoolyard and cleaned bricks. Just like the rubble women, who worked in all the destroyed German cities, we each got a hand tool to knock the mortar from old bricks. The clean bricks were stacked into neat piles. They would be used to repair damaged classrooms or to build new ones.

⌐⌐

Today about 1,000 girls attend the Ursulinen School. They are taught Latin, English, French, and Russian. The school has exchange programs with schools in France, Israel, Australia and Italy.

Joseph, our Polish worker, who protected me, visited us twice in the 1980s.

---

1. For an explanation of fringsten read: Cologne; After the War.

Aftereffects

Asked if her childhood experience affected her life, Annemarie answers:

"As a child I got to know the incredible destruction caused by war. I will never forget this. I am against all wars. I will always condemn and despise warmongers. When I see the news reports from Syria I feel sick and enraged. Why can't the people learn from the terrible events of the World Wars!

One of the consequences of war is that many refugees are fleeing the combat zones in search of safety. I experienced how we left Pulheim and came to Rabertshausen for such a reason. Even though our journey to safety does not compare to the fate of most refugees in Germany or Europe, it provided me with an understanding of the plight of refugees."

Annemarie and her brother Franz passionately embrace the cause of the Syrian refugees in Germany.

Cologne

During the War

On the night of May 13, 1940, Cologne experienced its first air raid; the second raid followed June 18, and the third August 2, 1940. By the end of 1941, Cologne had been bombed one hundred times. Many buildings were destroyed—factories, houses, shops, and even three churches—and many people were injured or killed.

The inhabitants of Cologne lived in constant fear of further bombardments, fervently searching for ways to protect themselves. More air raid shelters were built because the existing ones could accommodate only 15,000 persons. Most people took refuge in their basements. To ensure that they were able to get out if their basement door was blocked by rubble, underground passages were constructed between neighborhood houses.

On the night of Sunday, May 30, 1942, the bombardments escalated. The Royal Air Force used all 1,000 bombers at its disposal at once.[2]

> "The vehemence of the attack, which lasted about 90 minutes and involved 540 ton of explosives and 925 ton of firebombs, was horrendous. Over 41,000 of the city's 250,000 homes were destroyed or damaged, 2,500 industrial enterprises were hit, 45,000 people were made homeless, 469 were killed, and over 5,000 were injured.

2. Möring, *Cologne Cathedral in World War II,* 51–52

As Annemarie had seen from afar, the houses of Cologne were burning, while the cathedral, tall and dark, seemed to be unscathed. Yet it also had been hit by countless firebombs, which started 42 fires. Due to the vigilance of the firefighters, they were extinguished before serious damage was done.

The massive air raid a year later on June 29, 1943, had a similar but even greater effect:[3]

> "... Bombs (were dropped) in three waves: first came the high-explosive bombs and firebombs, then came the blockbusters weighing between 2,000 and 5,000 pounds, and finally more high-explosive bombs ... Large parts of the city were in flames at the end of the air raid. The violent fire that raged in the city generated a storm with strong gusty winds."

People were burned alive in the firestorm. Over 4,300 persons died and over 230,000 were made homeless. By the end of the war 20,000 civilians had been killed by bombs.

Cologne, View of the Cathedral, the Old City, and the Rhine River 1945

After the War

When on March 6, 1945 the seventh corps of the first US-Army marched into the city, Cologne was a ghost town. The old city was 90 percent destroyed; mountains of rubble and bomb craters made streets impassible; all the bridges over the Rhine were destroyed; and there was no running water, gas or electric power. Less than 40,000 people were living in Cologne. Before the war Cologne had had 770,000 inhabitants.[4]

Many people who had fled Cologne returned during the following months. They lived within the ruins, in basements, improvised huts, and lean-tos. Protection against rain or snow was insufficient. But worst of all,

3. Ibid., 69

4. An exhibit of the City Museum of Cologne, "Das Neue Köln 1945–1995."

the people were starving. The shortages were immense and lasted a long time. The normal rules of commerce and business no longer applied.

In his famous Sylvester speech of December 31, 1946, Cardinal Joseph Frings, the archbishop of Cologne said the following:

> *"We are living in a time when those in need may take what they need in order to survive and remain healthy if they have no means of obtaining it by their own labor or by begging."*[5]

The people of Cologne took notice of this sentence. If you stole coal from an unguarded truck or train like Annemarie and her siblings had done, you would say: "I fringste some coal."

It had been assumed the industrial sector had been the main target of the bombing campaign, while the destruction of the residential area had happened more or less as collateral damage. This hadn't been true in Cologne. Seven times more bombs were dropped on residences than industries.[6] As soon as May 7, 1945, the Ford factory in Cologne was able to manufacture trucks; and in fall of the same year, it had produced 500 of them.

Rubble Women at Work

It was the task of the rubble women to clean the mortar from old bricks for reuse and to remove the rubble. Yet, no team of women with all their effort could accomplish such a task in Cologne. A former mining train was used to take the rubble out of the city where it was piled into eleven mountains. The largest one, named Hercules Mountain, was 237 feet high and was later transformed into a popular recreational park.

It took twelve years to rid Cologne of its rubble.

5. Dux, *Cologne in the Early Post-War Years*, 20.

6. Reinicke and Romeyk, *Nordrhein-Westfalen. Ein Land und seine Geschichte*, 23.

Rationing of Food in Germany

Annemarie reported that she and her family did not suffer from hunger during the post–war period, but she had heard that many families in Cologne did. This was also true for the people of Berlin and most other urban areas in Germany.

Since the beginning of World War II and all through the war, Germany had food rationing. Every month a person would receive a rationing card with coupons for the amount of each food group or food items he or she was allowed to purchase. For instance, if your grocer sold you one hundred grams of sugar, he would cut the equivalent coupon from your rationing card. At the end of the day he had to paste all coupons received on a large sheet and turn them in to receive a new supply of sugar. Restaurants also had to collect food coupons for meals served.

The *weekly rations* between September 1939 and October 1944 varied as followed:

2400–2225 g. bread, 500–250 g. meat, 270–218 g. fat.

The allowed amounts of food had been adequate, but decreased in November and December 1944 and throughout 1945, when food allocations were no longer sufficient.

After the war the victors, the United States, Great Britain, France and Russia, were responsible for the food supply for the German population within their occupation zone. Consequently, food rationing varied in the different zones.

North Rhine Westphalia was comprised of the big cities in the Ruhr Valley as well as Cologne and Düsseldorf belonged to the British zone. The British military government continued the established rationing system, but the allocations were far below previous levels and could change monthly or weekly. In addition, some food might not be available at all and when new supplies arrived, hungry people waited in line for hours.

The following is an example of *weekly rations* for the average consumer of the Rhine-Wupper County (located between Düsseldorf and Cologne) for the weeks June 25 to July 22, 1945:[7]

2000 g. bread, 100 g. meat, 75 g. fat, 100 g. sugar, 2000 g. potatoes, and daily a 1/8 liter milk.

Today the average German eats 81 g. meat, 140 g. fat, and 93 g. sugar *per day*, which is more than what had been available for the whole week at that time.

7. VHS Arbeitskreis Geschichte, *Langenfeld 1945–1949* ,98.

In terms of *daily calories*, the following has been reported: In July 1946 the average German received:

1,050 calories in the British zone, 1,270 calories in the American zone, and 880 calories in the French zone. In 1945 the nonworking adult had received 900 calories in the Russian zone, which was increased to 1,250 in 1946.

It has been calculated that the average person needs 2,400 calories daily. A diet of 1,800 to 1,400 calories signifies hunger and 1,400 or less signifies extreme hunger.

School Lunch Program

The insufficient nutrition after the war endangered the health of the growing children. To address this problem, the British military Government introduced a school lunch program for all children between the ages of six to sixteen years in Cologne on December 15, 1945. In March 1946, it was extended to the entire British zone. Each child received half a liter of soup daily. Leftover army rations were used for the program. Soon Sweden and Switzerland contributed to the effort and children between three and six years of age, who attended preschool or kindergarten, were also included.

The American military government distributed school lunches starting on April 14, 1947. Because former president Herbert Hoover had promoted the program, it was named after him. As late as May 1949, a school lunch program was introduced in the French zone. The Russian zone had none.

We (the author and her family) lived in the British zone. I (the author) remember my siblings and me walking to school with our lunch pail. During recess, a big tub of soup was carried into the classroom and each child received a portion. Often it consisted of oats, rice, cream of wheat or noodles cooked in milk made from milk powder. I liked them all. The pea soup was also good, but I detested the pearl of barley soup. My friend Hannelore's family had been refugees from East Prussia. For them the school lunch was a lifesaver. Hannelore had an extra large pail. After she had eaten her soup, she would go back for a second helping, which she took home for her widowed mother.

Ingrid, center, with the children of her Irish guest family

Chapter 3

I Sat on my Suitcase all Alone

Ingrid, born November 1939 in Hambach, Germany; with contribution by Ingrid's mother, born 1915

AT THE TIME OF Ingrid's birth, her father had been the forester of Hambach in the Eifel, a low mountain range in western Germany, close to Belgium. The forestry office and the living quarters of Ingrid's family were located in the main house of the moated castle of Hambach. The estate included adjacent stables, barns, and staff housing. Surrounded by an idyllic countryside, the castle and village of Hambach could have been a picturesque setting for a movie or a honeymoon. Yet in 1944, it became instead the site of vicious battles.

Hambach was situated eighteen miles from the city of Aachen, five miles from the town of Jülich, and just two miles east of the small river Rur, which marked the border between Germany and Belgium. Unlike further south where the West Wall[1] fortified the frontier, this part of the border was not protected. For this reason the Americans might be planning to advance here into the Rhineland. To prevent this, the German military started an

1. A system of defensive positions along the western border of Germany.

accelerated program to strengthen the border in August of 1944. Soldiers as well as civilians were ordered to build anti-tank barriers and trenches.

⤿

Ingrid's first childhood memories begin at this time.

In the summer of 1944, I was four years old and my brother Helge was five. Ohmchen, as we called our grandmother, was living with us in order to help our mother. Ohmchen enjoyed her time with us. Often she took Helge and me on long walks through the fields and nearby woods. Then she might exclaim: "How lucky we are to live in this beautiful countryside away from the cities and the sadness of war!"

As far as I knew, the war was somewhere in Russia, because that's where my father was fighting as a soldier. He wrote letters to my mother and sometimes she would read them to us aloud. "I would like to be home with you," he would write. It had been a long time since he had visited us.

Later in the summer, many German soldiers came to our village, but my father was not among them. Then a truck with workers arrived, who went to work at the border. Everyone from the village and the forestry office was asked to help dig ditches. My mother and grandmother were excused from the work, because Ohmchen had become ill. A large open wound on her leg did not heal. The doctor had ordered bed rest for her, and Mutti, as we called our mother, had to care for her.

After the workers left, more soldiers and tanks came. A huge military truck drove into the castle yard. The driver explained to my mother that a military dispensary would occupy our farm buildings. The same day, military personnel moved in and set up a field kitchen.

"We have a slaughter-house here," Mutti exclaimed. She wasn't pleased when stray cattle were driven into the yard and slaughtered everyday. At the time, many cows were wandering around unattended, because farmers at the border had left their farms to escape from the fighting. I thought all the new activities were very interesting. I slipped into the farm buildings and watched the cooks as they cut beef into mountains of cubes, chopped vegetables at lightning speed, or peeled potatoes into rings. They dropped everything into huge steaming kettles.

Mutti and Ohmchen did not like for me to hang out in the field kitchen. "I bet you will catch lice from these workers," Mutti predicted correctly. Fortunately, she noticed the infection immediately and treated me before the critters could attack other family members.

Next, our main house became a military field hospital. The military physician moved in with us and the rooms on the ground floor became hospital rooms. Mutti and Ohmchen assisted as nurses. I remember them holding a flask with alcohol and rushing with it along the hallway from room to room. Helge and I were not allowed to enter the patient rooms, as my mother worried that we might become infected or that the sight of injured soldiers would traumatize us. Of course, we wanted to know what was going on and tried to catch glimpses through half-open doors. We saw men with white bandages lying in beds.

For Helge and me, the activities in the field kitchen and makeshift hospital were new and exciting. Yet for the adults, they were signs that danger was fast approaching. My mother told me later how frightening these weeks in the late fall of 1944 had been for her. The wounded soldiers told her that the front line was retreating; it was moving closer and closer to the border every day.

"Will Hambach become the new battleground?" she wondered. She was very worried about our future and started to prepare for the worst. She buried some family treasures and arranged for transport of our furniture to a safe area. Because low-flying enemy planes were patrolling the border and shooting at vehicles, the truck with our furniture left at night without headlights. Even trains used only minimal lighting. This made driving at night very unsafe, and a terrible train collision occurred that destroyed the truck with our furniture and killed the driver.

About two weeks later, three women from our neighborhood came to us and asked Mutti, if she wanted to drive with them to Jülich to go shopping. They had heard that the department store had advertised a fantastic sale. All merchandise would be reduced. It would be a great opportunity to stock up on some items. They liked to go with Mutti, because she had a car. That was very rare. All private cars had been confiscated by the military long before. We were allowed to keep a car for the official use of the forestry office. Private use of the car was not allowed and the unofficial use of our allocation of gasoline would be considered "theft of national property," which might be severely punished. Also the low-flying planes made the trip dangerous. Mutti contemplated this and said no.

The three women were not discouraged by Mutti's refusal. They wanted to have some fun for once and on the 16th of November 1944, rode cheerfully by bike to Jülich. On that day the Allied military planned enormous air raids on Düren, Jülich, and a few other small towns in the area.

Jülich was bombarded not at night but during the early afternoon. Did the three women take shelter in the air raid bunker under the post office in Jülich during the bombardment? Nobody who sought safety in that bunker survived, because a mountain of rubble blocked its entrance. We never heard from the three women again. For Mutti, it was painful to imagine that she could have been in this shelter, slowly suffocating together with her neighbors.

Mutti had no time to reflect on what might have been. After the dev-astating bombardments, events rapidly overtook us. The injured people and all survivors of Jülich were immediately transported to safe places in Germany. The forestry office, the field hospital, the field kitchen, and all of Hambach were evacuated. Anyone without a way to leave was transported by the military. My uncle came with a truck and helped us pack.

Everything useful was loaded. My mother added 100 pounds of po-tatoes, carrots, smoked ham, and the fresh meat of a hastily butchered pig. Even three live geese accompanied us. Mutti believed that "The more food we have, the friendlier will be our reception."

Moving day was another exciting time for Helge and me. Everyone was rushing around, calling, ordering, moving, and carrying. No one was paying attention to us, and we too ran here and there wherever we saw something of interest to us. No one took the time to think about or tell us how much the move would change our lives; change them forever.

Ohmchen, Helge, and I squeezed between boxes, bags, and folders with essential papers, into the backseat of our little Volkswagen bug. Mutti sat in the passenger seat and the military physician drove the car. My uncle trailed behind us in the truck with our belongings. In front and further be-hind us rumbled ambulances and medical vehicles that belonged to the field hospital. Traveling with the medical convoy probably was the safest way for us to leave.

I remember how uncomfortable we were in the back seat. Ohmchen moaned because after the long strenuous day, her leg wound was hurting. I whimpered because my toes were numb and aching from the cold. Helge sat quietly in his corner. We soon fell asleep, exhausted from the excitement of the day.

Like the truck that incurred the fatal accident, we were driving without light. Later Mutti told us: "I remember the drive as the most dreadful night of my life. Again and again I heard low flying planes overhead and saw their flares, which lit up the skies like flashes of lightning. I assumed that the en-emy pilots saw us and were following the convoy. Would they shoot at us? I was totally overcome by fear—believing that any moment might be our last."

At midnight, after we had survived the most dangerous part of our journey without incident, we left the convoy and took the road to Euskirch-en, where the owners of a country estate were expecting us. We arrived early in the morning and received a friendly welcome. Later in the day we learned that they were reluctant to provide shelter for us.

"We really do not have room for four people and all your belongings," they argued gazing at the loaded truck. "And even Euskirchen is close to the fighting. We ourselves have been considering leaving the area. We think it will be much safer for you to take shelter further east," they advised us.

After a night's rest, we travelled on. A colleague and friend of my father lived with his wife and three children in Dattenfeld, Siegerland, a beautiful rural region in the middle of Germany, far away from the western border. They might be able to take us in.

Unfortunately, the small forestry house was already fully occupied. The parents of the forester had lost their home in Bonn, the city south of Cologne on the Rhine River, and had moved in with their son. The forester was sorry that he had to turn us away. He helped as much as possible. "You can store the things you don't need immediately in our barn," he offered. He also provided a home for our geese. But how about us?

After a couple of days he heard that the family Grimm in Eitdorf, Siegerland was willing to take us in. "They live in a large villa and will have space for you," the forester assured us. Happily we drove seven more miles to Eitdorf only to be disappointed again. The family of the big house offered us a room in the attic. Resigned, Mutti and Ohmchen furnished and fixed it for us. It had little insulation and they worried how we would be able to stay warm during the approaching winter.

We had to climb the steep stairs to the large storage attic; from there a door led into our room. Helge and I thought that the attic was very interesting. Hidden behind some old furniture we found something very new—a large, lovely dollhouse! Three stories tall, it had many beautifully furnished rooms. The dainty sofa in the parlor had red velvet cushions and the shiny little coffee table in front of it was decorated with a white lace coverlet. A delicate chandelier hung over the dining room table. In the bedrooms little lamps sat on each nightstand. Helge noticed an electric outlet at the side of the dollhouse. Could the lamps in the house be turned on? We pondered this question a long time.

I was in awe of the wonderful house and often sat in front of it, taking in the many details. I would have loved to play with it, but never touched the precious furniture.

One day the dollhouse was gone. "Did Santa take it?" I wondered. "Maybe he will bring it to me!" With all my heart I wished for it to come true. On Christmas Eve, I found a funny, cute ragdoll on the table where Santa had left our presents. I loved my doll at first sight, hugged her, and named her Roswitha. Yet, I did not forget the dollhouse. It remained my Christmas wish ever after.

Mutti had decided to butcher one of our geese for Christmas and had talked about it with Mrs. Grimm. "May I roast the goose in your kitchen? We can eat it together at dinner," she had asked. Mrs. Grimm accepted the offer. We had our Christmas feast in the elegant and cozy warm dining room of our host family. The shared meal spread goodwill. When in January Ohmchen's wound flared up again, Mrs. Grimm suggested that she stay in one of their bedrooms.

For Helge and me, Christmas passed too fast. The weather in January was cold and miserable. One morning when we woke up, we noticed we were all by ourselves. The house was quiet. Where was our Mutti? When would she return? We felt utterly alone. Helge rested his elbows on the windowsill and looked out over the deserted street in front of the house. I joined him. How long did we stand there side by side at the window and wait? An hour or even more? It seemed like an eternity.

My mother had left very early to buy bread in a neighboring village, where she had heard that the bakery would sell some bread that day. She had hoped to be back in a short time but waited in line for many hours. Upon returning home, she saw our little faces in the window from far away. Even today, ninety-nine years old, my mother has not forgotten our anxious looks and the relief on our faces as she came home to us.

Shortly thereafter a letter arrived from my Aunt Irene, my mother's sister and Ohmchen's other daughter. "We live on the estate Naundorf by Schmiedeberg, about eighteen miles east of Dresden," she wrote. "We have no air raids and we have enough food. Why don't you come here and join us?"

It was a tempting invitation. What should we do? We had all our things here. We had also experienced that four guests are rarely welcome. Mutti and Ohmchen talked it over and decided to separate. Ohmchen would travel with me to Aunt Irene's and Mutti would remain with Helge in Eitdorf. Temporarily Helge stayed with the forester family while Mutti accompanied Ohmchen and me on the difficult journey to Berlin.

⌒

Ohmchen, Mutti, and I got seats on a military evacuation train on its way to Berlin. Most of the passengers were old people evacuated from a nursing home. They had already been traveling for eight days. Apparently, it had been difficult to find a new safe home for them. We sat tightly squeezed between the old folks. In the dim light of our compartment, they looked like ghosts to me. To Mutti and Ohmchen, they were people in need. They were busy accompanying or supporting them to and from the bathroom or helping in other ways. Once I noticed that the old man across from me

grabbed my mother's skirt and wiped his nose with it, while Mutti was helping another frail man to get up.

During the night, dark shades covered the windows so the planes would
not see any light and would not bomb our train. We traveled a day and a night
before reaching Berlin. To our surprise and delight, the train stopped at the
small station of Berlin-Eichkamp. Right there stood Aunt Irene's house and
luck had it that her husband, my uncle Walter, was home. He had remained in
Berlin because he worked as a technician at Radio Berlin.

Uncle Walter was glad to travel with Ohmchen and me to his family in
Naundorf. Satisfied that all went well, Mutti said good-bye to us and made
the strenuous trip back to Eitdorf.

Uncle Walter, Ohmchen and I reached Dresden in the early afternoon.
It was a nice, sunny afternoon and Ohmchen encouraged us to look around
in the city. Many stores had sales. She took the opportunity to buy a nice
blue blouse for me. Then Uncle Walter hurried us to move on. After a short
ride with the local train, we reached Naundorf.

Aunt Irene and my three cousins happily welcomed us. They had been
waiting for us impatiently. I knew my cousins well. Soon we four girls ran
off to check out all their favorite spots in or around the old castle, which sat
high up on a slope surrounded by fields. I was glad to be in Naundorf. The
estate reminded me of our forestry office in Hambach, the home we had left
three months previously.

Two days later on the night of February 13 to 14, Uncle Walter, Aunt
Irene, Ohmchen, and we children stood on the tower of the castle. Far
away on the horizon we saw the deep red glow of fire rising into the dark
night sky. Dresden was burning. The Allied military had flown the largest
air raid ever seen over the city. An enormous firestorm enveloped everything and everybody. We couldn't have known it when we watched the
glow. Maybe Ohmchen had a premonition of what was occurring. "You
may never forget this," she said to us. I never did forget what I saw that
night when I was five years old.

The next day, people were fleeing from the still burning city. They
passed by us on the road at the foot of the hill. Always curious, we four small
girls ran down the hill to the edge of the road. Quietly we stood there watching the strange procession coming from Dresden. Looking down in front of
her, a woman slowly pulled a handcart. An old woman crouched in it. Blood
soaked bandages were wrapped about her feet and one leg. Her eyes were
closed and her head wobbled each time a wheel hit a stone. Was she asleep?

An old man shuffled along in a tattered fire-singed coat leaning onto a
stick. A group of three women walked close to me. Two of them were supporting the one between them, who turned her head towards me. It was wrapped

in what looked like a white turban. One of her ears and a cheek were deep red and raw. She stared at me with eyes that had no lashes or brows. I shuddered. I stood there motionless until the women disappeared. Then I turned and ran up the hill to the house, never stopping until I found Ohmchen.

A week later, the Russian troops arrived. The women were very afraid of them and hid in the trench underneath the castle. I joined them. Lying on my tummy at the edge of the trench I looked through the tall grass as a long procession of vehicles and soldiers moved up the winding road to the castle. A ladder wagon with Russian women had pots and pans hanging from it.

The Russians confiscated the estate and all of us living there were ordered to leave. The Russian soldiers and women seem to be in a good mood. They did not threaten or harm us. There was a big commotion of them moving in and us moving out. The friendly Russian cook even gave me a fat sausage. "Don't eat it!" Ohmchen ordered, alarmed. A big worm crawled out of the sausage.

⌒

Where would we be able to stay? We were a large family of seven people. Luckily, the housing office moved us into a house in nearby Schmiedeberg.

Uncle Walter did not move in with us. Instead he built himself a temporary shelter in the woods. He had heard that the Russian military police conducted night raids of German homes, taking away the men, who they sent to Russian labor camps. They especially looked for men with exceptional skills like Uncle Walter to work in the Russian industry.

Sometimes in the late afternoon we went with Uncle Walter to his hideout. He had made a shallow pit under a big tree that he had padded with straw and blankets. The tree protected him from the weather but he must have had additional rain protection. Uncle Walter slept in the woods for many weeks, perhaps months, and thus saved himself from imprisonment.

Slowly life became normal again. It was summer and we four girls played together as happily as ever. The one thing that was bad, terribly bad, was the constant hunger. Our portions for each meal were so small that they did not fill us up. We were always hungry.

Schools opened again in the fall. My cousin Helga and I entered first grade. We had to learn reading and writing in German and Russian. Consequently, we were taught the regular Latin letters and the Cyrillic alphabet. I found this very demanding and difficult. We had a long walk to and from school. I remember how hungry, weak, and tired I felt climbing the hill to our house.

Once I came home from school too tired to eat, even though I was very hungry. Exhausted, I put my head on the dinner table.

"Ingrid, sit up straight!" my aunt admonished me.

"You can't order me to do anything. You are not my mother!" I blurted out defiantly. Aunt Irene looked at me astonished and hurt. I knew that Ohmchen would have corrected me sharply and ordered me to apologize at once. But she wasn't home that day, because she was helping a sick neighbor.

In the evening when they were alone my aunt told Ohmchen about the incident. They talked it over and sorted things out. They both agreed that it was time for me to return to my mother. I had been separated from her an entire year.

We had received a letter from my mother in which she wrote how much she missed me. She reported what had happened to her and Helge since Ohmchen and I left:

"During the winter of 1945, Helge and I froze in the poorly heated attic room and were glad when we could move to Dattenfeld. The father of the forester had traveled to Bonn to look for items in his damaged house. While there, he was killed during a bombing raid. Since only the grandmother lived with them now, they had enough room for Helge and me.

In April, the American troops came to Dattenfeld. They caused no harm. However, the forced laborers, who were released from their camps, threatened us. They broke into our neighbor's house, tied up the old couple, and stole everything. We were afraid we would be burglarized next.

The forester and three of his friends decided to guard the house at night. One of them, who spoke English, went to the commander of the American unit stationed in town and explained our problem. The commander was sympathetic and promised to help us. He sent troops the same night for our protection. As the Americans approached the house they noticed the forester who was guarding it. Assuming he was a burglar, they shot him. This was tragic for several reasons. The forester, who was part Jewish, had endured constant harassment by the Nazis and was looking forward to a new life; he died due to a simple mistake.

Mutti ended her letter by writing: "I wish very much for my dear Ingrid to come home." She did not know how to reunite me with my family. This proved to be difficult.

⌒

After Germany's surrender, the four victors divided Germany into four occupation zones, which were governed according to the laws of the occupying nation. Dattenfeld in the Siegerland belonged to British zone and Schmiedeberg was in the Russian zone. Germans were not allowed to travel from one zone to another without a special permit. The Russians, who guarded their border with the British, were especially strict. An additional problem was that long distance train travel was limited due to the extensive damage incurred to important rail lines.

Ohmchen dared to make the journey with me to the West in the summer of 1946. We travelled with a Red Cross transport hidden under a blanket as we crossed the border. We reached the large transit refugee Camp Friedland in lower Saxony, in the American zone. I have forgotten the details of our travel, but remember Camp Friedland well. It was swarming with people walking, waiting, rushing, or resting. Ohmchen searched for a place for us to sleep at night, for a way to obtain food, and for news from my mother, who was coming to meet us. It was confusing and I noticed it was difficult for Ohmchen to find her way around the crowded place.

I was sitting on our suitcase when Ohmchen was called to the camp office. "Ingrid, I have to take care of things. Stay here and wait," said Ohmchen and disappeared in the rushing crowd. First I was glad to rest a bit, but then I got bored. I sat on the suitcase waiting and waiting. Many people streamed past me constantly, without paying any attention to me. Where was Ohmchen? Why didn't she return? I felt deserted and alone. Maybe Ohmchen was lost! Panic was about to grip me. At the same time, I noticed sharp hunger pangs.

I peeked into the bag Ohmchen had pressed into my lap when she left. In it was the paper bag of cookies, which Aunt Irene had given to Ohmchen for her journey to Berlin. I took the bag out and smelled it, yum! I opened it and tasted a tiny crumb, yum! I ate a cookie. It crumbled in my mouth with a wonderful buttery taste, yum! Would I be allowed to eat another one? I ate it and then another, and another until they were all gone. A little bit of my tiredness and sadness vanished with each bite. When I dropped the last little crumbs into my mouth, a sweet sense of contentment washed over me.

When Ohmchen returned after many hours, she was relieved to find me sitting on the suitcase the same way she had left me. Would she miss her bag of cookies? I think she had more important worries. Mutti was supposed to come soon and meet us. We were concerned that she would not find us among the many people. I think we waited several days.

Suddenly, my tall Mutti stood before us with a happy wide-open smile. With her strong arms she lifted me up into the air, kissed, and hugged me. Just as exuberantly she greeted Ohmchen, her mother. What a happy reunion! Life was good again. Full of energy, Mutti and Ohmchen took care of the next hurdles. Mutti and I would travel to Dattenfeld, and Ohmchen would travel to Berlin.

Helge and I were happy to see each other again. Yet my father was not there to be greeted. Nobody knew where he was. Mutti had received his last letter from Russian in February 1945. We had not heard from him since.

Slowly I became accustomed to home. It meant living with the widowed wife of the forester, her three children, and their grandmother. Instead of a family, we were a group of three women, five children, and three generations. Many people lived in similar units at this time. It probably made it easier to cope with the hardships of the post-war years. For me, there were drawbacks. Helge, who had been my buddy, liked to play with the energetic daughter of the late forester, who was his age. I couldn't keep up with them and felt left out. I missed my cousin Helga.

Mutti worried about me. She realized how malnourished, thin, and unhappy I was. Just then, a letter from Peggy, her Irish friend arrived. As an unmarried, young woman, Mutti had spent a year in Ireland. She and Peggy had become close friends. "Our government is sponsoring a program for malnourished German children to come here for a year.[2] If you have Ingrid participate, I would love to have her stay with us," Peggy wrote.

~

On March 23, 1947, I boarded an Irish Red Cross train with many other German children that took us to the English Channel. We crossed it, took a train through England, and finally a boat to Ireland. It was a long journey to an unknown land. Many children around me were crying and sobbing when our train left Frankfurt. I felt sorry for the girl next to me, and I let her hold my doll Roswitha to cheer her up.

I was not sad, but looked forward to the adventure. Mutti had told me all about Ireland, Aunt Peggy, her house, her small children, and the beautiful Irish countryside. She had taught me some English. I could say: Good morning, thank you, please, and a few other phrases. "English is not hard to learn," she had said. "You will know it in no time." I was sure I would. A photo that a reporter took of me in London was published in the paper; it showed me smiling. Because of my doll Roswitha, I got extra attention. When I was not holding her, Roswitha peeked out of my backpack and her tag said: "Roswitha looks out, looks into the big world around." Helge had made up the verse and had hung it around her neck to bless my journey.

My happy anticipation was not disappointed. My host family welcomed me warmly. Aunt Peggy especially loved and spoiled me. Hunger was soon forgotten. The food was plentiful and delicious. I did learn English very quickly. I loved Ireland and everything Irish. When a year later my worried mother met me at the Frankfurt airport, I spoke only English. Since she was fluent in English, she didn't mind. She listened to my stories and was delighted that I had had such a good time.

2. The Irish government sponsored Operation Cloverleaf for 400 needy German children.

On our trip back to Dattenfeld a strange incident occurred. When we had to change trains, my mother had to use the bathroom at the station. Once again I sat on my suitcase all alone, surrounded by strangers. Again, I waited and waited. Our train came and the people rushed in. I sat on my suitcase. Where was my mother? The train left.

Finally my mother came running towards me. The lock of the public toilet had jammed and wouldn't open. Mutti later recounted:

"I called for help. I screamed. Nobody heard me. I was desperate to get out. I put one foot on the hinge, the other on the handle and swung myself over the door. I am still astonished that I got over without falling and breaking a bone. What a relief to see you quietly waiting on the train platform."

During my stay in Ireland, my father had returned home from a Russian prisoner of war camp where he had been held for almost three years. Altogether he had been away for six years. He had missed six important years of Helge's and my childhood. I greeted him with joy. He should have been a total stranger to me, but he wasn't. He was my father. I was so happy to have a father. Like him, I had been away from home a long time. Maybe this allowed me to understand him. Soon a loving bond developed between us. Unfortunately, Helge did not share my sentiments. Helge never developed a close relationship with our father.

My father did not like to talk about his years in prison. He mentioned that a small book by Schopenhauer and poems he was able to recite by heart helped him. In his later life, he suffered from periods of severe depression. There is no evidence that the war or his imprisonment caused it. Nevertheless, it is likely that these experiences contributed to his depression.

Aftereffect

"Have your childhood experiences during and after the war affected your life?"

Ingrid reflects and then answers:

"I have a reoccurring dream about a little suitcase. I am packing it. It stands somewhere. I am looking for it. In my dream I know that I very much need my little suitcase. I have to be ready to leave any time.

I think deep down I harbor fears that make it difficult for me to relax. Maybe I made some important decisions too quickly because I was afraid that otherwise I would be paralyzed by fear.

Since my childhood, I suffer from symptoms that the war could have triggered. For instance, it easily happens that I hold my breath. I would have a headache in school and would tire sooner than other children. Later it was noted that my blood pressure shows extreme fluctuations when I am tired.

A clear consequence of the war and the difficult post-war years has been my insufficient elementary education. Several times I changed schools and each time I had to adjust to very different requirements. The school systems of East Germany, West Germany, and Ireland had completely different curriculums. As a result, I do not have a solid foundation in many subjects. One needs this to sort out new information with ease. I am always ready to learn something new. Learning is fun for me. Nevertheless, I sometime feel too much floats around in my brain. Does this make sense?"

Blackout Measure in Germany during World War II

A general blackout measure was enacted from dawn to dusk after the first air raids on German cities. The measure assured that cities, towns, and vehicles were not visible to enemy bomber pilots. The purpose of the blackout was to protect civilians at night from air raids.

Every window had to have black blinds or black curtains drawn before the light in a room was turned on. Streetlights or any other outside lights were not allowed. Cities were not permitted to have lighted advertisements or lighted shop windows. In the evening, special blackout wardens would patrol streets and neighborhoods, and fine "blackout sinners."

In some cities, school children received glowing decals that they wore at dark. The decals would protect children from traffic on their way to school during early winter morning hours.

Trains, streetcars, and automobiles had to follow blackout rules. Headlights could provide only the essential light needed for safe driving. All windows, except for the front window, had to be blacked out. No light was supposed to be visible from the outside. This measure made driving at night less safe. The number of accidents similar to the one reported in this story increased.

The German blackout measure posed a problem that the Royal Air Force soon overcame to the detriment of the German civilian population. Britain developed light-emitting flares that when dropped from an airplane, would hang in the sky, and then slowly float to earth, illuminating a wide area on the ground.

Jülich

Jülich is a small town with a 2,000-year-old history. Archaeological excavations give testimony to the settlement. The Romans called it Juliacum. It was their way station when traveling to Colonia Agrippina (Cologne) on the Rhine River. Later it became the Frankish town named Jülich.

In 1543, a large part of the town's buildings burned in a raging fire. Duke William V decided to rebuild Jülich in the style of an Italian Renaissance city.

In 1930 efforts to renovate the old center of Jülich were proposed. Extensive plans were made and finalized in 1942 but not implemented due to the war. Jülich had 12,000 inhabitants at the time.

On November 16, 1944, 487 American Halifax and Lancaster bombers flew to Jülich. Between 15:28 and 15:50 they dropped 3,994 high explosive bombs and 123,518 incendiary bombs onto the small town. Afterwards, Jülich was totally devastated, 97 percent of the houses were in ruins. The bridge over the Rur, the streets, and the rail lines were destroyed. The entrance to the air raid shelter under the post office was blocked by rubble. It became the mass grave of those who had gone there for protection. The same fate was suffered by shoppers in Düren, who had taken shelter in a bunker under the department store. There too, the entrance was buried under rubble, trapping the people inside.

Three weeks after the bombardment, Jülich became the battleground for American and German troops. At the end of the war, the ravaged ground that had once been Jülich, had 100 inhabitants. Everyone doubted that the town would or could be rebuilt.

Jülich no longer existed, but the detailed plans for its renovation had survived. These plans made it possible for the town to be reborn to its original splendor. Today Jülich enjoys cultural heritage protection. It has about 33,000 inhabitants.[3]

---

3. Stadt Jülich, "2000 Jahre Jülich."

Anna on her first day to school

Chapter 4

Anna Grows up Fast

Anna, born 1934 in Cologne, Germany

ANNA IS KNOWN AS Anita Schorn. She wrote and published her childhood memories in 2000.[1] Ms Schorn allowed me to write a shortened version of her story and to translate it into English.

Anna was six and her sister Margot was thirteen years old when their mother died unexpectedly of a heart embolism during childbirth in 1941. At the time their father, a well-known musician, had already been drafted into the military. To take care of Anna and Margot, the parental grandparents, and their grown daughter Aunt Ija moved into the children's house in Klettenberg, a suburb of Cologne. Grandma (Oma) lovingly replaced the mother the girls had lost so suddenly and Grandpa (Opa) took over the role of their absent father.

Anna remembers:

After my mother's death, my dear Oma became the most important person in my life. Oma was always there for me. We spent many hours

1. Schorn, *Anna—erwachsen vor der Zeit*, 5–158.

together. When Margot was in school, Oma took me along to the grocery store, the butcher shop, the open-air market and other errands. Like everybody else we used rationing coupons for all food or clothing purchases.

In the spring of 1941, I started school. For the occasion, Aunt Ija took the day off from work at the big department store Peters in downtown Cologne. She and Oma accompanied me to the local elementary school. Oma had put a big silk bow in my hair and I proudly carried my large colorful cone filled with candy.[2] My new backpack, made of leather, was strapped to my back. As I walked its contents: a slate, a pencil box, and a small box with a moist sponge, gently rattled and the little rag Margot had crocheted for me, hung out to the side, bouncing back and forth. I would use the sponge to clean the slate and the rag to wipe it dry afterwards.

Many excited children and their parents gathered in the schoolyard. I recognized some playmates from the neighborhood. We were asked to line up in two rows and two teachers were introduced to us, a young woman and a very old one with her hair pulled into a tight bun. "Hopefully I will get the young teacher," I whispered to Aunt Ija.

Indeed the nice young lady was my teacher. She asked each of us to say our name. She greeted us, told us about school, and read a funny story that made us laugh. Then a photographer took our pictures. Thereafter, school was out and I happily walked home with Oma and Aunt Ija.

⌒

Soon after the war with England had begun, Cologne experienced bombing raids, but the suburbs without any industry like Klettenberg, where we lived, were not targeted. Yet, already in the fall of 1941 some bombing happened in Klettenberg and the close-by suburbs of Sülz and Lindenthal. While Oma, Opa, Aunt Ija, and the other adults of our neighborhood became very worried and anxious, we children thought of it as something interesting and exciting. My friend Gernot and I ran over to the busy main street, the Luxenburger Straße. We stood at the edge of a deep crater, amazed by the hole a bomb had bored into the asphalt. The powerful explosion had torn up the streetcar line. Several feet of iron track arched into the air. Some multistoried buildings had been severely damaged. Two houses had the walls that faced the street partially demolished.

"Gernot, look, we can see into the apartments!" I called out.

"Yes, and there are bomb shrapnel scattered around. Let's gather them," Gernot replied. Among the broken window glass and the rubble from masonry, we found oddly shaped, shiny metal pieces, remnants of

2. It is customary in Germany that on their first day of school first graders receive a special cone filled with sweets, which they will carry to school with them.

exploded bombs. We collected several. At home I put my shrapnel into an old cigar case that served as my treasure box. Later I might show them to other friends or trade them.

A few houses from us lived the Rosenbaums, a friendly young couple. The nice Mrs. Rosenbaum always talked to me and sometimes she gave me five Pfennig (cents). I used them to buy my favorite candy, "Spinnknöpp", a specialty of Cologne, similar to chewing gum. All of a sudden the Rosenbaums were gone. At night I overheard Aunt Ija telling Oma: "The poor Rosenbaums have been taken away."

"Why?" I wanted to know."

"They are Jews," was her tentative answer.

"What are Jews? Who took them away?" I had more questions.

"You don't understand these things yet," was the answer I received then and several other times.

Later at our play corner, I heard two boys insisting that Jews smell bad. When I told Oma about it she looked at me seriously and said: "What nonsense! The Rosenbaums were very clean and orderly people. My darling, you mustn't believe the rubbish children blab about." Today it makes me incredibly sad to think that our friendly neighbors belonged to the six million Jewish persons murdered by the Nazi Regime.

⌒

On and off over this year Oma suffered severe stomach pains. She was hospitalized for a week, but the illness continued. Opa and Aunt Ija were very worried about her. I loved Oma very much but worried less, because in spite of how she felt, she carried on her housework and mothering me without complaining. She was always ready to listen to me and to care for me.

The year 1942 brought the good news that our dear father (we called him Vati) would marry a young woman named Brigitte from Deutsch Krone, a small town in Pomerania, Germany. Margot and I didn't think it was good news at all. We fretted that perhaps this woman would be an evil stepmother. Margot was especially upset. Oma did her best to reassure us. "It will be for the best, believe me." But I sensed that even Oma was bothered by the fact that Brigitte was very young, just six years older than Margot.

In July, Opa and Oma traveled to the wedding and afterwards they, Vati and his new bride came home to us. "Well, Anna, here is your new mother," said Vati. Shy and embarrassed, I shook Brigitte's hand and curtsied. My new mother was nice and friendly, but as I silently observed her, I decided that my real mother had been far lovelier.

Vati's holiday soon came to an end. He had to return to his unit. He told us that the officer of his unit knew of his songs from the radio and recordings. He wanted him get a band together and perform for soldiers to boost their moral.

Brigitte stayed with us. She tried very hard to win Margot's and my confidence. She very much wanted to be a mother to us. Of course it took time. I think I warmed up to her first. Margot found it very difficult to relate to Brigitte.

In early 1943, the war became worse for us. Like other parts of Cologne, Klettenberg was bombarded almost every night.

As soon as the sirens screeched, we ran into our air raid shelter in our basement. Each one of us had a small emergency suitcase packed with important documents, some clothes, and special treasures that we took to the shelter. I never forgot my doll Ines and my doll suitcase.

We sat close together in the small shelter. Aunt Ija constantly whimpered and cried out loud when she heard the awful hissing sound of an approaching bomb and its loud detonation thereafter. Margot covered her ears tightly, desperately blocking out the noise, and I cried in terror. Brigitte, my new stepmother, would cradle me in her arms and sooth me. She had little patience with Ija.

"Pull yourself together, Ija. You'll drive us all crazy with your constant blabbering," Brigitte scolded her.

Once again we were sitting in our shelter. Grandma was quietly praying with her hands pressed together. "The bombs are closer today," Grandpa worried. Suddenly we heard the high-pitched piping noise of a bomb in flight and an extremely loud detonation very close by. An enormous thud made our house tremble. Mortar rained down from the ceiling and crumbled off the walls. Then silence. We sat still as if paralyzed.

We heard the faint call of our neighbor. Margot jumped up, ran down the narrow hallway and opened the iron door to our neighbor's basement.

"Are you alright?" called our neighbor.

"Yes, we are. How about you?" Grandpa replied.

"That was a close call, wasn't it!"

"It sure was."

The brief exchange took the edge off the fear that had grabbed us. The passageway between us and the neighboring basement had made it possible. We had installed it following the Fire Marshall's advice. It was a precaution that provided us with an emergency exit in case a bomb hit our house and rubble blocked our basement stairs.

Finally, the all-clear signal sounded. We rushed upstairs and starred at our living room. It looked as if an earthquake had hit it. The glass of our big windows overlooking the street and garden had been broken into a thousand shards that were scattered all over the floor. The lamp dangled crookedly from the ceiling. The cabinet doors had been flung open and some of the porcelain had fallen out.

In the morning we found out what had happened during the night. I was the first to see it. My friend Ingeburg came to the door and told me about it. Together we ran across the street and there it was — a huge crater in the ground. We starred down into the deep hole. An enormous bomb had bored itself into the soft dirt of the neighbor's front yard. How lucky we had been that the bomb had not fallen on any of the houses, maybe our house!

After this close call, we decided that during the next air raid we would go to the neighborhood bunker about 200 yards from our house. We would be safer there than in our basement shelter. It was a good plan, but how would we get there in time before it was full and the door was closed? We had heard that often the bunker did not have enough room for all the people wanting to get in.

Grandpa solved our problem. He had noticed that the signal lights from the nearby railroad tracks would go out before the sirens sounded. From Aunt Ija's room upstairs, one had a good view of the tracks and the signals.

$$\backsim$$

It became Margot's and my job to watch the lights. I would watch early in the evening; Margot's turn was later at night. When it got dark, I would put on several dresses on top of each other. Oma insisted that this way I would have enough to wear in case our house was destroyed by a bomb. So all bundled up, I went to Aunt Ija's room.

"Anna, remember not to turn on the light," Grandma reminded me. I knew that light was not allowed to shine outside, because it would show the bomber pilot the location of our house.

Quietly I sat by the window in the dark room and watched the railroad lights. I was aware of the importance of my job. I was responsible for our safety. Still, it was boring and difficult to stay awake. Again and again my eyelids dropped, and I had to arouse myself. I was glad when Margot came and shooed me away. With all my many layers of clothes on, I fell asleep in my bed. We all slept this way.

I remember well the night when I was sitting on my perch and suddenly the signal lights went dark. "The lights went out!" I yelled and raced down the stairs. The door of the kitchen and of the living room flew open.

"Good job, my watchman," praised Opa. We grabbed our bags that had been sitting in the hallway, and rushed off to the bunker. We were halfway there when the sirens wailed.

Grandpa leaned his shoulder against the heavy iron bunker door and pushed it open. Its dimly lit hallways leading to different-sized rooms were already teeming with people, and more were coming in behind us. The warden at the door told us to find a place. Pulling my ear a little, he cheerfully asked: "Have you already slept, little girl?" "I catnapped a little with one eye closed," was my reply and everyone around us laughed.

As the big door closed all gaiety disappeared. Frightened and quiet we sat in our places. Once in a while someone whispered. We listened. Through the thick concrete of the bunker we heard the muffled noise of planes and bombs.

The woman across from me gently cradled her little boy and whispered to the woman beside her: "It sounds like a squadron of bombers. I hope they will not carpet bomb us."

"What is a carpet bomb?" I asked Oma softly.

"It means that many planes drop bombs all at once."

We were always apprehensive when we walked home after the all-clear. Would our house still stand? Or would we come home to rubble and ashes? This time the house was unscathed.

﹌

Due to the constant bombardment of Cologne and other cities, the German government decided to evacuate all children from the endangered areas to the countryside. A letter came to us from the city of Cologne saying that a children's transport would take me to Saxony.

The thought that I had to leave my family was unbearable to me. I cried, hollered, and protested.

"Anna, you will be safe in Saxony. No bomb was ever dropped there!" Brigitte tried to reassure me.

"Think of it as a vacation," suggested Aunt Ija.

No one and nothing could persuade me. I did not want to leave and dreaded the moment.

If it could not be helped, and I had to go, I wanted Margot to go with me. But this was not possible either. Margot was fourteen years old and different rules applied to her. I was sad; I was very sad, and very upset. That night I crawled into Margot's bed. "Please let me sleep with you. I am so scared," I whispered.

Away from Home

I left home on a rainy day in April. My luggage was a small suitcase with my clothes and my big doll Ines. A tag with my name, address, and the destination of Zwickau, Saxony dangled from my neck. As I hugged Aunt Ija and grandpa, he said: "Anna, you have always been my sweetheart; now be a brave girl."

Grandma, Brigitte, and Margot went with me past my damaged school building and some flattened houses to the streetcar stop. In the twilight we saw the outline of the approaching streetcar and its thin beam shining through the slot in the front (a blackout measure).

The platform at the train station was filled with excited children and their chaperones. A woman dressed like a nurse and a girl in the uniform of the Bund Deutscher Mädchen (Association of German Girls) greeted me and took my hand. I pulled myself free, ran to Grandma sobbing and hugged her tightly. I did not want to let go of her. It would be the last time I saw her. When it was time to say goodbye to Margot, we fell in each other's arms and cried.

The train pulled out into the night. We departed late, because at night, trains were safer from bombing raids. Early the next morning we arrived in the town of Zwickau where two busses took us to the small town of Crossen an der Mulde, Saxony.

Tired after a night of travelling with little sleep, we were ushered into a classroom and sat down on the benches. A stern woman gave a short speech. Next the classroom door opened and a swarm of adults entered. They walked between the benches looking at us. An older couple stopped in front of me. They seemed to feel sorry for me sitting there with my tear strained face and my big doll Ines. The woman bent down and looked at my nametag. "So, you are Anna," she said with a nice smile. Turning to her husband, she said in her Saxon dialect: "Sure, Vati, it will be her or no one." He turned to me and asked in a friendly voice: "Would you like to come with us?" I nodded. I trusted them at first sight. The gray-haired woman had a lovely face and the man had the same mustache as Grandpa.

I had a wonderful time in the little country town. Aunt and Uncle Schreiber, my loving hosts, lived in the spacious apartment of an old fashioned house next to fields and meadows. I slept in the room of their grown and married daughters and was allowed to play with all the games, dolls, and puzzles they had left behind.

I helped Aunt and Uncle Schreiber in their garden, played with the neighborhood children at the creek, learned to speak Saxon, and felt well and happy.

Not all the evacuated children had found a nice home like I had. One of the girls from Cologne told me that she was home alone all day long, while her host parents worked in their grocery store. At night she had to paste rationing coupons onto large sheets, which she found tedious and boring.

For me school was boring. I was repeating second grade because there was no room for me in third grade. The little village school was overflowing with the newcomers from Cologne.

The Schreiber's were sad when my half-year with them came to an end. I was sad too, but I also looked forward to seeing my family again. But where was my family? My father had been transferred by the military to the south of France. Margot had been sent to a farm by the North Sea to do her obligatory year of household training. Only Grandpa and Aunt Ija lived in our house in Klettenberg. My dear Grandma had had an operation shortly after I left and had died from it. My stepmother Brigitte and my newborn half-sister Dagmar lived with her mother in Deutsch Krone, Pomerania away from the bombardments of Cologne. I too would live there. Aunt Schreiber traveled with me by train to Deutsch Krone and visited for two days before returning home.

⤶

Deutsch Krone[3] in West Pomerania is a small town of about 15,000 inhabitants situated between two beautiful lakes. On the second floor of the house at Scheerstraße 1, I lived with Brigitte, Baby Dagmar, and Omi Luschei, as I called Brigitte's mother. Brigitte's father, Opa Luschei, worked for the military administration and was seldom home.

Soon I felt at home in my new surroundings. I loved the Pomeranian winter with lots of snow and ice. Brigitte gave me her old sled, and whenever possible I sledded with the neighbor children or scooted on the ice.

At home I enjoyed playing with my little stepsister Dagmar.

As Brigitte had told me before I had left Cologne, no planes had dropped a single bomb either in Thuringia or here in Pomerania. I had forgotten all about them, when sad news arrived from Cologne. Aunt Ija wrote that our house in Klettenberg had been destroyed. A huge bomb had hit our neighbor's house and the resulting air pressure caused our house to collapse. It was all rubble except for the basement. Fortunately, Grandpa and Aunt Ija had moved to a small apartment outside of Cologne just weeks before.

Brigitte read the letter to me and sighed: "Our home in Cologne was destroyed; we have not heard from your Vati in weeks. What terrible times we live in!"

3. Today Walcz in Poland.

Sadness and fear gripped me.

My gloomy mood did not last long. I was attending school and worked hard to catch up with what I had missed in Crossen an der Mulde. Spring came and a dry warm summer followed. My friends and I enjoyed ourselves at the pool. Best of all, Margot joined us in June after her farm program ended. I was happy to be with her again. We went swimming together and I proudly showed her how I had taught myself to swim. At the end of play days with friends, I would share my news with Margot.

In the fall of 1944, young soldiers made trenches and tank traps close to our house. "Why?" we wondered. "Would there be fighting here in Deutsch Krone?" We hoped not.

Winter approached and with it Christmas. We had a simple but festive celebration. A few days later the holiday spirit was chased away by bad news about the war. The German army had been retreating from a Russian assault. Each day the fighting was moving closer to us.

Omi Luschei, Brigitte, and Margot would listen intensely to the radio and find the location of new fighting on a map that was always spread open on the living room cabinet. Often they would whisper the latest military advances to each other, because they did not want me not to worry, but of course I did. The tone of their voices told me that something dreadful was approaching, and fear crept inside me.

I saw sad refugees with their bundles coming through our town. They headed west fleeing the Red Army.

Fleeing

A few days later, Opa Luschei came home with a big suitcase. His workstation at the German-Polish border had been closed because of the advancing Russian military. He had heard terrible news about the treatment of German civilians by Russian soldiers. He insisted that tomorrow we pack all we wanted to take and leave the following day.

"But why such a hurry? We didn't get an official notice that we must leave our town, " Brigitte objected.

"Brigitte, by that time it will be to late to leave. Listen to me. You have to leave. Now it is possible that you will get seats on the train. When every one leaves, there will be pandemonium, trust me."

Opa Luschei was right; he had convinced us.

The next morning we started packing, which wasn't easy because Omi Luschei and Brigitte didn't want to part with many of their things. We could only take as much as we could carry and each item had to be chosen carefully. It was my job to take care of one and a-half year old Dagmar. This proved exhausting. Dagmar loved all the commotion and had fun pulling out what had just been placed in a suitcase.

That night I had bad dreams about Russians who looked like monsters and about soldiers fighting. I had never seen a Russian soldier, but all the nervous talk made me fear them.

It was still dark when we got up and ate our breakfast the next morning. Omi Luschei cried. All her life she had lived here; this was her home and now she had to leave —maybe forever. Opa Luschei put our luggage on the sled and walked with us to the train station. He would stay one more day, take care of things, and leave the next day. We would meet him again in Cologne.

In -4 degree Fahrenheit we and many other people waited on the train platform, stamping our feet and huddling together to stay warm. When we talked, we could see our breath like tiny clouds floating between us. When we finally heard the train come, Omi Luschei and Brigitte cried saying good-bye to Opa Luschei.

Luck had it that the door to an almost full train car stopped right in front of us. We all got in and people moved together giving Omi a place to sit with Dagmar on her lap. Margot and I sat on our suitcase.

"See you in Cologne," Opa Luschei called and waved as our train left the station.

Many more people had gotten in after us; even standing room was tight. We traveled all day. Sometimes the train would stop somewhere and we worried why. We were relieved when it continued after each pause. When I had to go to the bathroom, I had trouble getting there. One time people lifted me up and passed me from one passenger to the other.

Once a murmur went through the train. "We just passed the Oder," someone announced the good news. We believed that the Oder River would stop the Russian troops and we were safe. A few hours later the train stopped. Everyone had to get off, and we were asked to go to a nearby refugee camp. We were treated for lice even though we did not have any; we were given some soup and slept on straw mattresses.

The next morning an old bus took us to the village of Hildebrandtshagen, where we were assigned to stay with families. Brigitte, Dagmar, and I received a nice room in the house of a friendly elderly couple. Omi Luschei and Dagmar were sent to an estate, where they lived in a small attic room.

We stayed here for the next three months. I think we felt lucky to be in the countryside and not in Cologne, where the air war continued the destruction of the city. Yet, we had not escaped from the Russians. They did cross the Oder and soon would occupy our area. Fear spread. What should we do?

We had heard that people in town suffered less from the occupation than people in the countryside. We packed quickly and traveled the next day to Grimmen, the nearest town.

⌒

Grimmen was crowded with people coming, going or passing through. Horse drawn refugee wagons, refugees on foot, German military vehicles, and civilians from the area all mingled in the city square and streets.

At the housing office we were assigned to a house on a side street owned by two elderly sisters. They felt sorry for us, took care that each of us had a bed, and they let us use their kitchen. We quickly felt at home.

I would often do our food shopping in Grimmen. One morning I was sent to buy milk at the creamery, when I noticed a throng of people in front of the warehouse next to it. German soldiers were standing on the warehouse ramp passing out food.

I slipped through the crowd to the front. A soldier saw me, and with a big smile placed a large, round cheese into my outstretched arms. It was so heavy, it made my knees buckle a bit. Holding my gift tightly pressed against my chest, I wiggled away from the people, and rushed home as fast as I could.

"Next to the creamery they are giving away food! Hurry!" I yelled out of breath, as I stormed in with my cheese. Brigitte and Margot ran there and got a fifty-pound bag of brown sugar. For all our next meals we would have cheese and a slice of bread loaded with brown sugar.

Brigitte was not happy. "The soldiers are cleaning out their storage. This means they are leaving. What will happen to us?"

A few days later, I was sent to the bakery to buy bread. As usual, I had to wait in a long line in front of the store. Suddenly, someone called out, "The Russians are coming! The Russians are here!"

The line dissolved. People scurried away in all directions. I was pushed this way and that way. Not knowing what to do, I ran down a side street. But then, I stopped and walked back to the main street corner.

I hadn't heard any shots or seen fire. I slipped into the entrance of a house. A dangerously loud rattling sound made me anxious and curious at the same time. From the edge of the entrance, I peeked down the street. I saw tanks turning into the road and proceeding in my direction. My heart raced. The Russians were coming! It was too late to run home. I crouched down and made myself small—maybe invisible.

The Russian tanks rolled closely past me. After them marched men with machine guns. I was amazed that the Russian soldiers looked like people, people in uniforms.

I heard a creaking window being opened above me, and a white flag was pushed out. I realized I had to warn my family. Maybe they did not know that the enemies had arrived. I had to force myself out of my safe hiding place. I jumped up and raced home!

"The Russians are here. I saw them!"

How would the five women protect themselves from the victorious troops? Because Brigitte and Margot were the most endangered, we had to find a hiding place for them. Together we figured out a plan. Behind the house was a shed. Its steep roof met the house gable at an angle, so that the open attic space of the shed was hidden from view. We put a long ladder against the shed, and with blankets and pillows Brigitte and Dagmar made beds for themselves in there.

As it got dark Brigitte and Margot climbed into their loft. Omi gave them a tin plate and spoon to clank when they wanted to come down. Then she took the ladder away, and hit it in the shed.

Later at night we heard loud music blaring and hoarse singing. "The Russians are celebrating their victory," explained Omi.

The next morning when Brigitte and Margot were still sleeping in their hiding place, the doorbell rang and someone banged at the front door. Miss Mertens, one of the older sisters that owned the house, opened the door and four Russian soldiers with guns stormed in. Their leader stopped in front of Omi Luschei and asked:

"Where soldier?"

"Nix soldier!" stammered Omi and pointed to both of us.

"Where Frau[4]!"

"Nix Frau, only old Babuschka[5]!" answered Omi pointing to herself.

The leader ordered a search. The men stripped the beds, looked under them, moved the couch, ran to the other rooms of the house searching on and on. Dagmar started crying and I tried to comfort her. The soldiers did not find what they wanted and left the house.

What would happen if the soldiers came during the day when they were in the house, Brigitte and Margot wondered? Just in case, they wore old tattered clothes, pulled a head scarfs low to obscure their faces, and painted wrinkles on their forehead and cheeks.

In the late afternoon of the third day of occupation, the doorbell rang several times and again Miss Mertens opened the door. A Russian officer in a perfectly clean uniform and several soldiers stepped in. The officer glanced at Brigitte and walked into the next room. Margot was sitting there

4. Woman in German.

5. Grandmother in Russian.

at the sewing machine without painted wrinkles and headscarf. Her wavy, dark blond hair framed her face, softly lit by a small lamp. She was so concentrated on her work that she did not look up until the officer was standing right in front of her.

Then something extraordinary happened. The Russian man pointed to her sewing, smiled, and said something in Russian. He took off his right glove and courteously shook Margot's hand. Margot sat quietly and looked at him calmly with her dark eyes. The officer looked at the room, lifted his hand to a salute, and left the house with his men.
Astounded we looked at each other.

"Strange," Margot said with wonder, "I did not feel one bit of fear."

This time all went well, but now the soldiers knew that two young women lived in this house. The next time may turn out very differently.

↩

The next time was at night. I was helping Omi do the dishes by candlelight. We heard wild banging at the front door. Without thinking, I went to the door and unlocked it. A stinking, drunken soldier pushed me to the side; he swayed as he walked into the kitchen to Omi.

"Uri! Uri[6]!" he roared.

Omi hastily took off her golden wristwatch. He grabbed it out of her hand. He already had four watches on his arm. The soldier pushed Omi into the chair.

"Where Frau?" "Frau!" he demanded.

"Nix Frau! Only Babuschka," answered Omi with a shaky voice. Swaying to the left, the Russian pulled his pistol out of its holster and pushed it harshly against Omi's chest.

I starred at the gun frozen in fear.

"Where Frau!" he hollered.

Omi shook her head and shrieked out in desperation and fear: "Nix Frau! Only old Babuschka!"

With her white hair and ashen face, Omi looked frail and very old in the dim light. The soldier hesitated a moment, pushed her with the gun barrel, turned, and staggered out of the door.

I had watched it all terror stricken, unable to move. Now I jumped up and locked the door behind the intruder. I ran to Omi and hugged her sobbing: "Its all my fault. I let him in!"

"No, my child," Omi reassured me with a quiet voice. "If you had not let him in, he may have broken in with force. We were lucky, after all."

6. watch.

The next day, Brigitte, and Margot found safety in a guarded freight train. They lived there in very primitive conditions but it was safer than with us.

A few days later the long awaited news arrived: The war was over. On May 8, 1945, Germany had capitulated unconditionally.

Life became more normal and less dangerous for women. Brigitte went to the military occupation government to ask about possible safe travel to Cologne. She was told that the city was nothing but a heap of rubble. Instead of going to the West, people were encouraged to return to the Eastern provinces. Conditions had improved there, she was told.

What to do? Omi, Brigitte, and Margot decided that Omi would travel with Dagmar and me back to Deutsch Krone, and Brigitte and Margot would make their way to Cologne. As soon as they had found a place to stay, they would have Omi, Dagmar, and me come too.

I had not been asked and did not like the plan at all. I wanted to go to Cologne, but most of all I wanted us to stay together.

"Please, let us all go to Cologne or to Deutsch Krone," I argued and begged. But the three grown-ups had made a decision and would not listen to me.

Living as Refugees in Deutsch Krone (Walcz)

Sad and unhappy after saying good-bye to Margot and Brigitte, I sat with Omi and Dagmar on the train to Deutsch Krone. The train was nearly empty; only one other woman sat in our compartment. Omi talked to her and shared how much she was looking forward to being home again.

Arriving in Deutsch Krone, Omi's good mood faded away. The train station was crowded with people wandering about, congregating in groups or sitting on the floor next to their luggage and talking—talking in Polish. Instead of returning home, we seemed to have entered a foreign country.

Omi allowed me to check out her apartment, while she and Dagmar stayed with our luggage at the station. On my way, I passed houses with damage from shelling and a few that had been destroyed. All the houses on Scheerstraße were still standing and people lived in them. Some people talked in a strange language and I realized they too were Polish. No one paid attention me.

A bullet-riddled, wrecked tank stood on the lawn beside our building. The front door was missing, and the house seemed empty. I stepped into the hallway and listened. It was all-quiet. I looked around. The hallway and stairs were strewn with paper, trash, and dirt. The banister of the stairway had been ripped out and lay on the ground. Quietly, I sneaked up to our apartment. Its rooms were eerily bare. All furniture, carpets, curtains, or pictures were gone. Even the bathtub was ripped out. Dust flew in through the broken windows. Everywhere there was dirt and trash. Nothing reminded me of the nice home we had left four months ago.

I tiptoed through the whole house. It looked the same everywhere. Without being seen, I stepped out and ran back to the train station. When I told Omi what I had seen, she wept.

Where would we live now?

The camp for German refugees and returning Germans was in my old school building. It was full and only after Omi's pleading did we get two straw mattresses that at night we put in the middle of the otherwise totally occupied room.

The hygiene of the camp was disastrous; the toilets were clogged and unusable. All the people in the camp had head lice. After only a day, we too were scratching our heads.

Once a day a kettle with some sort of soup or stew was brought into the courtyard and people lined up for their share. That was all the food provided for the day. Every day Omi would go with us and look for something to eat. In the schoolyard the women had made a small fire ring with bricks. Omi cooked dandelions, nettles or other weeds as vegetables or made nettle tea. We were happy if we found some berries or fruit in neglected, overgrown gardens.

It got worse; a dysentery epidemic spread in the camp; many small children did not survive. Almost daily small wooden coffins were carried out of the building. To prevent infection, we stayed away from the camp as much as possible during the day. But then Omi worried that some of our few possessions might be stolen while we were gone.

⌒

"God help us, our Dagmar is sick! She has a fever and diarrhea," Omi cried out one night. "Anna, stay with her, I have to find the physician."

As we had feared, the physician's diagnosis was dysentery. "I am sorry, I have no medication right now," she told us. "Give her plenty of boiled water, so she won't dehydrate and give her nothing but oatmeal mush to eat." The physician gave Omi a note to get oatmeal from the kitchen.

Omi did as she was told, but Dagmar's condition deteriorated rapidly. Like a weak newborn baby bird she lay in Omi's arms. Stomach cramps made her curl up and instead of stool she eliminated bloody mucus. I was thinking of the small coffins and did not want to leave her side.

Day and night Omi cared for Dagmar. To bring her fever down, she put a cool wet cloth on her forehead and wrapped some around her calves. To relieve her cramps she placed a warm moist towel on her belly.

That night for the first time I had the terrifying nightmare that would stay with me for many years. A Russian soldier threatened a woman with a pistol. In my dream I could not recognize the woman, but I knew she was Omi. I watched as the soldier pulled the trigger and the shot rang out. Then I would sit up in bed screaming.

On the third day of Dagmar's sickness, Omi rummaged through her luggage. She pulled out my pretty embroidered Sunday dress, which had been Margot's first communion dress, altered to fit me, one of her dresses, and her golden brooch; she rolled them into a bundle.

"Stay here, Anna. I will go to the Polish market and get some food," she whispered to me and left. In exchange for the precious bundle, she returned with two handfuls of soup bones, half a loaf of bread, and two eggs.

With the bones and some herbs, Omi cooked a nourishing broth. With a spoon Omi would patiently feed the broth to Dagmar. A miracle happened. Slowly, but steadily Dagmar got a little better. Omi cooked the bones several more times. Everything that we could spare she took to the Polish market and exchanged it for food.

After twelve days Dagmar was still pale, weak, and nothing but skin and bones, but her eyes shone brightly, and she smiled again. How happy and relieved I was! Omi and I knew that Dagmar had survived.

The illness had weakened Dagmar so much that she had to learn to walk again. Even holding her head up when Omi carried her was difficult at first. On one of our walks I found an old baby carriage that Omi had repaired.

When I took Dagmar for walks in the baby carriage, Omi would go to the train station to find out about trains going west. A few times a week a train with German refugees passed through the station without stopping. Daily some trains with mostly freight cars stopped and throngs of Polish and Russian people would get on.

"We could mingle with them unnoticed," Omi thought.

"Anna, tomorrow morning we will leave here for good." I was excited when Omi shared her decision with me. Maybe in a few days we would be in Cologne.

Traveling West

In the morning we said good-bye to the friends we had made at camp, loaded our luggage into the baby carriage, and walked to the train station. Like the Polish people around us, we sat down on the station platform and waited. The first train that stopped carried Russian soldiers and no one boarded the train. One of the soldiers ran over to us and placed something wrapped in paper in Dagmar's little hands and then jumped back on the train. Omi unwrapped a cold boiled potato.

"Unbelievable!" she marveled at the friendly gesture.

After a long wait, another train arrived that had several low, open freight cars with people sitting on the platforms.

"Anna, let's get on," Omi decided and helped me climb in. A Russian militiaman in uniform helped Omi lift the baby carriage up.

"Please, sit next to us," Omi whispered to him in German. The Russian looked at her questioning and did indeed sat down beside us. Omi whispered to me: "Let's not talk any German and see to it that Dagmar is quiet." Fortunately, Dagmar soon fell asleep.

I knew we were in a dangerous place. The women at camp had told us stories about how Germans were robbed and killed. Some dirty men, dressed in rags that sat not far from us kept looking at our luggage. I believed that the presence of the militiaman next to us kept them away.

The train travelled slowly. At times it stopped, some people got off and others climbed on. For miles and miles furniture could be seen standing along the tracks—chairs, tables, sofas, cabinets, even a piano. Pointing to it, I looked questioning at Omi. "All things the Russian soldiers took out of homes. They will be shipped to Russia," Omi whispered into my ear.

In the evening more and more people left the train. When it was dark the train stopped and everyone jumped off and scattered. The Militiaman told us "gefährlich"[7] in German indicating that we too should get off, and he helped us. Suddenly he grabbed our small suitcase and disappeared with it.

"Omi, he robbed us," I sobbed and Dagmar cried too.

"Don't worry, we did not lose much," Omi comforted us. "Only Dagmar's featherbed and her potty were in the suitcase."

We saw some tall bushes, parked the baby carriage in front of them and crawled in. Hidden by the green branches, we lay down on the soft dry ground. Omi put her arms around us; from far away we heard some sounds and cries, and then we fell asleep.

---

7. Dangerous.

Early in the morning we woke up. I pushed the branches aside. Our baby carriage was there, but the train was gone!

On a track not far from us stood a long freight train. Some of the cars sliding doors were open and we notice movement inside. In the morning mist we walked over to the last car. At the narrow door opening stood a woman looking suspiciously at us. She and Omi stared at each other.

"Deutsch?" Omi asked hesitantly.

"Yes, we are German refugees," the woman answered and her frown disappeared. She told us that they had been traveling for many days. They were going west, but she really did not know where. Regardless of the many people sleeping in the freight car, the woman helped us get in.

"You just can't stand around here," she had decided and we were very grateful.

The people on the freight car were crammed close together. The smell of sweat, old cloth, and urine hung thick in the air. People were waking up as we got in. Two girls stretched and jumped out of the car soaking in the fresh morning air. A jolt of the train made the last sleepers sit up straight. The girls hurried back in. "Hurrah, we are traveling again!"

The train moved, our journey to the West continued.

"Omi, I am starving. Do you still have something to eat?" I begged. Omi rummaged through her bag and found a piece of bread and a carrot for Dagmar and me. Alternating, I took a tiny bite of the bread and then of the carrot. This way the food lasted a long time.

Later Dagmar cried because she was thirsty. Omi cut a bruised pear in half and gave one half to me. She sat Dagmar on her lap, rocked her gently and had her suck on her half of the pear.

With stops here and there, the train rolled on all day and into the night. Before sunrise the train stopped at the Oder River. Paramedics and nurses came to the train and took us to a large, well-organized refugee camp. I was glad to be there. It was good to feel safe, receive some food, and have a straw mattress to sleep on.

The camp was situated on the east bank of the Oder River close to a guarded bridge to the German town, Angermunde. We were not allowed to cross, because the refugee camp was on the Polish side of the river. After the war, the Oder River had become the new border between Germany and Poland.

⌒

I liked to hang out at the bridge, and wished I could cross over to the town on the other side. The Russian guard noticed me and waved indicating that I should come to him. When I shyly approached him, he gave me his empty water bottle and said "Wasser"[8] pointing to the guard on the other side. Surprised if I had understood correctly, I pointed to me and then to the other side of the bridge. The guard nodded. "Wasser!" he repeated, pushed me forward onto the bridge, and whistled loudly. Wow, I quickly ran over the bridge; the opposite guard filled the bottle with water, whistled, and had me run back.

The same guard was on duty the next couple of days. When he greeted me in a friendly voice, I ran over to him. "Wasser?" I asked. He laughed and handed me his bottle. When I brought it back all filled up, I got brave. Pointing to me and then across the river I asked:

"Angermunde?"

The young soldier smiled, then nodded, turned towards the river, and whistled twice to his comrade on the other side. I hesitated. He nodded again and waved me off. Like an arrow I zoomed over the bridge, and the other guard let me pass.

Catching my breath I ambled through the small town. How nice and orderly it looked. I stopped in front of a bakery and longingly looked at the displays. Through the open door streamed the heavenly smell of freshly baked bread.

Dressed in a spotless white apron the woman of the bakery came to the entrance.

"Would you like to have something?" she asked me in a friendly manner.

Embarrassed I shook my head. "I don't have any money and bread coupons."

"Are you from the refugee camp?"

I nodded.

"Stay here, don't go away. I will be right back."

She returned and pressed a large white paper bag with freshly baked rolls into my hands.

Blushing with embarrassment and joy, I curtsied and stammered: "Thank you very much."

On my way back I ate two of the delicious, crunchy fresh rolls and saved the remaining ones for Omi and Dagmar.

꜅

Omi was waiting for me with good news. "Anna, tonight a train leaves for Berlin. Let's hurry to get on." When we arrived at the station the train

8. Water.

stood there already filled with passengers. We still found seats, but sadly we had to leave the baby carriage behind.

For a long time the train remained in the station. It got dark and suddenly there was a commotion at the door.

"Robbers!"

A big man in the uniform of a train stationmaster pushed himself through our compartment. With his loud, booming voice he called out:

"Out of here, you thugs or I will take care of you!"

Amazing, with the power of his voice, he chased the thieves away. We children and women relaxed and the train started to roll.

In the morning the train reached Berlin, Germany and we left the refugee transport. We would travel on our own to Cologne. While Omi asked about travel information, Dagmar and I waited outside the station. I felt dizzy—maybe from hunger.

Two girls my age walked by singing. I looked at them sadly. Some time long ago I had sung the same song with my friends. That had been in a different world—a world were I had enough to eat, could take a bath, and wear clean clothes. Today I was hungry, dirty, and a million lice crawled in my hair. My head itched and hurt from my scratching.

Omi returned from the station and bought a hot broth for us that made me feel better. Our train would leave from another station. It was a long walk to get there.

We walked down a street were only two houses stood. All the others were in ruins or rubble. Women were congregating around a fire hydrant getting water. We too filled our old battered water container.

Omi saw a brand new stroller in a store window and walked in with Dagmar on her back. It was amazing: the saleslady sold her the stroller for money without the required government issued coupon. We sat Dagmar in the stroller, put our bags next to her, and off we went.

We were all by ourselves on the train. Omi sat across from me looking very tired. "Anna, I am sorry, but I can't travel further. I believe I am getting sick."

We got off at the town of Haldersleben, about one hundred miles west of Berlin. At the mayor's office Omi inquired about healthcare and asked for a room for us to stay. We were sent to a large farm where a tiny room over the entrance gate was assigned to us. The farmer's wife, angry over the assignment, took us to the room. Omi immediately lay down and rested.

The next morning my eyelids were puffed up and I couldn't open my eyes. Omi soaked my eyes with a wet cloth and wiped the dried puss from my lashes. Oozing boils covered my head and made me feel sick. Omi's condition had gotten worse. She had a headache, back pain, and seemed to develop a fever. Just then, when we were feeling sad, sick, and miserable, the public health nurse stepped in like an angel sent from heaven.

"Oh God, my poor child!" she exclaimed, when she saw me.

She examined Omi and determined that she needed to be seen by a doctor. Then she took care of me. Horrified, I watched as the nurse cut off my hair. She cleaned and disinfected the wounds on my skull and wrapped my head with a large bandage. "See, now you have a nice white turban," the nurse tried to cheer me up.

Hardly an hour later a big, elderly physician squeezed himself through our low, narrow doorway. He checked Omi and confirmed what the nurse had suspected:

"You have typhus and need to be admitted to the hospital as quickly as possible." He wrote the order. Then he looked at us and wrote another order for Dagmar and me: "To be admitted due to suspected typhus infection." Turning to Omi he explained: "I don't think your grandchildren are ill, but this way they will be taken care of for now."

In the Hospital

The hospital was temporarily housed in the Hindenburg, a large castle close to Haldersleben. It looked impressive as the ambulance drove us there.

"Do you think there are ghosts?" Omi had her eyes closed and did not answer.

Before the orderly rolled her away, she looked at us and said: "Be good! And Anna, watch over your little sister."

Tears welled up in my eyes and I hugged Dagmar tightly.

"Don't be sad. We will take good care of your grandmother," the nurse consoled me and took us to the children's ward. It was a large hall with many bunk beds along its walls. Dagmar and I got our beds next to each other.

Nurse Inge took us to the bathroom. In a big tub I took my first bath in many months. It felt so good. When it was Dagmar's turn she screamed and kicked. Nurse Inge and I had to calm her down and then she liked it too.

Later the hospital physician examined us.

"Totally malnourished, but otherwise they are fine," he told the nurse. "But with their grandmother being very ill, we will keep them here for observation."

Dagmar and I liked to be in the hospital. I enjoyed talking to children my age and playing with them. All the nurses loved Dagmar with her cute smile and sparkling eyes. I was proud of her and took good care of her. At mealtime I would feed her, take care that she always had her pacifier, put her regularly on the potty, and at night, Dagmar would sleep with me in my bed.

After a little while we heard that Omi was getting better. I was happy. Maybe Omi would soon be well and we would travel to Cologne.

The next day Dagmar and I had another physical and were tested for diphtheria. When the results came back, I was called into the physician's office and he explained to me: "Anna, you are healthy, but you are a carrier of the bacteria that causes diphtheria and you may infect others. Therefore, you have to be transferred to a different ward where you will receive medication that will destroy the bacteria. We will test you each week, and when no bacteria is found for three weeks in a row you will be released."

I could not believe what I heard. I was to go to a different ward! And Dagmar?

I jumped up. "But my little sister has to go with me!"

The physician shook his head. "No, that is not possible."

"I can't leave her alone! She is so little, I have been always be with her," I cried.

"Calm down, she will be well cared for."

I did not calm down. I was very, very upset. I cried and sobbed when nurse Inge had me pack my things together. Tears ran down my cheeks when I kissed Dagmar good-bye. She looked at me with her big brown eyes, not understanding why I cried.

The nurse took me to a room with five women. They were happy to have me join them and did their best to comfort and cheer me up. They succeeded. Within a few days I became accustomed to my new place. I helped the nurse pass out the food at mealtime and did little things for the women in the room. Nurse Ursula brought me some books to read and a jump rope. I enjoyed both.

One day nurse Ursula came into our room, and behind her in the hallway stood Omi. Seeing her, I cried out with joy. She looked pale and thin, but she was nicely dressed and her hair was pinned up. Because I was still contagious, we could not hug. Omi had to stay in the hallway and I in my room.

"Anna I am well again and will be released tomorrow," Omi told me. "Dagmar had been sick with chicken pox, but she too is better. Tomorrow we will go to the room we had rented in the farmhouse."

I wished very much to be released as well, yet so far the medicine I was taking had not destroyed the bacteria in my body. Each week I hoped for negative test results only to be disappointed. I was sad that I had to stay longer in the hospital.

⌒

Omi visited me a few more times. In the middle of November she told me the worst news ever:

"Anna, the government wants Dagmar and me to leave. Tomorrow a transport departs to the West. I am told it will be the last one. If we don't leave with it, we will no longer get food coupons."

"And I . . . ?" my voice faded.

"You know you can't yet leave the hospital."

"But I don't want to stay here by myself!" I cried desperately

Anna, you must understand this. I know you are a good and brave girl." Omi tried to reassure me.

"No!" I screamed beside myself. *"I don't want to be brave! I am not good at all! I want to get ouuut!"*

Nurse Ursula held me tight. I was shaking and sobbing in her arms. Shocked and concerned, the women in my room stood around us. They were feeling sorry for me and tried to calm and comfort me. Slowly I quieted down. Looking up, I noticed Omi was gone.

She did not come again, instead she sent a long letter that ended with the promise that she would try hard to come when I was well and take me to Cologne. I threw the letter away. I felt betrayed, abandoned, and alone.

Again and again the people I loved deserted me. Why did this happen to me? My sadness turned into rage. I swore to myself: "As soon as three negative test results showed that I was healed, I would leave for Cologne on my own. I would not wait a single day for someone from my family to come. If I had to, I would sneak away at night."

⌒

On my eleventh birthday on the 16th of December, the nurses baked a little cake for me. Everyone congratulated me, the women from my room gave me a card they had decorated, and from nurse Ursula, I got a book.

A day before Christmas I received the most wonderful surprise—a letter from my father. He wrote:

"We found each other, Brigitte, Margot, Omi, Dagmar, and Opa Luschei. We live in the house of the Essner bakery down the street from our destroyed house. Even though the upper part of the Essner house was destroyed, we patched up the first floor, so we can live here temporarily. Grandpa and Aunt Ija live outside of Cologne."

Father ended his letter with: "My poor child, how much you had to endure! We are all thinking of you." He had a twenty Mark bill enclosed in the envelope. I saved both carefully. The letter and the money were my most precious treasures and the best Christmas present.

In January and February, I received two more letters from Father and also one from Margot. Whenever I was sad, I would read them again.

The patients in my room changed. When eighteen-year-old Marianne was admitted, she became my special friend. Initially, when she was very sick and I helped her. I would bring her a glass of cold water, a towel or whatever she needed. Later when she felt better, she would cheer me up when my test result came back positive, which meant I had to stay longer.

When Marianne was well and leaving, she told me: "Anna, I have a plan for you. After you are released from the hospital, you come and visit me in Helmstedt. It's about twenty-five miles away from here. You can get there easily by train and our house is very close to the train station. You can stay with us and my father will help you to cross the border to the British zone."

Marianne wrote down her address and gave it to me. I saved it with my treasures.

                                 ↶

Two weeks later I was called into the physician's office. "Your last three tests were negative, Anna. You are healthy."

"Hurray!" I jumped with joy, ready to run out of his office.

"Wait, Anna."

I sat back down.

"I will write to your parents and . . . "

I shook my head and calmly told him: "I will leave tomorrow morning."

The doctor looked at me not believing what I had said. "My darling, you are only eleven years old!"

I explained to the doctor that I would take the train to Helmstedt, stay there with my friend, and then travel to Cologne.

He looked at me for a long time. He seemed to be impressed with my determination. "Hmm, I have to talk it over with the director of the hospital. You are an extraordinary little person."

In the afternoon, the head nurse brought me my release papers and gave me a big hug. "You are a brave little girl. My best wishes to you. Tomorrow morning you can pick up some travel food in the kitchen."

Everyone was amazed that I would travel on my own. They were happy for me and wished me well. But some people thought differently. "It is irresponsible to let such a young girl travel on her own," they said. I was glad that I was allowed to leave and happily packed my bundle.

I Traveled Alone to Cologne

Early the next morning I tied my scarf around my head and shouldered my bundle. After a last good bye to the patients in my room, I walked all alone out of the big gate of the Hindenburg castle down to the train station.

"A ticket to Helmstedt, please," I said and gave my twenty Mark[9] bill to the clerk at the train station. He gave me the ticket grumbling about all the change he had to count out. He gave me 16.50 Mark in return. The train arrived. The nice stationmaster lifted me up the two steps into the train, and off I traveled.

A few hours later I was in Helmstedt. Holding Marianne's address in my hand, I asked for directions and soon found her house.

"Anna, what a nice surprise!" Marianne hugged me delighted. Her parents, Mr. and Mrs. Schubert, also welcomed me warmly. Mrs. Schubert was especially nice to me. I enjoyed helping her in the kitchen when Marianne was at work. At night I slept in her older, married sister's bed. It was so soft and comfortable that I happily fell asleep without worrying about my nightmare.

Marianne's father was a paramedic and worked in the big refugee camp close to the train station. At breakfast the next morning, he told me about his work and said:

"Anna, you can stay with us as long as you want. But I know that you are eager to return to your family in Cologne. I will keep my eyes and ears open. Whenever I hear about a possibility for you to cross the border to the West we have to grab the chance. It may be all of a sudden on short notice. Do you understand?"

I nodded.

In the morning of my fifth day, I was spending time with Mrs. Schubert in her cozy kitchen, when suddenly Mr. Schubert rushed in.

"Fast, Anna, get your bundle! Soon a train to the West pulls in. In the last car are expelled Germans."

I was shocked. The news came so suddenly. Mrs. Schubert helped me gather my things. She quickly made me a cheese and ham sandwich for the journey, while her husband watched impatiently. We hugged with tears in our eyes.

Mr. Schubert grabbed my arm and pulled me across the street to the station platform. We stopped at the far end of it. Three Russian soldiers with their machine guns hanging over their shoulder patrolled the platform

---

9. The German equivalent of a Dollar.

and looked towards us. My heart pounded. I looked questioningly at Mr. Schubert. He made a reassuring gesture.

"Don't worry! I know them. We sometimes talk. I know some Russian," Mr. Schubert explained quietly.

I saw it first. "There comes the train!" I whispered.

Everything happened very fast. The train stopped. Mr. Schubert rushed with me to the last car, pulled its sliding door a crack open, and pushed me in.

"Farewell, my child! Lot's of luck!"

I saw one of the Russian guards run to Mr. Schubert and push his gun butt into his chest. Someone closed the door and the train moved on.

The refugees stood or sat closely together in the freight car. The air was so thick I had trouble breathing. Some light shone in through a small window up high. People who stood close to it would lift each other up to look out.

"We passed the border! It's true, we are in the West!" Someone called out the good news. An excited buzz went through the crowd.

The border! The Schubert's had explained to me this border within Germany. Haldensleben, where I had been in the hospital and Helmstedt belonged to the Russian occupation zone and Cologne belonged to the British occupation zone. The border between the zones was heavily guarded. No one was allowed to cross it without a permit. Mr. Schubert had helped me to cross it illegally. I hoped very much that he was not punished for it. I thought that would be terrible and unfair.

I moved to the wall, crouched down and took off my scarf. A man crouching next to me asked: "Well, son, where are you traveling to?"

I was surprised and looked into his unshaven face. Remembering my short hair, I answered embarrassed: "I am not a boy, I am a girl!"

"Well, alright. Are you alone?"

"No," I brushed him off, folded my arms over my knees, put my head down, and soon fell asleep.

A jerk woke me up. The train had stopped in an open field. People jumped off, stretched, caught a breath of fresh air or relieved themselves. I got off too. Then the train jerked again. It was about to roll on. Everyone rushed to the door. I was pushed in different directions but managed to get back on.

In the afternoon, the train ended in Salzgitter about sixty miles west of Helmstedt. The people from the refugee train car were taken to a camp and I walked with them. I was glad to be in the camp, where I got something to eat and had a place to sleep. I used my bundle as my pillow to keep it from being stolen.

After I received some bad-tasting coffee and a piece of bread in the morning, I left the camp and walked back to the train station. The ticket window was half boarded up with cardboard.

"I want a ticket to Cologne, please," I told the grouchy looking clerk.

He pushed the ticket to me. "Twenty-one Mark," he demanded.

"I only have 16.50 Mark," I answered desperately.

"Too bad, that's what it costs." He snatched the ticket away and closed the window.

Stubbornly I knocked again.

"What do you want now?" the clerk grumbled.

"How far can I travel with my money in the direction of Cologne?"

"To Wuppertal, there you have to transfer to another train."

"Then I'll take a ticket to Wuppertal."

He pushed the ticket and a little change towards me. Before he disappeared I quickly asked: "How far is it from Wuppertal to Cologne?"

"Too far to walk." The window banged shut.

I did not dare to knock again to ask where and when the train would leave. With my ticket and the 50 Pfennig (equivalent to 50 cents) change, I walked to the platform crowded with waiting travelers. I noticed that people looked at me. Two women asked:

"Child, are you all alone?"

I nodded and moved about. I felt uncomfortable when I was asked this question.

A train pulled in. I ran over to the conductor. "I want to go to Wuppertal. Can I take this train?"

"Yes, little Miss," was his friendly answer. "It's the right direction."

Relieved I boarded the full train. I stood in the hallway at the window looking out in thought. After a while many people got off and I sat down in a compartment with two elderly women.

Tired, terribly hungry, thirsty, and sad, I sat crouched in a corner and worried about how I could get from Wuppertal to Cologne.

"Child, are you all alone?" Again this question! And yet, the women looked at me so kindly. First I stammered but soon my words flowed out, and I told the two women all my problems, including how hungry I was.

The women were most sympathetic with my plight.

"You poor child, I am so sorry I have nothing to eat," said one of the women, "but I have some peppermint tea in my thermos. Do you want some?" Yes, I did. Thankfully, I drank the warm tea while the women looked through their purses. They both gave me 10 Mark!

I starred at the money in my hand and started to cry with joy and relief. At once my problem was solved! I was overwhelmed. I wanted to thank them so much and found it hard to find the right words. The women were touched. At the next station they had to get off. They wished me a good journey home.

It was evening when the train pulled into Wuppertal. The ticket office was closed and no more trains were leaving. I was very disappointed.

It was dark. The train station was deserted. I felt all-alone in this world as I walked forlorn down the train platform. In the moonlight I saw a community garden with a little shed next to the train tracks. I climbed over its fence and opened the creaky shed door. Feeling around in the dark, I found a folded reclining lawn chair and opened it. Cold and hungry I rested in it. I remembered my mother and longed for her. I knew she would not have abandoned me ever. At last I fell asleep.

The next morning I boarded the train to Cologne. Too excited to sit, I stood at the large window in the hallway and looked out. Finally, I was on my way home. My happiness had me forget my hunger. Why was the train moving so slow? It seemed to pick its way past heaps of rubble.

Suddenly, I saw the Rhine River and the two towers of the Cathedral of Cologne. I was home!

The train tracks ended east of the Rhine. With help from passers-by, I found the temporary bridge over the Rhine. Arriving on the west side, I was at a loss. Everything, including the streets, was covered with rubble. I asked two girls for directions to Klettenberg.

"Just follow us on this path to the Neumarkt. The streetcar to Klettenberg leaves from there."

I walked behind them watching my steps so I would not stumble over lose stones or rubble.

After I got off the streetcar, I walked down our street. Every house was destroyed. Only the basement was left of our house. I walked to the house where my family now lived. The windows were broken, bullet holes were everywhere, and the roof and upper floor had collapsed. It looked deserted. I stepped into the hallway and looked into an empty room. I walked up the crumbling steps. Again nothing. My legs trembled as I walked down. Had my family left? My courage and hope were leaving me.

Then I heard voices behind a rough hewn door. Maybe there is someone who knows where my family is. I knocked. The door opened and my father stood in front of me. He was thinner than I remembered. He looked at me like a stranger.

"Yes, child, do you want something?"

I starred at him. "Vati, don't you recognize me?" My voice faded.

Puzzled and surprised he asked: "Anna?"

I threw my bundle behind me and jumped into his arms.

Home at last!

Chapter 5

Hannelore and the Air War

Hannelore, born 1935 in Duisburg, Germany

DUISBURG, HANNELORE'S HOMETOWN OF almost half a million inhabitants, is located at the confluence of the Rhine and the Ruhr River. It is the most western city of the Ruhr Valley, a large densely populated industrial region of Germany. Other cities of similar size in the Valley are Dortmund, Essen, Oberhausen, and Mühlheim an der Ruhr. The Ruhr Valley is Europe's fourth largest urban area after Moscow, London, and Paris. During World War II, the Ruhr Valley was Germany's industrial center. The area with its coalmines, steel mills, and heavy manufacturing plants produced a variety of military hardware, including tanks, trucks, cannons, and airplanes. Consequently, the cities, industries, and their workers were major bombing targets of the Royal Air Force (RAF) during the war years.

⌒

Hannelore was nine years old when the bombing raids on Duisburg increased in 1942. She remembers:

We would listen intensely to the special radio station that provided detailed information about the ongoing air war. If we heard that a squadron of bombers was sighted over Amsterdam, we knew that they would fly to Berlin. It meant we could relax, go to bed, and most likely sleep through the night. If the radio announcer talked about sighting airplanes over Rotterdam, we knew that they most likely would come to us. So—let's be ready!

We had three levels of warnings. The early warning signaled that bombers were approaching. The radio announcer would say in a monotonous voice: "Enemy bombers approaching the Ruhr Valley." Since we lived in the most western city, we might be hit first.

Soon thereafter the sirens began to wail with a penetrating long-short-long burst indicating that planes were approaching the outskirts of Duisburg. Bombardment was imminent. Everyone had to leave the city streets and immediately find shelter.

When the sirens changed to three short screeching bursts over and over, the planes were overhead and dropping bombs. By this time everyone was in a bunker or shelter. After the planes left, the all-clear signal sounded. We were always glad to hear it. It said we could go home and back to sleep.

When we heard the early warning sirens, my older sister, older brother, my mother, and I would dash out of the house and sprint to the air raid bunker five minutes away. It was a windowless, five-story building of thick concrete. Each story was divided into narrow sections with triple bunks against the walls. The bunks had straw mattresses for the children to sleep on. The benches in the middle provided seating for the adults.

The air raid bunker protected us from bombs, flying debris of glass or metal, rubble raining down from buildings, fire that incendiary bombs started, earsplitting noise, and lung-busting air pressure produced by high explosive bombs.

In order to get our favorite place, we liked to be in the bunker ahead of the crowd. Each section had an airshaft close to the ceiling. I would climb onto the upper bunk near the airshaft. Frequently, I was asked by the adults to listen at the small opening. They would ask:

"Do you hear the droning of planes?"

"Do they sound close by or far away?"

"Do you hear detonations?"

I would listen intensely and report what I heard.

Even if we had heard the high pitch acute warning, no bombs might have been dropped, because the pilots were targeting another city east of us. When I did not hear much noise, we had high hopes for an all-clear signal that would send us home to sleep in our beds.

People were encouraged not to leave important documents at home, where they might catch fire, be buried under rubble, or damaged by water. They were urged instead to take them to the shelter. Adults and some children would carry small suitcases or briefcases to the shelter. A friend of mine had received a pair of beautiful black patent leather shoes for her communion. During the commotion and haste of getting into the bunker at the last minute, she lost one of her shoes. To this day, she is saddened by the thought of her lost shoe.

A woman rushed into the bunker only to discover that her children had not yet arrived. She asked the warden to let her back out. She found her children, but by the time she returned with them, the warden had locked the bunker's heavy iron door. The woman and her children had to endure the air raid outside.

My father never went with us to the bunker but stayed at home. Several times he was able to save our house from catching fire. The incendiary bombs might penetrate the roof or attic. If an explosive bomb shattered the windows, an incendiary bomb might land in a room. They would spray sparks that would start a fire and, if left unattended, would burn the house down. The bombs could not be extinguished with water, but had to be smothered with sand. My father always had a shovel and a bucket with sand ready. He might also use the shovel to throw one of the sparking sticks out of the house.

My father did not have to serve in the military because he worked in the defense industry. His work was strenuous and at times dangerous, but he liked it better than being a soldier.

↜

Due to the many air raids, the German government started to evacuate the children from the most endangered cities. My brother, along with his classmates, and teachers was evacuated to a youth hostel in the countryside. He lived and had school there until the end of the war.

My class was evacuated while I was hospitalized due to appendicitis. When I returned home, my parents looked for a safe place for me to stay. One of our neighbors, a policeman, had been transferred to Hoyerswerda in Saxony. He promised to find a place for me there.

In Hoyerswerda, I was far away from the bombing and the danger of war. I lived there almost three years. During those years I was safe but not happy. The family, who had volunteered to take me in, showed no interest in me. My foster father, a busy craftsman, was rarely home. My foster mother was a strict housewife. Even her son Hartmut, two years younger than I, had a hard life at home.

I went to school and read a lot at home. A letter or a package from my mother arrived every other week. She was a good seamstress and sent me pretty dresses she had made for me. My foster mother would admire the colorful embroidery and fine stitching and then conclude: "This dress is way too nice to play in." She would pack it away and I would never see it again.

It had not been possible for my mother to visit me. However, when it became known that the Russians might overrun Saxony, she travelled to Hoyerswerda to take me home. My foster parents let her know that she had come just in time. They were about to leave Saxony and had not planned to take me along. Would they have left me, an eleven-year-old girl, to fend for myself when the Russian troops arrived to take revenge on the Germans?

Our journey back to the Ruhr Valley was very difficult. Aboard extremely crowded trains we made it to Wolfenbüttel, which is about 200 miles northeast of Duisburg. My mother heard that the bombardments in Duisburg had further intensified and decided we should not travel home. Instead, we went to the local housing office and asked for temporary shelter. A small room was assigned to us.

My mother wrote letters to my father and siblings telling them where we were. Today it is a miracle to me that the postal service functioned at that time of total chaos. My sister, who had also been away from home, joined us in Wolfenbüttel. As soon as the war was over, we made our way back to Duisburg.

               ↜

My father had been drafted into the Volkssturm, the civilian defense corps, during the last few weeks of the war. Luckily, he evaded being captured and put into a prisoner-of war-camp. Equally lucky, our house was still standing in spite of all the bombing. It stood alone surrounded by ruins and rubble. We felt extremely fortunate that during the coming hard times, we had a roof over our heads, furniture, household items, and clothes. We had so much more than our neighbors, who had lost everything.

I remember playing with friends in the rubble. One of the houses in our neighborhood had been literally split in half. A kitchen cabinet stood on the third floor of the remaining half of the building. Did it harbor something interesting or delicious? We knew how dangerous it was to climb into ruined houses, as they might collapse any time. But we were just too curious! Carefully we made our way to the cabinet. It was empty.

The time after the war was very hard for the residents of Duisburg. The stores were empty. Many people starved. Again my family was more fortunate than most of our neighbors. I don't remember going to bed hungry. We had chickens and a small garden. My mother would sew for other people and frequently received some groceries in return.

Duisburg

Because Duisburg was on the approach path of British bombers on their way to the Ruhr Valley, the city had almost daily air raid warnings between 1942 and 1945. According to the official count Duisburg experienced 311 air raids.

The most devastating bombardment occurred on October 14, 1944 when 2,000 planes attacked Duisburg in three waves. They dropped huge explosive bombs weighing up to eight tons each. The bombardment resulted in 3,500 deaths. Approximately 8,000 of Duisburg's registered citizens died during the air raids in World War II. Statistics were not kept for travelers or forced laborers who perished during the raids.[1]

By the end of the war, 80 percent of the residential buildings were destroyed or severely damaged. Large sections of the city had to be rebuilt, including the infrastructure.

In all of Germany almost half a million lives were claimed by the bombing.[2]

Unexploded Ordnance

The author talks about a recent experience:

Again and again I searched the list of departures from John F. Kennedy International Airport for Air Berlin 7451 to Düsseldorf, Germany. I had arrived at 3:10 PM from Columbus, Ohio. According to my itinerary, my check-in time for flight 7451 was 4:10 PM. That was now! Why was the flight neither listed on the board nor at its gate? When I left this morning everything seemed fine. I had received the boarding pass with my seat assignment. What was going on?

"No, flight 7451 has not been dropped," explained the traveler standing next to me. "Air Berlin will be two hours late and depart from gate six instead of eight." He showed me the updated information on his boarding pass. Relieved I walked over to gate six, where the flight was indeed announced.

I had to hurry to let my brother know about the delay. Otherwise he would get up extra early to pick me up at the airport. It was an hour's drive from Rheinberg by Duisburg, where he lives, to Düsseldorf. Unfortunately, at this time, I did not have a cell phone.

Planning ahead, I took a seat across from a woman, who was talking on her phone. After she was done, she gladly sent my brother a text message. Then she told me something astounding. Our plane had been delayed due to a bomb explosion in Düsseldorf.

"A bomb attack in Germany! We really live in insecure times," I thought to myself.

"How bad was the terror attack?" "I heard a bomb exploded!" "Were people hurt?" I showered my brother with questions when I met him in Düsseldorf. He grinned, "A bomb was defused. This is almost a weekly occurrence in the Ruhr Valley. Unexploded ordnance from World War

1. Mohrs, "Bombenkrieg über Duisburg."

2. Bessel, *Germany 1945*, 3.

II are found during building projects and must be defused. Yesterday a
1,000-pound bomb was found by workers digging a trench in the Neusser
North City. Five thousand people living in the surrounding area had to leave
their homes for two hours, while the bomb was defused. During the same
time, air traffic in and out of the airport was disrupted. Aviation officials
restricted access to the airspace as a precaution."

I was very surprised. Almost seventy years after the end of World War
II, bombs were being found! I had never heard about this and felt out of
touch with what was happening in the country of my birth. I still remembered an accident when a group of children played with an unexploded
bomb and were hurt. But that had been in the summer of 1945 and not now.

The website of the city of Duisburg confirmed what my brother told
me. A section titled: Discovery of ammunition/bombs stated:[3]

> "Even today, more than six decades since the end of World War
> II, all sorts of military ordnance are found almost daily during
> excavation work. An ordnance may be a bomb, a grenade, am-
> munition, ammunition parts as well as weapons or weapon parts,
> which were left behind by the German or Allied armed forces . . .
> If the ordnance can't be handled, it has to be defused, and if this is
> not possible, it has to be safely detonated."

Thanks to the newest techniques the old bombs are being removed
without harming the public. Yet, defusing or detonation of unexploded
bombs continues to be a dangerous assignment for firefighters. Since 1949,
more than one thousand have died doing this job. Also, it may happen that
an old bomb explodes before being sighted.

On Friday, January 5, 2014, I listened to the radio and heard the
following announcement:

> "In Euskirchen, Germany the operator of earthmoving equipment
> hit a bomb that exploded and killed him. An additional thirteen
> people were injured. The air pressure produced by the explosion
> damaged nearby houses, shattered a shop window, blew shingles
> off roofs, and indented the side of a parked car. According to re-
> ports, the detonation was noted as far away as six miles."

Experts assume that there are still 100,000 unexploded ordnance buried in German soil. Chemical reactions due to the age of the bombs make
them especially dangerous. Erosion of the metal casing may trigger an explosion. The effects of World War II will be noticed for a long time to come.

---

3. Duisburg "Bürger- und Ordnungsamt."

Almut

Chapter 6

Here and There and Anywhere

Almut, born November 1941 in Düsseldorf, Germany, and her mother Ada, 1909 to 1994.

Prior to Almut's birth, the war had disrupted her family's life. In 1939 her father, Helmut, had been promoted to a position at his employer's office in Amsterdam. He and Ada, Almut's mother, were looking forward to moving with their baby Konrad, Almut's 2 1/2 year older brother, to the Netherlands. They cancelled the lease on their apartment in Düsseldorf and then—World War II broke out. Helmut was drafted into the German military as an air-traffic controller in the air force. Initially, he was employed nearby and was able to visit his family frequently.

Without a place to live, Ada decided to move into her mother's house. It was vacant because her mother was visiting Ada's younger brother in Buenos Aires, Argentina. Caught by the outbreak of hostilities, her mother barely managed to return to Germany in December of 1939.

For the next three years Almut's family lived with her grandmother in her stately house in Düsseldorf. This is where Almut spent the first year of her life. When the British Royal Air Force began bombing the cities along

the Rhine, Grandma built a bomb shelter in their basement. Often Ada
would put her small children to bed at night in the bomb shelter.

In 1943, the air war intensified and women with small children were
urged to leave Düsseldorf. Ada moved with Konrad and Almut into a vacation house of relatives on a farm in Dhünberg, in the hilly countryside
southeast of Düsseldorf. It was a lovely, safe place for them to stay. In her
memoir Ada describes how Konrad and little Almut enjoyed visiting the
neighboring farmer and his farm animals. Because they were not too far
from the city, Ada was able to visit her mother occasionally. A day after a
cheerful visit, her mother died unexpectedly of a heart attack.

Without the support of her husband, Ada had to cope with the loss
of her mother. Helmut was now stationed in East Prussia and three days of
leave was all the military granted to attend the funeral.

More bad news followed. Four weeks later, her mother's house in Düsseldorf was severely damaged during an air raid. Later the city house of
the relative, who owned the property in Dhünberg, was also hit by a bomb
and they needed to move into their vacation house. This necessitated that
Ada and her children find another place to live. In her 1973 memoir, Ada
described her eighteen months-long journey through war-torn Germany
as she struggled to provide for her two small children. Her daughter Almut
contributes to this narrative what she remembers.

Ada[1]—Ellen, my oldest sister, accompanied us on our long trip by
train to our aunt Alice in Braunwalde[2] in Posen where she lived on a large
estate. At this time, eastern Germany was still peaceful.

Our dear Aunt was always cheerful and caring. It was important to her
that children were well mannered and well educated. I had nothing to do
but care for Konrad and Almut. The large, spacious house on the estate with
its beautiful garden was a paradise for the children and me.

Almut—One day a big soldier in full uniform appeared. I was scared
and hid under the table. Even though I was assured that this stranger was
my father, I was not convinced and still frightened.

Ada—But then we were a happy family for 24 hours.

In Braunwalde, we shared the estate with other permanent guests: a
family from Berlin and a professor with a secret mission. Employed by a
chemical institute, his assignment was to improve human nutrition.

The following events cast dark shadows: waves of families wandered
aimlessly past the estate. They were refugees or evacuees from Ruthenia,

1. Translated by Sieglinde Martin.
2. Today Bronikowo in Poland.

White Russia, and the Black See, who were asked to return to their home-land and who were also fleeing from the Soviet Army.

A foreboding of doom gripped us, but nobody wanted to admit the fear. "We are in no danger", pronounced the Starost (County Commissioner) even though we could hear the subdued rumbling of the approaching front line.

Quickly hay wagons were covered with tarps. At night they were loaded with provisions, tools, and valuables.

In January of 1945, on a bitterly cold morning, three wagons, twelve horses, and many people departed Braunwalde. Taciturn and quiet, filled with hidden fatalism, we joined the flow of families seeking safety. At the pace of a slow walk we moved west for many days and nights participating in an endless wagon trek that snaked through the endangered countryside.

Almut slumbered most of the time; rocked to sleep by the soft swing-ing of the wagon. Konrad and I often walked alongside to keep warm. Aunt Alice, wrapped in furs, occupied a commanding seat. My cousins, Gerda, Wilhelm, and Ilse each steered a wagon. On the second day we lost two horses when the brakes failed as we travelled down a slope. More horses succumbed due to sub-zero temperatures, snow, and ice.

In Sogan am Bober (a village in Silesia) children sprinkled ashes to keep our horses from sliding, and the women distributed steaming hot soup at the side of the road. It was a feast that made us feel like victorious gladia-tors. In Grünwald in Silesia, (today Zielenic, Poland) we spent the night in the warm waiting room of the train station. We rested our arms and head on the wooden table and slept. The floor was already occupied by other participants of this human migration.

Sometimes we spent the night in country estates or castles. Their gates and doors were open to all as a resting place. The owners were already trek-king west, just like us. They had left their homeland. In their rooms and halls strangers slept on straw mattresses and helped themselves to provisions for the coming days. The final goal of our trek was the estate of the family von Kehren by Luckau in the Spreewald district about sixty miles south of Ber-lin. The castle of the estate temporarily housed the National Library. The generous von Kehren's had furnished a huge hall with bunk beds, where we slept like in a youth hostel. Sitting at long, wooden tables we ate hardy, plentiful meals. A large supervised play area in the garden let the ten chil-dren from our trek and those of other refugee families forget the miserable trip. After eight days we said good-bye to Aunt Alice and I travelled on my own with Konrad and Almut to Lalendorf, a village close to Güstrow in the state of Mecklenburg, Germany, where my sister Hilde lived on a large farm.

It was a harrowing journey north through bomb-raged Germany. Konrad was five and Almut was three years old. They each had a band-aid with their name and address pasted onto their backs in case they were lost during our four-day trip on extremely crowded trains. Amid the turmoil, Almut and Konrad were surprisingly calm. They trusted in the security I provided. Their unwavering sureness made me confident and totally fearless. With the courage of a wild creature, I hid my children under me as we lay in a field outside of Magdeburg (in Saxony-Anhalt, Germany). The night sky glowed red from fire that spewed sparks and shards. The city was being destroyed by a devastating air attack.[3]

Almut—We always trekked ahead of the front. Many people, who didn't have little children to care for like my mother, carried a lot more belongings with them. While on a crowded train, a painting fell from the luggage compartment overhead onto my head. Luckily I got away with just a bump.

When somebody asked Konrad and me where we came from or where we were heading, we answered with an elusive: "Here and there and anywhere."

Ada—We stayed only a few weeks with my sister in Lalendorf. When the news came that the Russians were approaching the village, the people made barricades and grenade launchers were distributed to the men of the Volksturm (civilian corps of teenagers and old men) and to the village women. Hitler's portrait and book were thrown into the kitchen fire. I did not want to be part of this. Daring the journey into the unknown with Konrad and Almut, our few possessions packed into bags, a knapsack, and a suitcase, we fled to the West. It was April of 1945.

We traveled by train from Güstrow west to Lübeck in Schleswig-Holstein, Germany. The distance was a mere eighty miles, but it took us five days and nights to get there. Squeezed between people, we sat on our luggage on a freight train. Again and again the train made long stops; long enough for travelers to relieve themselves, to refresh themselves at a brook or lake, or to make a fire and cook food in a tin can. Before continuing, the train whistled and everyone nimbly climbed back on board.

Almut—One morning at the first light of dawn, the train stopped again. Most people were still sleeping, but I had to go urgently. So, we got out and as my mother was busy taking care of me, the train left with all our belongings on board.

Ada—The approach of low flying enemy planes caused the train to leave quickly without first blowing its horn. Our luggage traveled on while we stood

---

3. Ninety percent of Magdeburg's inner city was destroyed by an air attack that night.

there forlorn. Luckily, we three were together, and each of us wore a pouch with money, passport, and other important items hidden under our clothes.

We walked along the train tracks until we came to a signal station. I explained our misfortune to the signalman and he had good news for us. The signal some yards ahead no longer functioned and the train in route had to stop there. We hurried on. The train arrived and did stop. It was a military hospital train.[4] I walked to the locomotive and called out to the engineer. After listening and looking at me with little Almut and Konrad clinging to my skirt, he got down, went to the administration car and had two officers come out. They deliberated and we were allowed to ride in the laundry storage car right behind the locomotive. It was filled with blankets and mattresses.

The roofs of the train cars were painted white and marked with a red cross. The low flying planes did not respect it. As soon as we heard the rapid firing of their machine guns, we put mattresses on top of us. What a relief it was, when this dreadful noise stopped.

This train too travelled very slowly due to the many obstacles in its way. The nice engineer provided us with pea soup and bread.

Shortly before Lübeck, the train tracks were blocked. This was as far as the trains could travel. The officers ordered us to get off quickly. Then we had a wonderful surprise. Right ahead stood our original train. The same people were still on it and our luggage was with them! I shouldered my knapsack and left the remaining luggage with them. Carrying Almut, who was ill and keeping Konrad close by, I walked into Lübeck, trying to find a place for us to stay.

It was the second of May 1945. The city was flooded with refugees from the East fleeing from the Soviet army. From the West and South, the American troops had advanced and were ready to conquer the city. Cannons blasted and tanks rattled. The people of Lübeck huddled in their houses behind locked doors. I remember walking with my two children through deserted streets. As it became dark, the noise of the fighting was accompanied by flashes from rockets and the beams of searchlights.

I wanted to avoid going to a refugee shelter. The sight of my appealing children opened a door for us. A family took us in for the night and several nights to follow. During the day we were not allowed to stay in the house. We took long walks between gardens and alongside the Trave River towards the harbor. Along the way we got to know Mr. Gaul, the skipper of the "Anna-Alida", a tanker, which supplied the nearby power plant with oil. Mr. Gaul offered to let us stay in the vacated shipmates cabin. I borrowed a

---

4. Chapter 13 provides information about military hospital trains.

two-wheeled cart from a gardener, retrieved our luggage from the train, had Almut and Konrad sit on top of it, and off we went to the tanker.

We lived for five months on the Anna-Alida. She pumped oil from other vessels to the power plant, continuously vibrating and chugging. A thin layer of brown oil made the deck slimy and slippery. At the bow was the roomy two-storied cabin where Mr. Gaul and his family lived. Our cabin was at the stern. A steep staircase led down to two rooms with portholes. A large bed served Almut and me and Konrad slept on a cot. The kitchen had a coal-fired range and everything needed for cooking. There was a table, a bench, electric light, and water. It was really nice and comfortable. We got coal from the power plant and had warm water to shower.

Mr. Gaul was a really nice person—always in a good mood, ready to joke, clever, and canny. He fished eel and other fish in the Trave and shared his catch with us. He also made soap with the dead dogs, cow heads, and other ghastly things he fished from the Trave. With his knapsack filled with soap and coal, he biked into the countryside and returned with bacon and potatoes. Mr. Gaul officially declared me his skipper mate, and I received the appropriate rationing cards for Almut, Konrad, and me. They entitled us to buy milk and larger portions of severely rationed foods.

Almut—When Mr. Gaul boiled the carcasses to make soap, a horrible smell waffled over us. Luckily, I couldn't yet understand what was going on.

Everyday my mother brushed my hair and every time I made a big fuss because it hurt so much, and she would say: "Now let's throw these tangles of yours out of this porthole, 'whoosh-di-woop' and all is well again." And it worked.

That's how we lived relatively well for quite a while, until it was time again to depart.

Ada—One day in the fall of 1945, Helmut appeared on the Anna-Alida. Released from captivity, he had returned to his father in Düsseldorf, read the postcard I had sent there, and immediately set out to find us. Together we traveled back to our hometown on a coal train. At the end of the day, two big and two small black people walked into my father-in-law's house in a western suburb of Düsseldorf. We stayed only a few days because the house was occupied by many strange people. To reach the city of Düsseldorf, we had to cross the Rhine in a rowboat as all Rhine bridges had been destroyed.

Almut—The war was over and we were back in Düsseldorf. We lived in an almost undamaged, formerly one-family house that we shared with four other parties. Our apartment was half of the second floor, separated by a curtain made of military blankets. Later I had a suit made from these blankets with knitted sleeves, neck- and waistbands that was warm and chic but very itchy.

Konrad and his friends had a lot of fun playing in the ruins and going on adventurous discovery excursions that were not always completely without danger. I was still too small, and also a "girl", to participate in the excitement. Instead, I observed the rubble women pounding mortar off bricks and the little trains with their tipper wagons, which carried the debris away. I found this very interesting and fun to watch.

During this time, everything was scarce. Konrad and I collected all cigarette butts we could find on the street for my father, and in the attic he grew a few tobacco plants. Now and then he rolled himself a cigarette, which he did with great pleasure.

In our neighbourhood was a British Occupation building. The English officers were always very nice to us children and sometimes gave us chocolate or chewing gum. One of them showed me his pocketknife and said: "knife." This was the first English word I learned. The search for butts was also very successful in front of that building.

One day, I slowly walked up the wide staircase to our apartment taking one step at a time. I leaned forward taking care not to loose my balance. Usually I held onto the railing but today my arms were full. They held something warm, heavy and precious—a live chicken!

My mother looked at me and the chicken incredulously. She asked me where I got it and I answered with big eyes: "I wanted to see if there was a chicken under the old car, and there it was," as if it was the most natural thing in the world! I did not make the connection between the chicken and the most delicious soup we ate that night.

During these lean times I became ill with tuberculosis. At the age of four, I spent four months in a sanatorium, which was located outside of the city. There, in a bright room with plenty of windows, cribs were placed side by side. We received good food and were not allowed to get up, we had to rest, not an easy task for little children. Visitors were not permitted, but sometimes my mother came with Konrad and we could wave through the window. Konrad liked to wave so vigorously that his mittens flew off his hands. It made me burst out laughing and he did it again and again.

Aftereffect

The war never was mentioned at our home. I learned that my father was captured by the French early in the war. He worked as radio operator during his captivity.

His brother did not fare as well. He was drafted at age eighteen, was captured by the Russians, and imprisoned in Siberia. One of the last to be released, he did not return until 1950, bald and broken. He lived with us for many years to come.

Today I avoid movies, books, and discussions about war as much as possible.

Frugality and "not wasting anything" is probably common to our whole generation.

Chapter 7

My father Came Home Sick

Manfred, born 1935 in Hoyerswerda, Saxony, Germany

MANFRED GREW UP IN the town of Hoyerswerda in the eastern German state of Saxony. When in early 1945 Allied bombers targeted the town, Manfred was nine years old. He and his mother lived by themselves in their apartment on Schillerstraße. Manfred's father, who had worked in the office of taxation, was now a soldier and his older brother attended a boarding school for gifted children.

⤳

Manfred shares these childhood memories from the war:

During the air raids, my mother and I, and the other residents of our apartment building would rush into the basement. We had rolled a big bolder for extra safety against the basement window. Before 1945, our town had never experienced any air attacks. Even now my mother did not take the threat very seriously. When we had reason to believe that the approaching planes were targeting the neighboring town of Lauta and its aluminum plant, we might not seek shelter in the basement.

The night Dresden was bombed, I was outside. Looking down the street between the rows of houses, I saw a fiery red sky in the distance. The glow from the burning city of Dresden was visible in Hoyerswerda, more than thirty-five miles away.

When we heard that the Russians were coming to Hoyerswerda, Mutti and I fled together with some of our neighbors. Pushing our luggage in an old baby carriage, we walked west on a footpath because the roads were too dangerous. We came across German tanks and soldiers in the woods, who were withdrawing their positions to the west. When we had to balance on beams to cross a stream we could not take the baby carriage along and left it behind.

79

We did not get far. Word came to us that the Russian army had overtaken us and we decided to turn back. My mother thought that it would be too dangerous to return to our apartment in town. Instead, we went with some friends to a small house on the outskirts. However, the Russian troops came there as well. One of the soldiers asked our old neighbor to unlock her suitcase, which she did. While the Russian dug through her possessions, I noticed a watch fall from a bundle of socks. Quickly and inconspicuously I slipped the watch into my pants pocket to keep it from being stolen. Yet, the Russian had seen me. "Uri, Uri,"[1] he yelled. I had to give him the watch.

During the following days and weeks Russian soldiers broke into our apartment several times and took whatever they wanted. Then slowly their conduct became more orderly. Once when a common soldier tried to rob us in the street, an officer came by and prevented it.

There were shortages of all food items after the war. However, we did not starve because we had a garden behind the house where we raised potatoes, tomatoes, and many other vegetables. It helped.

∽

"When my father . . . " Manfred interrupted his narrative. There was silence followed by soft weeping. Later he continued: I was playing soccer with some friends in the yard. Suddenly one of them called out: "Manfred, here comes your Vati!" I saw a tall thin man approaching us. It was my father.

Towards the end of the war my father's unit had been sent from Russia to western Germany. He had been taken prisoner by the Americans and detained in an open-air prisoner of war camp. It consisted of a barbwire enclosure and had no barracks or facilities. The prisoners were exposed to the weather at all times. My father said it rained so much that the clay soil became squishy and made holes where they stood or sat. Their food rations were minimal.

My father returned home ill. He never recovered. His health continued to deteriorate and he died in 1950 at forty-four years of age.

Prisoner of War Temporary Enclosure (PWTE)

The prisoner of war camp, where Manfred's father was detained, was one of nineteen American Prisoner of War Temporary Enclosures or PWTEs. In Germany they were called Rheinwiesenlager (Rhine meadow camps), because most of these camps were located in the flood plain of Rhine River.

As Manfred had been told by his father, the camps were large barbwire enclosures where the prisoners lived outdoors. The enclosure had no

1. Watch.

barracks or any type of shelter such as tents, tarps or blankets and no water or facilities. The prisoners were exposed to the sun, rain, wind, or storms twenty-four hours seven days a week. To protect themselves, the prisoners dug pits with their hands. Initially, food rations were extremely limited.

The PWTEs existed from April until September of 1945. At the end of the war in May 1945, up to 3.4 million German soldiers and auxiliary staff were held in the camps. Women, men from the Volkssturm (civilian defense corps), and youngsters from the Hitler youth groups were released after a short internment.

Germany's Prisoners of War

During World War II the German treatment of prisoners of war sharply differed by their nationality. Initially, prisoners from western countries were treated according to the rules of the Geneva Convention. Later their status was formally changed to that of civilians and as such they were detained as forced laborers. They were ordered to work in Germany, where they were frequently employed according to their skills, replacing German workers drafted into the war. Even as forced laborers, the western prisoners of war were treated considerably better than prisoners from the Soviet Union.

The Russian soldiers detained during the German invasion of the Soviet Union in 1941 became the victims of an unspeakable war crime committed by the German military. The 3.5 million prisoners were held in open fields without protection from cold, heat, rain, and snow with minimal food rations. Two million Russians died within months. The survivors and any later prisoners were sent to forced labor camps in Germany, where they worked in mines and large military factories. In many instances, their working and living conditions continued to be intolerable. By the end of the war, 1.3 million Soviet prisoners had died in Germany.

Marianne

Chapter 8

My Goldfasan¹, it Will Pass . . .

Marianne, born December 1934 in Berlin, Germany.

WHEN THE WAR STARTED in 1939, Marianne was four years old. Early in the same year her father had unexpectedly died of an illness at age thirty-nine. His stellar career in finance, which advanced him to the presidency of a Berlin bank, had promised his wife and Marianne, their only child, a comfortable life and bright future. With his death their fortunes dwindled.

No longer privileged, Marianne would grow up with a single parent, a fate many of her contemporaries soon experienced as a result of the harsh war that was about to begin.

↪

These are Marianne's recollections of growing up during World War II.

---

1. Means golden pheasant, a unique term of endearment used by Marianne's grandaunt.

I have many memories of the war and the years that followed. Some are sad, but I have funny ones too. Let me give you an example:

We were in the air raid shelter of our apartment building in Berlin, while outside there was an incredible noise. Bombs were raining down. The entire building shook and bits of mortar fell from the ceiling.

"Would the ceiling hold?" we worried. It held.

The air raid sirens sounded the all clear. Finally we could leave the shelter. Everyone was anxious to see whether their apartment had survived the raid unscathed. We were about to rush out, when the shelter warden yelled:

"Stop! No one leaves! First the building must be checked for incendiary bombs. They need to be extinguished immediately."

"Emil, you go and do it!" he ordered the only other man in the shelter.

The elderly Emil nervously looked for his steel helmet, which would protect him from burning debris or falling blocks of mortar he might encounter.

"Emil, hurry! Run!" the warden hollered.

"I can't find my helmet," Emil winced and wasn't running at all.

"Then take this!" the warden blurted out. In a fit of rage he had taken the old pot from the near-by camp stove and slammed it over Emil's head.

The pot fitted well on Emil's head. Too well.

"I can't see," Emil wailed. The pot covered his eyes and he could not tip it back.

"Get that pot off!"

It did not come off. Emil's head was stuck in it. He looked hilarious. We children laughed and laughed while the adults tried desperately to pull the pot off. Instead, the handles broke off, resulting in more shrieks of laughter. Finally, when several women pushed up the rim in unison, Emil was freed from his confinement with lots of cheering from us.

The nervous mothers were angry with us. They did not think it was funny that our house could burn down due to the delay.

Fortunately, this did not happen. None of the small incendiary bombs had bored into the attic or flown through a broken window into a room and created a fire.

Back in our apartment, we tried to fall back asleep. I don't know if we did after all the excitement. I do remember that in the mornings after an air raid, we children would run outside and look for bomb shrapnel. These shiny metal pieces had all sorts of shapes. I collected them in an old cigar box and traded them with other children. We had little treasure boxes with our most beautiful or most unusual shrapnel.

The heavy bombing frightened my mother. Before the next air raid, she took me to a special Kinderbunker, an air raid shelter just for children.

We would sleep there on narrow double or triple bunks, while some women watched over us. In the morning my mother would come and pick me up.

During my third night in the children's bunker, Berlin was hit by a devastating bombardment. The extra thick wall of the bunker protected us from the ear-splitting noise around us. We heard dull roars and an impact. The bunker lights went out and the emergency lighting came on. I think I fell back asleep until loud banging and bursting woke me the next morning.

The emergency lighting was still on. The sparsely lit bunker looked spooky. "I hope Mutti comes soon," I thought. But neither she nor any other mother came.

Our mothers were standing outside, impatiently waiting, and watching as the emergency crew cleared away the rubble blocking the entrance. During the raid last night, our bunker had been hit and pieces of wall had crumbled in front of the entrance door. It took all day to free the entrance.

Finally, the warden opened our door. Happy to escape from the dark dungeon, I flew into my mother's arms. Mutti hugged me tight and said:

"Never ever will I take you here again. Never again will you be in a bunker by yourself. If we have to die, we shall die together."

⌒

It was impossible to get away from eminent danger in Berlin. My mother was determined to leave Berlin and move to Stieglitz[2], a small town in the eastern German state of Pomerania, where her cousin, my aunt Ursel, lived. Stieglitz had never been bombed.

My young, unmarried aunt was a teacher in the elementary school. She lived in the schoolhouse and so did we during our year in Stieglitz. I loved my aunt Ursel and thought it was marvelous to have her as my second-grade teacher.

We felt safe in the small town. I was free to run and play without my mother having to worry. Air raid sirens never woke us up at night. Well rested, I would get up in the morning and enjoy the day.

At the end of 1944, the eastern front of the war moved closer to Pomerania. My school closed and became a transit camp for people from Germany's eastern border and ethnic Germans from the Soviet Union fleeing from the fighting and the advancing Russian troops. Straw mattresses were spread out in the well-heated schoolroom and lots of soup would be cooked for the refugees.

I remember a very cold winter evening when a trek of farmers from East Prussia arrived with their loaded wagons pulled by small rugged Panje

---

2. Today Siedlisko, Poland.

horses. The men walked beside them. The women and small children sat quietly on the carriages. The wagons moved slowly into the schoolyard. Stiff and half frozen, the women climbed from their seats and helped the children down. I observed one woman, holding a baby in her arms, being helped down by a man.

I ran ahead of them into the school where Mutti, Aunt Ursel, and other volunteers took care of the travelers. You could tell how glad they were to step in the warm bright room. Slowly their bodies had to adjust to the warm temperature. Their skin would prick like pins and needles as their blood flowed again though their small vessels. Hands and feet had to slowly thaw or the pain would be unbearable. Tears rolled down the children's cheeks as someone helped them to carefully pull off their frozen mittens.

The young woman with the baby in her arms remained by the door. Aunt Ursel encouraged her: "Why don't you let me hold your baby, while you take off your coat." Without a word the woman held her baby even tighter. She did not want to let go of her child. I saw the baby's pale white skin and heard someone whisper: "The child is dead."

⌒

Shortly thereafter we left Stieglitz. Before our departure, my mother wrapped our feather blanket in a sturdy cloth, tied it securely and mailed the big bundle to Berlin. It did arrive there, which seemed a small miracle at the time.

We could take only our most essential things on our journey. Even my dolls had to remain in Stieglitz. The night before we left, I put them to bed nicely and gave each a last good night kiss. I placed our alarm clock on a shelf of the tiled stove. "Maybe we will be back soon," I thought.

I remember well the cold clear January morning when we walked to the Stieglitz train station. Hoarfrost made the tree branches glitter in the morning sun. How beautiful it looked! I would have liked to stop and marvel at the enchanted world around me, but Mutti urged me to hurry. That was not easy for me. My school backpack filled with our fine silverware was weighing me down. I was wearing so many pants, skirts, dresses, and sweaters on top of each other that I could hardly move. My mother was carrying a very large travel bag. That was our entire luggage.

The station platform was filled with people when the train pulled in. It was already full and only stopped because someone had pushed a cart onto the tracks. The big throng of people around us wanted to get on. I noticed that nobody stood far down by the last train car.

"Come Mutti, let's run there!" I cried out excitedly and pulled my mother along. Well, this last car was totally occupied. But we were lucky. A soldier opened the door and let us into the military train car taking troops to Berlin. The men seemed pleased to have us in their midst. They moved together to make a little room for my mother with her bag piled on her lap. I sat on the lap of a nice soldier right beside her. The car was so full with people and luggage that the door no longer closed all the way and had to be held shut with a military belt.

We had hardly settled down when the train left. The station platform was still crowded with people who had not gotten on. Would there be another train coming for them? Rumors had it that we were on the last train out of Stieglitz.

The train seemed to travel forever. Once it stopped in the middle of nowhere. "Low flying planes!" shouted the conductor. Everyone got off and tried to hide under nearby bushes. Luckily, it appeared to be a false alarm. The train whistled, which meant: "Get in fast! The train will leave." It was not hard for me to climb back in, but Mutti needed help to get up the first high step. I believe we traveled all day and the following night until we finally arrived in Berlin.

Berlin looked sad. So many houses were destroyed. The Berliners said they lived in a city of warehouses —"where is my house, where is your house?" With so much destruction it was difficult for us to find a place to stay. My dear grandaunt Hedwig invited us to stay with her in her one room. Of course, we were crowded, but I did not mind. I loved Aunt Hedwig and was glad to be with her.

Her room was in one of the old apartment buildings in Berlin's working class district. Neighbors on one floor shared a toilet on the landing, half way down the staircase, with the neighbors on the floor below.

"Marianne, please go to the toilet and listen if an air raid is being announced," Aunt Hedwig asked me one afternoon. She was hard of hearing and constantly worried that we would miss an early warning.

Sitting on the commode, I listened to the neighbor's radio. Only music was filtering through the wall. In front of me pieces of newspaper were speared on a nail —our toilet paper. I started to read the story on the top piece until it was cut off in the middle of a sentence. Annoyed that I could not find the continuation, I gave up.

"No air raid was announced," I reported back to my aunt. All good for now.

Perhaps it was the next night that we were all gathered in the basement. Aunt Hedwig sat on an old rickety chair and I crouched on a stool facing her. As the bombardment started I put my head snuggly into her lap. Her thighs protected my ears from the thundering reverberations. Auntie stroked my head muttering over and over: "My Goldfasan, it will pass . . ." I felt calm and safe, in spite of the calamity overhead.

Suddenly the basement wall towards the neighboring house burst open. Dust and smoke streamed in. The neighbors climbed through the opening, coughing, and gasping for air. Quickly we opened our basement door. The smoke dissipated. The air raid was over and no one had been hurt, even though the neighboring house had been hit.

Shortly thereafter, good friends of my mother decided to get out of Berlin and offered their apartment in Wilmersdorf, a nice central district of Berlin, for us to stay in. Mutti gladly accepted, but I was sad to leave Aunt Hedwig's cozy place. I would miss her comforting presence during the following weeks.

The battle over Berlin was imminent. A large part of the remaining German troops had gathered to defend the capital city. In addition, all civilian men between sixteen and sixty years of age were ordered to join the Volkssturm—the civilian defense corp. How much of a help they were was questionable.

Mutti and I observed men of the Volkssturm build a barrier for tanks and armored vehicles across the main street not far from our apartment building. They dragged boulders from the rubble, iron rods, and grids from the destroyed building into the street and piled them up into a large wall. Surely, no tank would get through. Were we safe?

A few days later the huge Soviet tank, called Stalinorgel (Stalin's organ) rolled towards the barricade and with deafening blasts shot its way through it within five minutes. It was free rolling for all vehicles thereafter.

From April 16 to May 2, 1945 the German and Soviet troops fought fiercely. When on the 8th of May the German government surrendered unconditionally, 10,000 German soldiers had died in the battle over Berlin. Over 2.5 million Soviet fighters stormed into the defeated city where at the time 2.7 million people lived—mostly women and children.

Mutti and I, and most of the inhabitants of the large apartment building had been living in its basement for days when the Russians moved in. Nothing and no one was safe from them. They entered each house, each apartment, and all basements, including ours, where we were huddled together. "Uri, Uri,"[3] "Frau, Frau"[4] they called, taking everyone's watch and pulling the women out of our shelter, including my mother. We children, several old men, and old women were left alone.

3. Watch, watch.
4. Woman, woman.

At the time I did not understand what happened to the women during that night and the following weeks. I wondered why all the women were wearing old drab dresses, hid their hair under dark headscarves, drew folds on their faces, and a neighbor started to limp pitifully. Later my mother told me: "I was relatively lucky because one of the officers took a fancy to me. I was declared to be his girlfriend and no common soldier dared to touch me."

⌐

Slowly some order returned to the city as most of the fighting units were pulled out, with only the occupation forces remaining. Berlin seemed to be nothing but rubble. No other German city had endured more bombardment and the final street fighting had done the rest.

We lived on Kaiserplatz 7,[5] which is called today Bundesplatz.[6] The main building facing the street was destroyed. We had to climb through the ruin and over the rubble to reach the courtyard behind it, where we entered the rear tenement house, in which we lived in an apartment on the first floor.

The courtyard was our nice protected play area. On a lovely summer day in 1945 my friend and I played there. We had no toys or dolls to play with and used a stick to draw a house on the dusty ground. We were about to add a garden using leaves shredded into tiny pieces to create a lawn and bushes.

My mother had a good view of the courtyard from our kitchen window. She was glad to see us play so contently. "Almost like in peacetime, long ago," she may have sighed. It was a fleeting impression, erased when a young Russian soldier with a Kalashnikov over his shoulder entered the yard and looked around bored.

"What is he here for?" Mutti wondered. "I hope he leaves soon." Just then she noticed he had stopped opposite from our play corner in front of the ruined house. He seemed to canvas his surroundings. Slowly he let his machinegun slide down his shoulder. He released the safety catch, raised the gun, and aimed in our direction.

The shrill scream of my mother, as she flew out of the house, and the firing of the gun, seemed to occur all at once. Surprised we looked up. A cat, which had been slinking along an exposed beam of the ruined house, fell to the ground. Sadly we looked at the dead cat.

My mother too felt sorry for the cat, but, of course, was more relieved that the bullet had struck the cat and not her kid. Kid or cat! In those days disaster could strike anyone. The fear of mothers, of the people around,

5. Emporer Place.
6. Federal Place.

penetrated each day, all events. This time fate had saved us, but what about tomorrow?

My mother's scream and the terror she had felt, did it live on in her soul? After a reflective pause, Marianne continued.

I am glad I was a child at the time. I took the events as they unfolded and did not worry about the future. The shooting had not especially frightened me. For an adult, who recognizes danger early, who weighs future difficulties, and has to plan the means of survival for herself and her child, life was tough.

I too liked to plan, but my plans were not burdened by long-term goals and responsibilities. For me, planning was fun and emerged from the events of the day.

Already the next day presented an emergency needing my help. The three little kittens, orphaned by the death of their mother, appeared in the courtyard with heart-rending meowing. Hungrily, they wandered about missing their mother. How could they survive? All the persons we knew, as well as Mutti and I, experienced hunger every day. Who would have something left over for kittens?

I knew of a tent kitchen for common Russian soldiers not far from us. At certain times, troops would receive a meal there. With our pot I lined up behind the last soldier. When he had been served I held out my pot silently and looked at the Russian mess worker. He hesitated and then dipped his ladle deep into his pot and poured a generous serving of thick noodle soup into my pot. Thankfully, I curtsied and careful not to spill a drop, I started on my way home.

I had not gone far, when I noticed something peculiar. A pair of boots was sticking out from under a tarp. Placing my pot to the side, I curiously lifted the cloth. Dread and horror crept up inside me. A dead Russian soldier was lying in the grass. I shrieked and then cried. When I was finally home and told Mutti about it, tears continued to flow down my cheeks. Most likely my mother consoled me. I remember we contently ate the thick noodles. The kittens got the broth, licking it up eagerly. The story had a happy ending. Within a couple of days we found people who took the kittens in.

Another time a group of soldiers butchered a pig in our courtyard and had a grand feast. One of my friends and I noticed that they buried the pig's remains in a corner of the yard. As soon as the soldiers had left, we hurried to the spot and unearthed all usable pig parts: ears, tail, snout, bones, and so on. Our mothers washed them and cooked them in a big pot to a rich soup with bits of meat and plenty of fat. All our neighbors ate and enjoyed some soup. Fat had been scarce for a long time, which made the soup special. But it caused a problem: after doing without, our stomachs were no longer able to handle the fat. The next day we had diarrhea.

⌒

The people of Berlin were starving and so were Mutti and I. I collected melde, (the botanical name is ariplex sagittata) a common weed in Germany. Mutti cooked it and we ate it as a vegetable. It tasted terrible. Only the very youngest plants were tolerable. I would gather them on the side of the streets, in abandoned lots and between rubble.

Fruit tasted better than weeds. To pick an apple from a tree was stealing. I was allowed to take only the ones that had fallen. A quick shake of the branches resulted in extra good apples or plums that fell to the ground, allowing me to take them.

If some flowers stretched their necks out of the garden fence or were in reach of my hand, I picked them if no one was looking.

"See Mutti, I got a bunch of flowers for you," I would call out happily as I burst through the door. Mutti was often sad and wept. I wished to cheer her up. Mutti smiled and admired the daisies. But then she looked at me sharply and probed: "Where did you get them?"

"Mrs. Pitschikajelski gave them to me," was my white lie, because Mutti would no longer enjoy the flowers, if she knew I had taken them from someone's garden. My mother did not know that no Mrs. Pitschikajelski lived in our neighborhood. I loved the name. Mrs. Pitschikajelski was very generous and fitted well into my stories.

My mother had the firm moral conviction that you don't steal, while I thought a little stealing was ok, if you do it for a good purpose. Once my mother tolerated that I filched something for us.

We had noticed that the three-person family, who lived in the room next to us, always had enough to eat. The woman worked as a cook for the Russians and took food home from her job. She kept it in a locked chest, which stood in our common hallway.

All three people of the family worked during the day. After they were gone I had an idea. I took the key of our linen closet and stuck it into the keyhole of the chest. I turned the key and . . . surprise, surprise . . . the lid of the chest popped up. There was a whole pound of margarine with only a little taken off so far. Quickly I ran to our place and came back with a small plate and a knife. Carefully, I peeled back the wrapping paper, sliced off a fat strip, neatly rewrapped the margarine, put it back in its place, and relocked the chest.

Hurrah, we had margarine to spread on our slices of bread. I ate mine with gusto. Mutti ate hers also, but wept at the same time. She ate and wept.

I don't know if it was then or another time, that she said: "Marianne, you are a terrible child, but you know how to organize things. You got this from your father."

Organizing was fun. My playmate Werner and I managed to get into the basement of the bombed out main building. We checked it all out. Underneath where a coffee shop had been, we found a bucket and dragged it outside. Carefully blowing the dust off the lid, we read: "Strawberry Preserves." We could not believe our luck. As we carried the bucket home, its wire handle cut into my hand, but the pain couldn't diminish the pride and joy I felt. Everyone living in our house got some marmalade.

I was always on the lookout for possibilities. Sometimes Mutti and I visited Papa's grave. Then Mutti would tidy up the gravesite: picking off dead leaves, pulling weeds, and watering the plants. I would check out the big wire basket with garden trash. Usually I would find a few nice flowers hidden in a wilted bouquet or wreath.

"Mutti, I got flowers for Papa's grave, aren't they pretty?"

"Need is the mother of invention," says an old proverb. At school we had no notebooks. Never mind. Mutti helped me make one. We folded large sheets of paper in half and stacked several on top of each other. Mutti took a needle and sturdy thread, pushed the needle down through the papers and up along the middle fold; repeating it several times, she wove the pages together. Then the ends of the thread were neatly tied together. With a ruler and pencil I drew lines on each page and my notebook was ready for writing.

◁⁀

Hunger was a constant plight for most of the people in Berlin and for us. When in June 1945 the shuttered stores opened again, their shelves were sparsely stocked. The essential items were especially missing. For instance, you might be able to buy cinnamon, but no sugar, baking powder or flour.

A little later we again received rationing cards similar to those used during the war except for a significant difference: The allotted amounts of basic food items were much smaller. The rationing card for non-working housewives and office workers provided such small portions that the Berliners dubbed it the graveyard card.

Frequently, even the allotted amounts were not available in stores at a given time. People would barter for food or try to buy it on the illegal black market, where it was up to one hundred times more expensive than in regular stores.

For us the situation was especially difficult. Besides getting low value rationing cards, we might not even have the money to buy our allotted amount. During the war my mother had received a pension, but now with the collapse of the German government she got nothing.

In the fall of 1945 and the winter 1946, our nutrition was so poor, that my mother developed hunger edemas in her feet. A sickening smelly fluid would seep out between her toes. I know this exactly as it became my job to wrap her toes each day. I wished I did not have to do this, but I did, and I comforted my mother when she moaned. Every step was painful for her. By doctors order she had to stay in bed for a long time. This meant that I had to take care of our everyday needs. Today I wonder how I did it.

The only positive aspect of Mutti's illness was, that she was excused from working as a "Trümmerfrau"[7]. In 1945 the Soviet governor of Berlin ordered all women between the age of eighteen and forty-four years of age to clear away the rubble of the destroyed buildings and to clean the bricks, so they could be reused. Women who refused the service would not receive rationing cards. My sixty-three-year-old grandmother volunteered to work as a rubble woman. For her service, she received a small amount of money and a slightly better rationing card.[8]

During the months of my mother's illness, I suffered from scabies, a contagious skin condition. It is caused by a mite, which borrows into the skin. It leads to constant itching of the effected areas. Cleanliness is the best defense against an infection. The only soap we could buy was dark and rough. I did not like to use it —so the mites multiplied.

To make our misery complete, the winter of 1945/46 and the following winter of 1946/47 were very cold. Like most people, we suffered from the cold because little heating material was available. When we woke up in the morning we could see our breath. There was a film of ice on our blanket. To stay warm, my mother and I would sleep under the same large down blanket. It was the blanket that she had mailed from Stieglitz. How could we have survived without it?

There were days when I never felt warm. One of those days I remember well. Mutti was sick in bed and I had to do an errand. An icy wind blew snow dust into my face as I was climbing over the rubble to get to the street. Upon my return, the front door had been blown open and snow was covering our entrance hall.

7. Rubble woman.

8. The service of the rubble women was very much needed as in all of Germany four million houses had been destroyed and another four million severely damaged. The women were recruited for the cleanup not just in Berlin, but in all of Germany; because so many men had died in war or were in prisoner-of-war camps, seven million more women than men lived in Germany at that time.

To the right was the door to our apartment. I was in a hurry to get in, because I felt a strong urge to use the toilet. I tried to unlock our door, but it did not open. The lock was frozen shut. I blew warm breath onto the key, then crouched a little and blew into the keyhole. That's when it happened—my bladder relaxed and something wonderfully warm ran down my legs. Here I was, locked out, with tears streaming down my cheeks, I had peed into my pants, and at the same time I was happy about the brief moment of gentle warmth.

In spite of the medical help, my mother recuperated very slowly. In the spring of 1946, she was no longer confined to bed and took care of things. She got medicine for me and the terrible scabies problem went away in a relatively short time.

City Street in Berlin

Mutti knew that we had barely survived the past winter. Never again did she want us to be in such a predicament. Pushing her scruples aside, she decided to deal on the black market. And who would have known—she showed good business skills. Apparently, I had not just inherited these from my father, but from her too.

Frequently, Mutti's black market dealings became a family operation involving my grandmother, grandaunt Hedwig, and me. Aunt Hedwig sewed a big bag out of an old military coat. She used the shoulder boards with the military rank insignia and repurposed them as handles. I would stick my arms through them and carry the bag like a backpack.

Mutti found a source for oatmeal. Together we traveled there, had our bag filled to the top, and I carried it home on my back. Mutti filled the oats into many small paper bags, which she sold for a small profit. Usually all bags had been already pre-ordered by friends, relatives, or neighbors.

The same was true when my mother got hold of a big parcel filled with Cadbury Chocolates. Twenty customers were waiting for their delivery. I counted them and excitedly exclaimed: "Mutti, you got twenty-one bars!" Not believing me, Mutti recounted. Indeed she had twenty-one bars. She kept the extra bar for us. Each day, she would break a piece off for each of us. We ate it with delight—our special little feast of the day. Ever since, when I hold a Cadbury or similar chocolate bar in my hands a picture of this first bar appears before my eyes.

Sometimes Mutti made bad trades. An example was the bottle of oil that a farmer sold her. With it and the potatoes she got, she planned to fry potato pancakes —a specialty to which she invited Aunt Hedwig and two friends. She prepared a batter of grated potatoes, heated the oil, and added a spoonful of batter. The oil acted strange. Its drops did not bounce on the hot surface and it smoked enormously. Also the fried pancakes did not taste as we remembered. Regardless, we were hungry and ate them. The following day we suffered from bad diarrhea. Instead of cooking oil, my mother had gotten machine oil.

Mutti's trade was limited to small-scale food purchases and bartering. Her gains were not big; for instance, it was not enough to buy new shoes for me. Nevertheless, it helped us to survive without the deprivation we had experienced before. Never again did my mother suffer from hunger edema or I from scabies. Her trading business most likely improved my mother's mental health too. She rarely cried now or not at all.

⏝

The West German currency reform in June 1948 changed everything. (See: One city—two currencies) In exchange for one Reichsmark we each received forty Deutsche Mark (DM). A week later we could exchange another twenty Reichsmark for twenty DM. All other saved money lost its value 100:10 and later to 100:6.5.

A day after the currency reform, the former bare shelves in stores were filled with goods. "Where does all this stuff come from?" we wondered.

Apparently, rumors of the imminent reform had leaked out and merchants had horded the items until they could sell them for the new currency, which was ten times more valuable than the old Reichmark.

The Soviet Union instituted a similar currency reform a few days later in East Germany and East Berlin. Because they were unable to print the new bills due to a paper shortage, they used value added stickers on the old ones. We called them "wallpaper money."

Stalin wanted to prevent the DM from becoming the currency of East Berlin and East Germany. Because the allied nations, which occupied

Germany, could not come to an agreement about the currency and other issues, Stalin closed the borders and blocked all surface shipments of goods to
West Berlin. In order to supply us with the necessities for survival, the Western powers established the "Berlin Airlift." (See: Supplies from the skies)

Initially we were afraid that we would again experience very hard
times. How could it be possible to supply two million Berliners with everything they needed by airplane? To our surprise and relief, the Americans
with the help of the English and French made it happen.

To lighten the planeload, many food items flown in were dehydrated.
We had dehydrated potatoes, turnips, and carrots. The dry carrots were
small sticks, which tasted wonderfully sweet. I also found the milk powder
to be very tasty.

"Marianne, don't get into the milk powder!" my mother admonished
me sternly and wagged her index finger in front of my nose. The minute she
had shut the door behind her, I dipped my spoon into the delicious powder
and with relish put a heaping spoonful into my mouth. "Mutti will not notice a little less milk powder in the can," was my reasoning. Wrong! The door
opened. Mutti had forgotten something and asked me about it. Bubbles of
almost dissolved powder spilled out of my mouth as I was trying to answer.
My mother was not amused.

We fondly called the airplanes, which brought us all the goods, "Ros-
inen Bomber" (Raisin Bombers). They constantly flew in and out of Berlin.
Once I got to experience them first hand. Mutti and I visited an aunt, who
lived very close to the Tempelhof airport. We sat on her back porch to enjoy
a cup of coffee—or at least tried to do so.

Every three minutes a huge cargo plane roared so low over us, that
we instinctively pulled in our heads. The noise swallowed up our conversation; the air pressure made the coffee table wobble, and the dishes clink. We
quickly held onto our cups to make sure that the precious coffee did not spill
onto our clean dresses.

Aftereffect

"Did your childhood during the war leave lasting marks?"

"I don't like to be in a confined space," Marianne answered. "If a small
room is also poorly lit, I can't tolerate being in it for any length of time.
I have to get outside where I can breathe freely. I believe my experience
of being in the Kinderbunker, when the door was buried beneath rubble,
caused this."

"I can't throw away any food. This is impossible for me after I had experienced so much hunger and frequent shortages. By the way, this is not unusual for my generation. All my friends feel the same way."

"Again and again I become fully aware of the abundance around me. I look at the fruits, vegetables, breads, and baked goods in our grocery stores and markets and marvel at God's plenty. Like a child, I enjoy the wide selection of clothes, shoes, and household items. How wonderful to look at it! I savor it all. I enjoy life and wish it will continue to be full, rich, and peaceful."

The Black Market

After the war an illegal Black Market flourished in Berlin and all of Germany due to the severe food shortages and the extremely small food rations set by the Allied powers. In order to survive and to provide for their families, people had to barter privately or on the Black Market.

In spite of being illegal, everyone knew where to find the local Black Market. All cities and towns had places where Black Market traders would gather. Depending on the degree of law enforcement, traders would carry their wares concealed in their coat pockets, in briefcases, bags, or boxes or would display them openly. Instead of money, American cigarettes might be used in trades.

While professional black marketers became rich and powerful, most participants of the Black Market like Marianne's mother would trade in low volumes in order to survive. Others might bring valuable objects, such as inherited family treasures or items they could do without, to the Black Market and trade them for food.

The following are some of the Black Market prices:[9]

A loaf of bread 35 Mark; a pound of butter 250 Mark; a pound of bacon 200 Mark; one pound of coffee 500 Mark; one American cigarette 5 to 7 Mark. Meanwhile the monthly earnings of a German mineworker were around 200 Mark.[10]

In addition to undermining the moral of the regular working person, the Black Market made the Reich Mark worthless, fostered criminal activities, severely interfered with regular business, and stifled the economy. Reform was needed. Without it Germany would not have been able to rebuild its cities and industries.

---

9. Simon, in Grontzki et al.,*Feuersturm und Hungerwinter*, 261.

10. Gaflig in Grontzki et al., *Feuersturm und Hungerwinter*, 245.

One City—Two Currencies[11]

Three years after Germany's unconditional surrender on May 8, 1945 and the resulting occupation by the four victorious powers, Berlin experienced a crisis that from today's perspective appears as the first great conflict of the Cold War. The Soviet blockade of West Berlin confronted the Western powers with virtually insoluble problems. While the causes of the blockade were varied, the immediate occasion was currency reform.

The victorious powers had been forced to tackle the currency in Germany since the end of the war in 1945. A drastic glut of money, a lack of acceptance for the currency, and flourishing black market made reform a matter of urgency. The withdrawal of the Soviet representative from the Allied Control Council in March 1948, however, rendered a joint approach by the four victorious powers unthinkable. The Western powers announced the currency reform on June 18 and it was implemented two days later. As an immediate response, the Soviet military administration interrupted passenger traffic to and from Berlin on June 19 in order to protect itself from the expected flood of now worthless Reichmarks. A currency reform for the Soviet occupation zone was decreed on June 23. In Berlin the Western powers refused to recognize this "East currency." Instead they adapted the currency reforms enacted in the Western zones, so that beginning on June 25 the German mark of the Bank of the German States (West DM) also became legal tender in West Berlin. Berlin was now divided not only into four occupation zones, but also into two currency zones.

Supplies from the Sky[12]

Apart from the mentioned blockades of street traffic on June 19, between June 19 and 29, 1948 the Soviets also successively blocked all routes by land, rail, and water between West Berlin and the three Western zones. Only the air corridors on which the four victorious powers had agreed in the Air Agreement of 1945/46 were unaffected. For that reason the three Western powers began the Airlift to Berlin to supply the city and its approximately two million inhabitants with the necessities. It was an ambitious plan never before attempted on this scale and it was unclear whether it would work.

11. Alliierten Museum Berlin, *One city—two currencies.*
12. Alliierten Museum Berlin, *Supplies from the sky.*

On July 28, 1948 the first American and British aircraft landed at Tempelhof and Gatow airfields with goods for the people of Berlin. Many other flights followed, but nobody could predict how long the blockade would last. For that reason, the western powers initially planned to supply the city into the winter. The aim in the first weeks of the airlift was to fly 4,500 tons of goods into the city every day. This was raised to 5,000 tons a day in the autumn of 1948. Coal to meet the city's energy needs made up a large proportion of this tonnage.

In October U.S. General William H. Turner was appointed to head the Combined Airlift Taskforce (CALTF), which had its headquarters in Wiesbaden. He perfected the Airlift. The American military governor of Germany, General Lucius D. Clay, ensured the necessary political support of U.S. President Harry S. Truman. Clay continually requested more and larger aircraft to use in the Airlift, and Truman approved them.

In the first months of the Airlift, the French occupation power participated with six airplanes. The urgently needed third airport in Tegel in the French sector was completed in November 1948. Some 19,000 workers built it in record time, taking just three months. The British mobilized their Royal Air Force and contracted with an additional 25 charter companies to fly mainly oil and gasoline into the city. Aside from their circa 23 percent of the total Airlift tonnage for freight, the British were also responsible for the lion's share of passenger transport during the blockade. With their C-54-transport planes, the U.S. forces provided the largest air fleet for "Operation Vittles," as the Americans called the mission. In spring 1949 the operation to supply Berlin was working so well that on some days more goods were flown into the city than had arrived before the blockade by road, water, and rail.

The Western powers used the media very effectively to publicize this outstanding efficiency. The continuing positive reporting on Allied tonnage and the growing reputation of the Western powers were certainly part of the reason for the lifting of the Soviet blockade on May 12, 1949. Despite the end of the blockade, the Airlift continued for another four months into late summer 1949. The historical events known as the "Berlin Blockade" and the "Berlin Airlift" are thus chronologically not wholly identical.

The lifting of the blockade and the end of the Airlift solved the first crisis of the Cold War by logistical means – without military force. This did not, however, mean that there were no casualties of the Airlift. At least 78 people died in airplane accidents. Their names are engraved on the base of the Airlift Memorial in the Berlin district of Tempelhof.

Brigitte

Chapter 9

How I Saved my Mother's and Grandmother's Lives

Brigitte, born September 1942 in Berlin, Germany

"WHEN I WAS JUST two years old, I saved my mother's and grandmother's lives", Brigitte told me:

It happened in 1944, when Berlin was bombed almost daily. As soon as the sirens wailed my mother and grandmother would run with me across the street to the air raid shelter under the large church, where we stayed during the bombardment until the all-clear signal sounded.

One time when Mutti was hurrying with me past the warden of the shelter, he stopped us.

"Is your child sick?" he wanted to know, "What does she have?"

"The doctor says Brigittchen[1] has measles", answered my mother truthfully.

---

1. Diminutive of Brigitte.

"Measles! Don't you know they are contagious?" he exclaimed. "No, you can't take your sick child into the shelter."

Dejected, Mutti and Oma rushed back into the basement of the apartment house we lived in. It did not have the extra sturdy walls and the double thick cement ceiling like the shelter, but it had to be sufficient for right now.

The bombardment started. The planes seem to be right overhead. With ear-splitting blasts the bombs crashed down in our direct vicinity. How relieved Mutti and Oma must have been when the terror stopped and our apartment building had not been hit. But the church across the street had been severely damaged. It must have been a powerful 4,000-pound British "blockbuster" bomb, which had caused the walls on one side of the nave to collapse into a massive mountain of rubble. The entrance to the air raid shelter was buried under it.

During the following days, a rescue crew worked nonstop to free the entrance. Unfortunately, their equipment was unable to remove the enormous pieces of church masonry. They could not save the many, trapped people. For the refuge seekers, the shelter became a mass grave in which they slowly suffocated. If I hadn't caught the measles we would have shared their fate and I wouldn't have grown older than two years.

Mutti and Oma had not always gotten off lightly. The apartment building my grandparents had lived in previously had housed a leather manufacturing business on the first floor. During an air raid, an incinerating bomb sparked the flammable chemicals of the factory. A fierce fire broke out that soon engulfed the entire building. My grandparents lost everything. Oma had to deal with the accident by herself, because my grandfather was in the military. Homeless, she was lucky to be assigned to a room in the rear tenement house.

Two weeks later, Mutti and I moved in with Oma, because we too had become homeless. A bomb had damaged the apartment house we had lived in to the extent that it became uninhabitable. The stairway had remained intact, but might collapse at anytime.

Against orders, my mother had climbed to the fourth floor, where we had lived and checked out our apartment. She found her fine china unscathed in its cabinet. Proudly she later recalled how she managed to save it.

"My dear neighbor helped me. We found several clothes lines, which we tied firmly together. I tied the rope to the handle of my shopping basket and went up to our apartment. One by one I loaded some cups or plates into the basket and let it down slowly. My friend would take the items out, and I would pull the basket back up. We worked until even the large beautiful coffeepot was retrieved without a nick or scratch."

Today the precious service sits in my china cabinet. Every time I look at it, I am reminded of how my mother saved it from our ruined house. I never use it. I think it is something like a holy relic for me.

After I had recuperated from the measles, Mutti decided to leave Berlin. It had been very confining for us to live with Oma in a single room. Also, it was not safe there. The continued bombing raised the odds that a bomb would also hit the house she lived in. We knew people, who had lost everything due to bombardment not just once but two or even three times. And as we had just experienced, air raid shelters did not guarantee survival.

My parents had good friends in Finowfurt, a small town close to Eberswalde, about sixty miles northeast of Berlin. They invited us to stay with them, which we gladly accepted.

↶

My earliest memories begin around this time. I recall a jam-packed train with people sitting on the roof and standing on the outside steps by the door.

It must have been during the early Russian occupation of Berlin, that I sat with Oma in a basement and Russian soldiers burst in shouting: "Uri! Uri!" Nothing bad happened to us as far as I know. My mother must not have been able to find a place for us to live in Berlin and we were evacuated to Leetza in the Wittenberg district in Saxony-Anhalt about seventy miles southwest of Berlin.

I remember well an event when I was almost three years old. In late August of 1945, I was playing in the courtyard with neighborhood children, when a tall, slender man stepped in, crouched down to me and asked: "Where is your Mutti?" As soon as I answered he disappeared into the house. "Brigittchen, that's your Papa," called out my older friend. Quickly I scampered after the man. Looking up the stairway I saw Mutti and Papa standing by the open door to our apartment hugging each other.

How happy my parents must have been to see each other again. Until the moment my father stepped into the courtyard, he had not been sure how we had survived the war. And my mother—she had not heard from him and had feared the worst. And the worst had almost happened.

My father recounted how he had been taken prisoner at the Czechoslovakian border. With many other German prisoners of war he was loaded onto a freight train on its way to France. What would await them there?

"A friend and I decided to flee. Close to Fulda[2] we jumped off the train and ran for cover in nearby bushes. Shots rang out. Luckily we were out of sight when the guards fired."

---

2. A town in the German State of Hessen.

They managed to disappear within the German civilian population and reached the nearby city of Kassel. By telling an official a good story, my father received the required papers allowing him to travel from Kassel to Berlin. With this document, Papa was no longer in danger of being recaptured like a fugitive slave.

In Berlin, my father found Oma, who told him where we were. Now he wanted us to move back to Berlin and made it possible for us to do so. The housing office allotted us one and a half rooms in an apartment with four and a half rooms in East-Berlin. We shared the kitchen, bath and toilet with a woman and her teenage son as well as another woman with three children. How much privacy did we enjoy in our one and a half rooms? Yet, we did not complain about our tight quarters, as we knew that many people in Berlin made do with even less space. We lived there for the next five years.

Soon my father found a job. This too was enviable, because most Berliners had none right after the war. What work did my father do? He shoveled coal for the Russians. That was a surprisingly lucrative job at the time. Everyday Papa returned home with coal in his lumpy briefcase. It was more than we could use. Mutti happily exchanged our surplus coal for whatever we needed. Coal was worth more than gold.

Thanks to the coal my father earned, we survived the next years of severe scarcity from 1945 to 1948 without going hungry or suffering from the cold. Compared to our neighbors, we were doing well.

Once I became acutely aware of what our neighbors were experiencing. Mutti had spread butter on a bread crust and handed it to me. I walked out with it looking for my friends. Before I reached them, an older boy ran past me, snatched the bread out off my hand, and gulped it down immediately. "Was my crust his only meal that day?" I wonder today.

During the record cold winter of 1947–48, coal was especially valuable. Berliners went to extremes in their search of heating materials. They screwed the wooden slats off park benches and dug up roots of tree stumps left behind by legal or illegal lumberjacks felling trees in the Grunewald— the beautiful forest of Berlin. We heard of a well-to-do family who cut up their fine furniture to use it as firewood.

My mother's bartering business was thriving. She had enough money to buy tickets to the fancy Faschingsball[3] for Papa and herself. Unfortunately, they did not get to go because the hastily repaired dance hall burned down before the event. Instead, they went to the movies, leaving me at home alone.

"Brigittchen, you may listen to the Little Sandman radio program. Afterwards you go to bed and sleep tight", Mutti had said before leaving.

---

3. Carnival Dance.

I was five years old and had other ideas. I locked the door and decided to stay up until my parents returned. In spite of my effort to stay awake, I got so tired that I fell into a deep sleep; a sleep so deep that I did not hear my parents knocking, when they returned.

They pounded against the door—I did not wake up. They called my name—I did not wake up. Even when my mother went to the neighbors above us, leaned out of their window and let keys, tied to a string, clank against the window over my bed, I remained asleep. Finally, Papa borrowed a saw, cut out a square in the door, reached in, and turned the key. "Mutti, who ruined our door?" I called out, when I finally awoke the next morning.

In August 1948, my brother Hans Jürgen was born. A few months later he got sick with double pneumonia, which triggered bronchial asthma. Gravely worried about his health, Mutti took him to our grandparents in West Berlin, convinced that he would receive better medical care there. Fortunately, Hans Jürgen recovered. He continued to stay with my grandparents for a long time, because they were able to take better care of him.

We struggled during the following years. My father lost his job in 1948 after the German currency reform and was unemployed. Eventually he entered a retraining program to become a shoemaker. He made sturdy leather shoes for me, which I did not appreciate. Due to a severe shortage of footwear, my friends wore crudely made wooden sandals held together with cloth strips and I too wanted those. Only later did I learn that they were very uncomfortable.

Was it my disapproval or the extreme low pay, which made my father want to quit this line of work? Before the war he had been a policeman in a district, which now was in West Berlin. If we lived there, he most likely would be able to regain his former job.

Our grandparent would have liked for us to live close to them and would have helped us to move. Yet for political reasons, our move from East to West Berlin was next to impossible. Instead of just changing our address within Berlin, we might as well have planned to emigrate to a different continent. In order to move we needed a permit. In order to obtain the permit we needed an application. And for the application we had to meet certain requirements, which we didn't. In short, we would never get the needed permit to legally move to West Berlin. Consequently, my parents considered leaving East Berlin illegally in the summer of 1953.

Our departure had to be prepared very carefully. No one, not the co-workers, neighbors, or even our best friends, could know about the plan. Only total concealment would assure that the feared Stasi, the East-German secret police, would not hear about our intentions, foil our plan, and punish us severely. I was ten years old at the time. My parents let me in on their plan, trusting that I could keep the secret, which I did.

⌐

Then, an unexpected event occurred. On July 16, 1953 workers in East Berlin started to protest against their work conditions. The protest spread like a wild fire. The next day, July 17, over one million citizens of East Berlin and East Germany took to the streets demanding better working conditions and democratic freedom.

My father and many of his colleges at work took part in the demonstrations at the Brandenburger Tor[4], the main passage between East and West Berlin. Overwhelmed by the protesters, the guards retreated, and for the next few hours people could pass freely through this artificial border. Some families seized the opportunity and travelled unhindered with all their belongings to a new life in the West.

Before we could do the same, the tide changed. I remember being out in the street not far from our house and seeing Soviet tanks rolling towards the border. What was happening?

Later Papa came home and reported: "It's turning ugly. Several of my buddies were taken into custody. I am glad I could get away in time."

The Russian tanks and troops had moved against the unarmed demonstrators. Fifty people died and many more were injured. Sweeping arrests were made. My father heard that one of his colleagues had killed himself while in police custody.

After it was all over, the Soviet Administration sealed the border. No one was allowed to pass in or out of East Berlin. Had we missed our chance? It was a hard blow, especially for Mutti, because Hans Jürgen still lived with my grandparents. We had visited him every weekend. Even though we had not been allowed to move out of East Berlin, we had always been able to cross the border freely as long as we carried no luggage or anything indicating a household move. We waited weeks and weeks. When would we see Hans Jürgen again?

How relieved we were, when after six long weeks of uncertainty the border was reopened. Again, my mother could commute to work by the most convenient route, which took her through part of West Berlin. She noted that during the very early hours, the Vopos, as the Berliners called the East German police, were not yet on duty.

Taking advantage of this fact, Mutti left our house early in the morning with two large bags filled with household items and walked in the first grey

4. Brandenburg Gate.

daylight to the U-Bahn Station (subway station). She got off close to our grandparents place, emptied her bags at their house, and continued on to work.

Mutti did this many times. When she returned home from work the controlling Vopo would notice her large bags and check them, only to find them empty. Once when his boss came along, Mutti brazenly complained to him: "Why does the Vopo look into my bags every day? He knows they are always empty!"

"Well, my sweet woman, maybe he likes to look at the owner of the bags," was his amused answer.

Another time, Mutti stuffed bedding into our baby carriage and between the pillows she hid her precious white china, which she had saved from the bombed-out house.

Papa did his part. One Saturday he stuffed the brass rods of our bed under his shirt and down one pant leg. Like an injured war veteran, he limped with a stiff leg to the U-Bahn station and travelled to Oma and Opa. He couldn't strap our two upholstered chairs to his waist and hide them. So he mounted one onto his bike and rode to the border.

"My father-in-law will re-upholster the chair. May I take it to him?" he politely asked the guard. Just as friendly, the Vopo let him pass.

The next Saturday he told the same story to the guard at a different crossing and again he was allowed to proceed.

The following weekend we left our almost empty rooms in East Berlin for good.

Aftereffect

"Did the war and the period after the war influence you later in life?"

Brigitte reflects: "I know about the war and the bombing through the accounts of my parents and grandparents. I had been too young to remember it."

"Due to the shortage of school buildings and teachers after the war, I had a poor elementary school education. This was compounded by our move to West Berlin. The curriculum of the two parts of Berlin could not have been more different. In East Berlin we learned Russian, in West Berlin we were taught English and French. When I entered school in the West I had missed the introduction to both languages, and had to catch up on my own without any help. In general my schooling had been insufficient. Later as an adult, I noticed large gaps in my knowledge of history and sciences."

"Because we moved frequently, I had no childhood friendships which lasted into adulthood. When we moved to West Berlin, we left our neighborhood abruptly without saying good-bye. All our ties to the people we had known were severed. This was sad."

The Divided City

When in May 1949 the part of Germany that was occupied by Great Britain, France, and the USA was united and the Bundesrepublik Deutschland or West Germany, was founded, its constitution claimed all of Berlin as part of its territory. Later in October 1949 the eastern part of Germany, occupied by the Soviet Union, became the Deutsche Demokratische Republik, or East Germany, and it too claimed all of Berlin as part of its territory making Berlin its capital. In reality, East Germany governed the eastern section of the city, which came to be known as East Berlin, while the western section of the city was regarded as part of the West, called West Berlin.

The border between the two Berlins no longer just divided different occupation zones, or two cities, or two countries, but two worlds. The border was part of "The Iron Curtain," which at the time divided the world into two spheres of influence—the West and the East—capitalism and communism. When later in 1961 the infamous Berlin Wall was built, it merely confirmed the existing facts.

Anyone who wanted to move from East Germany, which included East Berlin, to West Germany or West Berlin, needed an official permit to do so. Illegal relocation to the West was punishable by law and usually resulted in a prison term.

In order to leave the country legally, one had to submit an application for permanent emigration, which was considered an "Unlawful Request." The secret police were informed of your intention and summoned you to a "frank discussion" about your reasons and motives for wanting to leave the country. Usually the applicant would be demoted immediately or lost his job. All educational opportunities for him or his family would be curtailed. His children would no longer be allowed to attend high school or a university.

Applications from persons who were or had been members of armed organizations were instantly rejected. For others, the application process dragged on for months or years. During that time, the applicant suffered from further discriminations and harassments, which were intended to induce him or her to withdraw the application.

Persons who tried to legally leave East Germany argued that article 13 of the UN Universal Declaration of Human Rights of December 10, 1948 applied to their request. It states:

Everyone has the right to freedom of movement and residence within the borders of each state.

Everyone has the right to leave any country, including his own, and to return to his country.

The declaration had been drafted by nine UN member states including the USSR. Therefore, East Germany was bound by it as well. Not wanting to defy the international community, as well as for other internal reasons, some legal exit permits were granted

Christa, right, with her father and her sister

Chapter 10

The Bank Vault Was our Air Raid Shelter

Christa, born December 1936 in Ranis by Plößneck,
Thuringia, Germany

THE HOSPITAL IN THE small town of Pösneck in the state of Thuringia had a rather mediocre reputation. Therefore, Christa's father, the vice-president of the Deutsche Staatsbank (German National Bank) of Pößneck, decided that for the birth of their second child, his wife should go to the superior hospital of nearby Ranis. Here Christa was born two years after her sister Helga.

Christa enjoyed talking about her childhood:

My earliest memories are from the fall of 1939, when I was three years old. I stayed at my grandfather's house, while my parents and my sister Helga vacationed at a Baltic Sea resort. Helga had been sick and the doctor had recommended it for her recuperation.

Deemed too young to come along, I did not witness, but was later told, that an urgent message had been sent to my father at the resort. It asked him to immediately report to the military. He was slated to serve as a non-combat officer in the regional military administration stationed in Kassel, Hessen. Because he had a heart ailment, he fortunately never had to serve in a combat mission.

My mother continued to live with us in Pößneck, where we occupied the spacious, third story apartment over the Staatsbank provided for the bank's vice-president. It was a nice place for us to grow up in, but we missed our father whose military duty kept him in Kassel. I was the reason that we stayed with him for several weeks.

During the summer of 1941 both of my legs were very seriously infected. I was an active, energetic little child and had cut deep gashes into my legs. It hurt when Mutti cleaned them with iodine and wrapped my legs with bandages. According to the doctor's order, the bandages were changed each day and more iodine applied, which made me scream in pain for all to hear. As the treatment continued on the following days I tried to escape before the procedure started, kicking, and yelling even louder.

My wounds did not get better. My legs swelled and I was hardly able to walk. The danger of blood poisoning was very real, because antibiotics were not yet available. My mother was desperate, when she called my father.

"Trude, come with the girls to Kassel. Our army physician knows best how to treat wounds. I want him to take care of Christa," my father decided.

"Fill the tub with warm water and add curt soap. Have Christa soak in it twice a day," the nice physician ordered. I did not mind this treatment. It was soothing to sit in the warm soapy water. Slowly and steadily my wounds got better.

During our stay Mutti, Helga, and I lodged with an elderly widow, who was my father's landlady. Our father, always wearing civilian clothes, took us to see castles, to visit beautiful parks, and other interesting places. These were good days. The war seemed far away. He was our "Vati." I got an inkling of what a family was supposed to be like.

About eight months after our visit, Allied planes heavily bombarded Kassel again and again. The city of over a quarter of a million citizens was reduced to rubble with about 50,000 survivors by the end of the war. My father stayed there until the bitter end. We never visited him in Kassel again.

Bombers had not reached Pößneck then. We lived peacefully in the large bank building in the center of town. To get to our apartment, we walked up its formidable stairway and passed by the bank president's apartment on the second floor until we reached the third floor landing. From there I would run ahead through a narrow, long hallway with doors to two large rooms and a toilet on the right side. At the end of the hall I reached the door to our place: a small, dim entrance hall, leading to our large center hall (in German a Diele) with doors to the kitchen, living rooms, and bedrooms. One of the bedrooms had been converted to a large bathroom. The building had central heating, which kept us comfortable all year around.

Our maid helped my mother with her housework. Sometimes we had a nanny too. She would wear a shiny white apron and a little bonnet. When she took us, dressed in matching dresses, into the living room where mother's guests had gathered, they would exclaim, "Oh, Trude, you have the sweetest girls!"

Little did they know about Helga and my escapades.

Germany was at war, but we lived comfortably. Surely, food was rationed, but the allotments were sufficient, and if we needed more, we would buy it directly from nearby farmers. Nevertheless, because my father was a participant, the war was very real for my mother.

Only twice in my life did I see my mother weep. The first time occurred on the 22nd of April 1942. She stood at the window looking forlorn, while tears streamed down her face. I snuggled up to her.

She told me that Germany had attacked Russia and that we would lose the war and that we would suffer for the sins of our country. Of course, I did not understand this fully then, but it filled me with an ominous sense of unease.

Towards the end of the war in early April 1945, Pößneck and other towns around us became the targets of US bombers. We assumed that the railway crossing close to the center of our town and a nearby underground ammunition factory were the main targets.

As soon as the air raid sirens screeched, we ran all the way down the stairway to the basement of the bank. The large underground bank vault was our designated shelter. There we stayed until the all-clear signal sounded.

One time we were not fast enough. The airplanes were already over us, as we were rushing downstairs. A huge detonation occurred close by. The air pressure from the blast pushed Helga and me against the railing. Without looking to see if we were hurt, Mutti called out in panic: "Keep running! Keep running!" We did. Safe in the vault we had plenty of time to look at our bruises. The bank president, his wife, and grown daughter, as well as the old bank custodian and his wife, were already in the shelter, when we burst in. Again and again bombs exploded in our vicinity.

The thick walls of the vault trembled. The heavy binders, lined up on a sturdy shelf on one side of the room, flew towards us like missiles. Luckily, no one was hit. We were frightened by the incident; especially so the wife of the director. The emergency water bucket was empty. Mrs. Bank President put it over her head for protection. How funny she looked with her head stuck in the bucket and its handle decorating her bosom. Helga and I looked at each other giggling softly, ready to burst out into laughter. A stern look from our mother told us that we were out of turn laughing at the old lady. During the next air raid we had to wear combat helmets, which also looked very much out of place and ridiculous on all of us.

Frequently the bombers just flew over us on the way to another target. The air raid warden had explained to us: "During flight the bomb makes a high pitched noise. This is followed by a pause and then the bomb will explode. If you hear a piping noise, the bomb will hit elsewhere." I would listen carefully, which alleviated my constant fear.

I often thought, "What will happen, if a bomb hits the bank?" "Would we be able to get out of the vault or would we be buried alive?" It was not the image of being dead, but of how we would die that concerned me.

Once we were in the vault a long time, and when Helga and especially I got restless, our mother went with us for a short walk outside. Strolling along the wide Linden Alley, a menacing roar approached us. Mutti grabbed our hands and pulled us under a nearby bush. A low-flying plane seemed to brush the tops of the stately Linden trees. We stayed hidden until the plane disappeared, and then hurried back to the vault.

During the bombardments, several buildings next to us, as well as next to the railroad station were destroyed. Fifty-seven persons lost their lives. The wife and daughter of our grocer were among them. They had been at home, when their house was hit. How sad this must have been for the grocer, who had stayed at his store in spite of the danger and had survived. I did not dare to look into his eyes, afraid to see his sorrow.

We knew the end of the war was near. Unexpectedly, one day, our father appeared in the doorway of the vault. His unit had come through town fleeing from the occupation forces, which had taken over Kassel. Vati hugged and kissed us. Putting his arm around her, he left with Mutti. A little later I found her sitting in an empty bank office. She wept. I wiggled onto her lap. "Christa, maybe this was the last time we saw Vati," she muttered.

How dangerous would it be for him to travel in a military convoy? Anytime a low flying plane might spot it. The combat zone was now close to us. Already enemy shelling reached our town and our building. We spent most of the time in the vault. I just hated that room.

᮫

Then it happened: The American troops moved into Pößneck. Helga and I stood at the side of the street and watched. In the first vehicle next to the American commander sat our mayor holding a white flag of surrender.

Next, large tanks and military trucks rolled down our street. Some vehicles stopped in front of the bank.

An hour or so later my mother went to the apartment of the bank president to hear about any news. To her surprise, the family was packing their belongings. "We have to leave in half an hour," the president explained. "The Americans confiscated the building."

Too concerned with their own fate, they had not shared the news with us. With no time left to argue, my mother rushed upstairs. She hastily packed our essentials into two suitcases.

The Americans came on time. While they moved in, we sat on our suitcases on the sidewalk. A dear neighbor, living across the street from us, invited us to stay overnight in her guest room. We gladly accepted and lived there until the Americans left.

The American troops and their commander were friendly to us. When my mother noticed the next day, that in the rush she had forgotten essential things, they allowed her to retrieve them. Concerned she noted how much the officers had changed our apartment.

One of the officers enjoyed talking to us. He called Helga and me "Red Skirts" and told my mother that back home in the US, he had two girls our age.

I had an encounter, which deeply impressed me. While I was playing outside, my ball bounced away and rolled across the street under a jeep parked in front of the bank. I ran after it, but then stopped hesitantly. No, I did not dare to get close to the vehicle with a big black man sitting in it. Never before had I seen a person with black skin. The soldier had observed me, got out and squeezed his large frame under the car. Holding my ball in one hand he dived into his pocket with the other. With a big smile he stretched both arms towards me. One open palm held my ball, the other a piece of gum. "For you, little girl," his gesture and twinkling eyes said. I approached him and took both. "Danke schön,"[1] I thanked him with enthusiasm. Then I turned on my heels and raced home in a flash. "I have to tell and show it to Mutti and Helga," was all I could think of.

After about three months, the Americans left Pößneck. As had been agreed by the USA, USSR, and UK, the administration of Thuringia was transferred to the USSR on July 1st, 1945.

Mutti was surprised and pleased to find everything in its place, after we moved back into our apartment. Our rubber duckies serenely floated in our bathtub. Was it a little gesture from the Americans to make us feel at home again?

1. German for thank you.

The people of Pößneck waited with apprehension for the arrival of the Russian troops. I sneaked out of the house and ran to the edge of town to watch them move in. So many times I had heard terrible stories about the Russians. I wanted to see them with my own eyes. I was surprised, that they did not march in formation, but wandered in groups—almost like visitors— and looked like ordinary men in uniform.

Luckily, the Russian Commander liked the hotel across the street from us better than the bank building. So we were allowed to stay in our apartment. Only the two rooms off the long hallway to our apartment would be used as living quarters for various officers. They came with a permit from the commander, which they had to show my mother prior to moving in. The arrangement was acceptable to us, as we only had to share the toilet off the hallway with them. Mutti took care that we had potties in our bedrooms, so we didn't have to go into the hallway at night.

Helga and I had nicknames for our Russian roomers. "Ivan the Stingy" asked our mother to fry bacon for him, while his girlfriend stood besides her, watching that not a single piece would be diverted into our household.

We giggled when we saw another officer with his pistol strapped over his pajama bottoms march to the toilet in the morning. I don't remember what we called him. Maybe "Gregor-ready to shoot at poop?"

"Peter-the-Handsome" was in love with my mother. He wanted to marry her, he told us. Then we would all move to Russia. There we would live in a fine house, where the light came from the ceiling and the water from the wall.

Once our doorbell rang at night. My mother opened the door and several drunken soldiers pushed their way in. I don't know how my mother got rid of them. Did the officers hear the commotion and take care of it? I don't know. I do remember that the commander ordered my mother never to let drunks into our apartment. "How I am going to do this?" she wanted to know. Fortunately, never again did a drunk come all the way up to the third floor.

Another officer had a very handy girlfriend. She had a car and would drive around the countryside and barter food from the farmers. Sometimes she would invite Helga and me to come along. We loved these fun trips. The girlfriend always managed to get lots of good things, which she generously shared with us. Mutti was thankful for everything we brought back.

After the war, all food items were rare. We suffered from hunger.

Sometimes the parents of our former maid sent us some produce from their farm. This suggests to me that our mother must have treated her well. Mutti never ever wanted us to go to bed hungry. Whenever and wherever food was available, she would purchase it. If none was sold, she would barter for food. Anything she felt she could do without, she sold for food: clothes, jewelry, handbags, pictures, and even our piano. How sad she looked, when her much beloved piano was carted off on a farm wagon.

I had my own ideas of how to get something to eat for us. Helga did not dare to, so I went on my own. Just nine years old, I shouldered my knapsack and scoured the neighborhood for edibles. I would gather apples or other fruit, which had fallen from a tree. Like other people in town, I gathered shafts of wheat from a harvested farm field.

Once I spied a heap of potatoes sitting at the edge of a plot. Excitedly I filled my backpack to the rim. Hurrying home I imagined how happy Mutti would be, when she saw what I had found. At last I reached our stairway. Wow, I wasn't prepared for how much the heavy knapsack pulled me back. Barely in time, I grabbed the handrail to keep myself from tumbling downstairs.

Mutti was grateful for all I brought home, but I knew she was uneasy about my adventures. Maybe it would have put her at ease if I had told her that when I had stolen cabbage from a field, I had met my teacher. He had probably seen me in the act and I had been deeply embarrassed. Later it had occurred to me to ask myself: "What was he doing there?"

Due to the shortage of coal, our central heating system was no longer running. Nor could Mutti cook on our gas stove, as there was no gas. She used the old-fashioned coal kitchen stove for cooking and heating. During the winter our large kitchen was the only warm room. We felt fortunate, when we had enough wood or coal to heat it, and maybe our living room as well at Christmas time. Our bedrooms were not heated at all. On especially cold winter mornings the urine in our potty was frozen.

I tried to "find" some coal. I went to the train station where goods were loaded and transferred. A coal car sat on a sidetrack. I climbed in and stuffed the briskets into my knapsack. Excited by my find, I filled it without thinking how I could carry the load home. Well, I didn't have to worry about it.

A policeman spotted me: "Down from the truck!" he called. I obeyed as fast as I could. Small and guilty I stood in front of him. What would happen to me? Were tears welling up? I can't remember. He looked at me and ordered: "You better hurry and put the coal back on the truck." I did while he watched me. That was it—he hadn't even pulled my ear. Relieved, I ran home to safety. Later I found out that people stealing a little to survive were usually not punished.

⌐

It was in the fall of 1945 that Helga and I were playing outside. We noticed in the distance a truck loaded with men. We assumed they could be

German prisoners of war, because during the past weeks several groups of men had come home.

"I bet the truck will stop at the corner by the post office," Helga reasoned. "Let's run, maybe Vati is one of them." We raced there, reaching the flat bed truck just in time to watch incredulously as our father climbed down. We rejoiced and flew into his arms. He hugged and kissed us both at once. What a happy coincidence. A movie director couldn't have timed it better.

"Won't Mutti be surprised?" We couldn't wait. Finally we climbed the stairs and leaned on our doorbell. "Hans!" exclaimed Mutti and literally sank into my father's arms. Her knees had buckled. With great effort and our help, Vati kept her from falling.

Aftereffect

Asked how her childhood during World War II had affected her, Christa responded with emphasis:

"I am against war. I am against all wars, wherever they are fought. All my life I have been an anti-war activist and have taken part in many demonstrations. I belong to the local peace organization and regularly take part in our Saturday rally."

"In 1950 when our teacher told us that war had broken out in Korea, my classmates and I were extremely alarmed. She calmed us down by assuring us that Germany had nothing to do with it. "It will never come here," the teacher convinced us by showing on a map, how far away Korea was."

"Also, I am against all stereotyping and vilification of nations or persons by religion, ethnicity, nationality, creed, or color. As a young girl I was told Russians were bad, but the Russians I got to know, were not bad at all. Indeed, the Russian commander of the occupation forces in our town was a good man. He was concerned about our well-being in spite of what the Germans troops had done to the Russian people during the war."

"Pößneck had an almost 500-year-old tradition of the whole town celebrating Christmas Eve together. The Russian commander made it possible for us to celebrate it again in 1945 with hope in our hearts. A Christmas tree was set up in the town square. After dark on Christmas Eve, Helga and I walked to the square with homemade, lighted lanterns accompanied by our parents. All around us, shining lanterns floated through the dark. We gathered around the tree, listened to our mayor speak of peace and hope, and then we sang "Silent Night" together. I will never forget the beautiful sounds and sights of this celebration. It was and will be forever my most memorable and meaningful Christmas."

Erika and her brother Werner Christmas 1942

Chapter 11

We Ate Oatmeal in our Hiding Place

Erika, born November 1935 in Düsseldorf, Germany

ERIKA AND I HAVE known each other for over fifty years. However, there are things we never talked about. I am interested in childhood memories from World War II and the immediate time thereafter. "Did the war affect you growing up?" I ask. "Oh yes, of course it did," is her reply.

↬

This is Erika's story:

I remember when my three-year-older brother Werner and I slept on straw mattresses in the air raid bunker. My eyes were closed, but my ears were alertly tuned in to my environment. I heard my mother and the other adults talk. They sat on benches in the middle of the room, as there was no bunk bed available for them. Today when I ride on a senior citizens tour bus, I close my eyes, relax, and hear fellow travelers talk in the background, I am transported back in time to the air raid shelter of my childhood.

Before the war, my father had been a civil servant of the city government of Düsseldorf. In his position, it became more or less a requirement to be a member of the NSDAP (Nazi party), even though joining it had always been voluntary. My father declined to follow this unwritten rule, which resulted in a more and more unpleasant work environment. To escape from the harassment, he volunteered for military service. Today such a choice may appear counter-intuitive, but it really was not back then. Soldiers had shown their patriotism by enlisting. There was no requirement or subtle pressure for them to join the party.

Initially, my father served in Düsseldorf. I remember strolling along the pedestrian walkway on the dam on the Rhine River and seeing him guarding the Rhine bridge below. I had a piece of candy saved in my coat pocket. I threw it down and watched it land not far from my father's feet. He did not pick it up, wave to me, or call thanks. I felt disappointed and rejected. "Why doesn't Vati like my candy?" I asked my mother. "Mein Schätzchen[1], he is not supposed to do something like that; it's against military rules," my mother explained.

On Easter of 1942, I entered first grade—a big event in a little child's life. I had hardly adjusted to it when my mother moved temporarily with Werner and me to Arnsberg in Westphalia, Germany. The military had transferred my father to the town and had promoted him to be the regional paymaster. We were very glad about this, because Vati did not have to serve in combat and never did so throughout the war. However, at times his "desk job" placed him very close to the front line exposing him to the danger and the hardships of regular soldiers.

After a six months stay in Arnsberg, my mother returned with us to Düsseldorf, where we experienced almost daily air raids. In the summer of 1943, downtown Düsseldorf became the target of a devastating bombardment. Fortunately, our house had not been hit as we lived in a suburban area. I remember, however, walking with my mother and Werner along a street with burning houses on both sides.

We were on our way to the main railroad station of Düsseldorf to take a train to Weida in Thuringia. All women with young children were asked to leave the city for safe havens in rural Germany. The small town of Weida and its surrounding area had not experienced any bombing. Its residents had been notified by the government to house a number of the evacuated families from Düsseldorf.

The housing office of Weida assigned us to two small attic rooms without running water. Mutti was not happy about it. How would we stay warm in these rooms without proper insulation during the harsh winter of Thuringia? What could be done about it?

1. My dear one.

My mother talked to a woman in a similar situation, and they devised a plan of action. Together they traveled back to Düsseldorf and shipped their furniture to Weida. At the housing office in Weida my mother explained, "My furniture does not fit into our assigned rooms and can't be brought up the narrow staircase. What can be done about it?"

Consequently, the office assigned us to two rooms on the first floor of a big single-family house. The drawback was that again we had no running water. At certain hours during the day, we were allowed to draw water in the spacious kitchen. The rest of the time the kitchen was locked. We were allowed to use a toilet in the basement. I remember that the young woman, who had just married the owner of the house, was very unfriendly to us.

Weida was a small, picturesque town with an eight hundred year old history. Google map shows its narrow streets with two-storied timber houses with red tiled roofs. One would think that I enjoyed going to second grade in this peaceful, pretty setting. Sadly, this wasn't true.

Each morning I dreaded school. Two popular girls in my class had singled me out for their type of fun and teasing. Pretending to be very nice, they would ask: "Erika, why don't you show us your math work so we can compare it to ours." I did as they said and later noticed that they had deliberately put mistakes into my assignment. Sure, I was upset, yet must have handled the situation appropriately. Eventually, I became friends with the girls and was invited to a birthday party.

Nevertheless, I continued to be afraid of school. Frequently we had to learn poems by heart, which was something impossible for me to do. Imagining being called upon to recite a poem and immediately stumbling over the first line, terrified me. I devised a strategy to prevent this. I would show Werner each new poem and ask him to read it to me with good pronunciation; then I practiced it on my own. When our teacher asked the next day: "Who wants to read the poem to us?" I would raise my hand. This way I made a good impression, and the teacher would not call on me later to recite the poem.

⏝

At the end of the war, even Weida experienced a few air raids. A week later, American troops occupied the town. They confiscated the big house we lived in. Right away we had to move out, and were assigned to a temporary shelter; thereafter we had to move two more times.

Only after we moved to Mrs. Fiedler's did we feel at home in Weida. My mother had become friends with the young woman, whose husband was serving in the military just like our father. She lived by herself in a small house next to the gate of a factory. Most likely she was happy to have our company during these uncertain times.

At the Berlin conference in June 1945, the Americans agreed to transfer the occupation of Thuringia to the Soviet Union. They withdrew their forces on July 1, 1945.

When we heard Cossack songs, we knew the Russians had arrived. A couple of days later, Russian soldiers pounded at our front door. Mrs. Fiedler resolutely refused to open the sturdy door. "Go next door to the factory! You'll find more there," she called out. Apparently, they did as they were told. Our door was never broken down. We felt very lucky.

Perhaps the change of the occupation forces caused the severe food shortages we experienced. We did not have enough to eat. Werner and I were always hungry.

Because the schools had been closed since the end of the war, we spent a lot of time at home. Our favorite game was to build a tent in the kitchen. We would drape blankets over a couple of chairs, taking care that the covers would reach the floor and the tent would be directly in front of the kitchen cabinet. We crawled into our tent house, quietly opened the lower cabinet door, and carefully lifted out the oatmeal box. Hidden from Mutti and Mrs. Fiedler, we munched dry oatmeal. Most likely, the two women were glad to have us play so nicely without loud arguments or fighting. We always took care not to eat too much, so that our little feast wouldn't be noticed.

My mother had had financial problems since the end of the war. Previously, she had received financial assistance from the German government because our father was a soldier, and monthly my father's former employer, the city of Düsseldorf, had sent us some money. Now my mother received nothing. What would we do when our savings were exhausted?

One day Mutti came home with a big stack of newspapers. She showed us how to deliver the papers to the customers. Thereafter, it became Werner's and my job to deliver the daily papers. In this way, we contributed to our finances.

～

Our greatest worry was for our father. We had not heard from him for many months. "Is he still alive? Has he been taken prisoner?" we wondered. In 1943 when our father served in Russia, he had been infected with typhus and had spent several months in a hospital. After he recuperated, he had resumed his duty. It was unknown to us, where he had been stationed last.

Mutti wrote letters to our relatives, telling them where we lived and how we were doing. Because Thuringia now belonged to the Russian zone, we could not mail letters to the West. Mutti gave our mail to people traveling to the West and asked them to mail them for us. This way our news and address reached our grandmothers.

After a few months, we received the most wonderful news from our grandmother in Krefeld. Our father had arrived there. He was weak and emaciated but in good spirits. He had been taken prisoner by the Americans and detained in a Rheinwiesenlager, an open-air temporary enclosure for prisoners of war, near the town of Remagen. After his release, he had walked to Krefeld.

How did my father manage to do this? MapQuest calculates that it takes twenty-seven hours to walk from Remagen to Krefeld. This applies to a fit hiker with good boots and clothes in peacetime, and not to Vati's condition back then. He was 6 feet tall, but weighed a mere ninety-nine pounds.

Vati recuperated at grandma's house and then planned and prepared to take us home. He managed the difficult task of getting the required permits for us to cross from the Soviet Zone to the British zone.

It was a happy reunion when Vati arrived in Weida. Soon our belongings were packed onto three handcarts. In the morning, we walked with them to the train station. We knew that the train would be extremely full. While we waited on the crowded platform, our biggest worry was that we could loose sight of each other, become separated, or one of us would not get on the train.

As the train pulled in, people pressed against the doors. Vati helped Mutti and me get a seat in a freight car. Werner squeezed himself into what had been a dog transport box. After he had taken care of us, no space was left for Vati. He climbed onto the roof, where he would sit or lay during the journey. Fortunately for him, the train did not go fast.

We traveled many hours in the freight car. It had no toilet facilities. Women and children used a bucket that was secured in a corner. Men would open the sliding door a crack and relieve themselves.

Finally we reached Helmstedt, the border town of the Russian zone. Everyone had to get off the train and go through security and inspection. We were treated for lice and our papers we checked. We boarded a passenger train to my father's mother, our Oma, in Westphalia.

A few months later, we returned to Düsseldorf. The house we had lived in had been totally destroyed. The housing office arranged for us to sublet two rooms of a three-room apartment belonging to a bachelor. Understandably, he was not happy that four people were invading his space. Our rooms had no water, only his did. We had to put our bucket in front of his door, and if he were inclined to do so, he would fill it—maybe after some hours.

To our great surprise and joy our condition soon improved. Our father was rehired by the city of Düsseldorf and was provided with an apartment—an entire apartment just for us! No more begging for water and sharing the toilet. The apartment was in a building that had survived the war. It had central heating.

We felt very fortunate during the very cold winter of 1946/47 to have a warm place. Vati's salary was sufficient to buy the food available in regular stores and maybe an extra loaf of bread from the Black Market, even though I do not know this for sure.

Most Germans had it much harder. I believe we had to thank our father for the advantages granted to us. He had been one of the few civil servants, who had resisted the pressure to join the party. Therefore, he did not have to go through a denazification process before his reemployment. The Allied Powers had instituted this process to find out a person's degree of participation in the activities of the Nazi party. Only non-members or members proven to be nominal party members were allowed to hold any position of responsibility in the local or national government of post-war Germany.

Aftereffect

"Did your childhood experiences during the war affect your life negatively?"

"I don't believe so," Erika replied. "During the war and immediately thereafter we lived in constant fear—fear of bombs, fear of the American troops and fear of the Russians. Today it is different. Today I have a positive outlook on life. What happened then is history. Today I live in the present."

Erika adds: "Some children had much worse experiences than I did and they still suffer from aftereffects. My cousin was in her house when an incendiary bomb set it ablaze. She was rescued barely in time. Even today, my cousin will have a panic attack when she sees fire."

Nadia with her mother 1942 or 1943

Chapter 12

Nadia the Lost Child

Nadia, born October 1938 in Krekhaev, Ukraine

THE TRUTH IS, NADIA was never lost. When the bombs destroyed part of Oskar-Helene-Heim, the well-known orthopedic Children's Hospital in Berlin Dahlem, Nadia had been evacuated with all the other patients. What was lost was her hospital chart, and with it, the knowledge of her birthday, place of birth, nationality, ethnicity, and religion. The bombs, the frightful events—or was it her fever? — erased Nadia's early memory. Later she could not remember her mother or the words of her native language.

The only existing document from Nadia's early years shows the name and address of a forced labor camp in Berlin. It also provides her mother's and her name, and states that in October of 1944, Katarina B. had taken her daughter Nadeschda (Nadia) B. to the hospital because she could not walk any more.

⤶

Nadia now lives in the United States. She told me the story of her childhood in English with a slight eastern European accent:

My first memories are from Berlin, Germany. I must have just turned six years old. I lay in a hospital bed, along with many other sick children, in the infectious disease ward of the Oskar-Helene-Heim hospital in Berlin. I had been diagnosed with tuberculosis coxitis. The bacteria had for the most part bypassed my lungs and settled in my right hipbone. It had destroyed it to the degree that I was no longer able to walk.

I spent many months in the hospital. Often at night air raid sirens woke us up, warning us of an approaching air attack. Being close to the window, I would see the anti-aircraft searchlights sweeping the black night sky. It was eerily frightening. Next the sirens would wail an air raid warning. The bombers were overhead, and the nurses rushed us to the hospital basement. This was a precautionary measure, because the hospital had a big white cross painted on its roof, marking it as a hospital and therefore, by war convention, it was safe from air attacks.

One night bombs hit the hospital and partially destroyed it.[1] After the raid we were carried outside. I remember lying outside on the lawn on a stretcher. Light rain drizzled on me, and I saw the hospital burning.

We were loaded onto a train, which was packed with patients, three bunks high. Another girl and I lay on the bed in the middle. Below us were two other girls. On the top bunk lay a badly wounded soldier from the wing of the hospital that treated soldiers. He was bleeding so profusely that his blood seeped through his mattress and dripped onto our sheet. When the nurse noticed it, she placed us in a different bed.

The train took us out of Berlin headed for Yugoslavia, but halfway there, a Russian train blocked our tracks. When the Russians entered our compartment, the nurse told them, "We have a little Russian girl here." They were pleased to see me, and one of soldiers gave me a nice stuffed bear.

I had had it only a short time when the nurse took it away from me. She had noticed that we had head lice, and my bear, stuffed with straw, had them too. Kerosene was doused over our heads, which were then wrapped in a towel. We had to sit still while the kerosene irritated the skin of our heads terribly, but killed the lice. My poor bear was burned.

Our train went to a town in Sudetenland, which was German at the time. We stayed there until July 19, 1945. After the end of the war, the Sudetenland became part of Czechoslovakia. Therefore, it is most likely that the hospital train took us back to Germany. Where did it go? I was a sick child

1. In 1945 the Oskar-Helene-Heim was hit by firebombs. Fifty percent of the hospital was destroyed.

and do not remember. My official records are blank. Who gave us supplies and food? Somehow we survived.

In January 1946, I was back in Berlin and was admitted to the Städtische Krankenhaus Zinnowwald (municipal hospital of the Zinnowwald district of Berlin). I must have been in poor health, because I remember little except that in the fall of 1946, a Russian officer came to take me out of the hospital and repatriate me to Russia. I threw such a fit that he left me and went away.

The hospital administration must have functioned minimally at the time. It was not until a year after my admission that my hospital chart was completed. I liked the hospital social worker and was pleased when she sat down at my bed. She opened my chart and asked,

"Nadia, when is your birthday?"

"I was born in the fall," I slowly answered while racking my brain, but no date was emerging.

"Well, I am an autumn baby, too," the social worker encouraged me. I was eight years old and smart. The social worker must have reasoned, "If I give her some time she will remember."

"When is your birthday?" I asked her instead.

"On November 4th."

"November 4th." is a good date," I thought and confirmed to her: "November 4th is my birthday, too."

The social worker penned the date into my chart. Since then I have celebrated my birthday on November 4.

"Nadia, where were you born?"

I shrugged my shoulders.

"Nadia, where are you from?"

Again, I had no answer. The social worker looked through my documents.

"I think you are from Russia," and she wrote "probably born in Russia" into my chart.

"Nadia, what is your religion?" When I again remained silent she wrote "unknown" and closed my chart.

Now it was official. I was Nadia B., the orphan from Russia who was lost in the chaos of World War II. Later when children asked me about my parents I often told them, "My parents were the czars of Russia."

More items had been entered on my chart: *Mother and child spoke Russian at admission . . . The mother never came to visit the child.*

Later the following was added to my chart:

> "*In September 1947 a Russian Liaison Officer came to the hospital with the intention to repatriate the child. Because of her violent*

protest he left her. In September 1947 she was visited by a Lieu-
tenant of the Soviet Military Administration accompanied by a
Russian physician and an International Red Cross Child Search
Officer. The authorization was given by the Russians that the child
could remain in the German hospital. Afterwards the advice was
given by the Child Search Officer that the child should be trans-
ferred to the US Zone where she could receive better treatment."

On July 12, 1948, American military personal burst into my ward, rushed me out of the hospital and flew me to Frankfurt, in the American-occupied zone of Germany. I heard someone say, "I bet tomorrow the border (between East and West Germany) will be closed forever."

⌐⟍

In Frankfurt, I was admitted to the Sachenhausen Hospital for further treatment. In Berlin, I had already had several surgeries and I had more in Frankfurt. My right hip, my right knee, and my right ankle all had been operated on. My right hip joint was fused, which took away all hip movements, but made it more stable for standing and walking. After each surgery, I had to wear a cast for weeks or even months. The situation was the worst after the hip surgery, because my cast was huge. It covered my leg, wrapped around my hips and came up to my waist. I had to be in bed with it for up to two months. It was really bad. Afterwards I had to learn to walk again.

Treatment for tuberculosis was easy in comparison. Because no antibiotics were available at the time, the doctors tried to build up the body's normal defenses with good nutrition, rest, and exposure to fresh air and UV radiation. I remember getting a spoonful of cod liver oil every night. We all hated it, but there was no way around it. We all had to swallow it each day. The nurses had insisted, "it contains the vitamins and the substances you need for healing," and they were right.

In Frankfurt my meals were good, because the physicians wanted me to gain weight. Even better were the treats the American servicemen brought us when they came to the hospital with CARE packages. They contained useful items like soap, toothpaste or toothbrushes, and all the sweets your heart desired—chocolate, candy, cookies, and chewing gum.

I thought this was marvelous and felt very grateful to the soldiers. Each week I looked forward to their visits, and so did my best friend Halina. We decided that when we were big we were going to go to America.

I made good progress in Frankfurt. My TB tests started to show negative results. After I was out of the cast, I learned to walk and climb stairs. I spoke German like all the children around me, and with the help of individual bedside tutoring, I also read German. (Unfortunately, I lost the ability later.)

After a year the physicians judged my treatment to be successfully concluded. Because I was so thin, they had decided not to send me to an orphanage, which were overcrowded and of poor quality at that time in Germany. Instead, I was admitted to the International Red Cross Children's T.B. Hospital in Kempten, a rehabilitation center for tuberculosis patients. Kempten is a picturesque resort town at the foothills of the Alps in Germany.

It was nice in Kempten, but not as much fun as in Frankfurt, because Halina was not there. No child in Kempten could replace her.

The International Tracing Service had not been able to find my mother or any of my relatives. I was now officially a DP (Displaced Person), a designation for anyone from another country, who was stranded in Germany after the war. Children who had no one in their home country to return to were sent to host countries for adoption or placement with foster families. Children under 12 would be placed in nearby countries like Switzerland or Ireland. Older children might be sent overseas.

I was 12 years old. When my caring caseworker in Kempten asked me where I wanted to go, I did not have to think twice. "To America," I burst out instantly. This was not what had been tentatively planned for me, but my clear goal must have impressed her. "Hmm, let's see what I can do for you," she promised.

She kept her word and worked hard on my behalf. The good news arrived. "Nadia, the US Jewish Refugee Organization has agreed to take care of you," my caseworker was happy to tell me. "Get ready to leave. The next transport will take you to the receiving camp in Munich. God bless you!"

There were constantly new children arriving and others departing at the very large refugee camp for DP orphans in Munich, which processed around 5,000 children for emigration to the United States. We were housed in US Army barracks and received our meals in the mess hall. At night army cots were set up in the auditorium. We each got a pillow, sheets, and a blanket and settled down for the night.

To be among so many children was confusing, but I was glad to be there and very happy when I spotted Halina among all the strangers. We had so much to talk about! Halina already had an American family who wanted to adopt her. I envied her and knew that for me things would not be as easy. Indeed, Halina's papers were processed quickly and she left the camp before I did.

Because the fate of my parents was unknown, my departure from Germany had to be publically announced. My name and the names of other departing children were read on the radio at certain intervals during the day for a set number of days and notice was given that anyone having concerns about us should call the refugee agency in Munich. If nobody called within the set time frame, we were allowed to leave. A military transport plane flew us to Reykjavik, Iceland, and then on to New York.

In the US

I was twelve years old when I arrived in New York early in the summer of 1951. I spoke no English; yet, I was excited to be in the country I had heard so many wondrous things about.

I had to spend the first few weeks on Ellis Island with other immigrants suspected of harboring infectious diseases. My papers certified that my TB was healed, but the US Immigration Services wanted US physicians to verify this. Several times I was taken to a New York hospital for x-rays and various tests.

The camp in Munich had prepared me somewhat for all the confusion, the coming and going of people, eating in a mess hall, and sleeping on cots that were set up at night in a long, wide hallway. But so much was strange to me.

A nice man gave me money to buy myself something at the camp store. I looked at the odd piece of paper, not understanding what he wanted me to do with it. I later gave it away. For the past six years I had been in many different German hospitals and had received whatever I needed. I had never bought anything or used money.

The hospital laundry service had provided me with the only clothes I wore. After wearing them for several days, someone from the laundry dispensed a fresh set.

"Here, Nadia, is your underwear, top, skirt, socks, and pajamas." I would be handed a neatly folded stack. On Ellis Island this never happened.

I observed mothers and older children washing some of their clothes at night, hanging them to dry from the rod of the their cot, and wearing them again the next day. I started to do the same. For the first time in my life, I took care of my own clothes. This was a small beginning of what was heading my way.

⁀

"Nadia, would you like the pink pajamas or the ones with the yellow stripes?"

"How about the sleeveless airy night gown for warm nights?"

"Do you like white underwear or the ones with the pretty pattern?"

I did not understand a word of what the nice lady, Miss Miriam, was asking. But it did not matter. Every time I touched one of these soft beautiful things and looked at her, she would take the item and slip it into her shopping bag.

This morning the caseworker from Ellis Island had taken me to the Jewish Children's Home in the Bronx. It was a special home for Jewish children coming from Europe. It was meant to be a place to recuperate from the hardships we had endured, such as the persecution, the concentration camp, and the loss of our parents. The safe and secure environment of the home was meant to soothe our souls, to let the joys of childhood emerge, and for us to learn about life in America.

The housemother had shown me and a couple of other arriving children around the home.

"And, Nadia, this is your bed," she said pointing to a real bed. It was not a cot or a bunk but a bed with a bouncy mattress, nice sheets, a fluffy blanket, and several soft pillows! Never in my life had I slept in a bed like this, and only three other girls would sleep in my room.

"Here are your drawers and your closet," the housekeeper continued. When she saw my puzzled look she added, "Miss Miriam will take you shopping and you will have things to put in there." I did not understand her words, but her smile told me that more good things were coming my way.

"Miriam, our newcomers have nothing. Let's get them the basics and a few outfits to start with," recommended the housemother, and off we went to Macy's department store. It was a shiny, bright place full of wonders.

"Hold onto the rail and step," Miss Miriam said and demonstrated. It was scary, but after the two other girls, I dared it and like magic the metal steps took me up to the girls' floor.

"Take a big step!" Miss Miriam helped me get off the escalator.

"We still need some dresses for you girls. I think over there is a good selection in your sizes."

Like little ducklings we followed Miss Miriam past tables with stacks of sweaters in all colors and a glamorous life-size doll that looked like a real person. I looked at her standing very still and smiling.

"Do you like the dress the mannequin is wearing?" Miss Miriam asked and pulled one from the rack just like it.

"Now, you have to try it on."

Incredulous I stood in front of the full-length mirror in the dressing room. The dress fitted well, and I marveled at how nice I looked. Only the brace and the heavy brown orthopedic shoe on my right leg did not fit the picture.

More things disappeared into Miss Miriam's shopping bag. After she bought a bottle of hair shampoo for each of us, we headed home.

"Time for dinner," she declared. "I bet you are hungry."

Mealtime held more surprises for me. There was no line at a counter dispensing our plates of food.

"Nadia, sit here with these nice girls," the housemother told me and obediently I sat down on the upholstered chair at the round table with five other girls. The table was set with a plate, silverware, napkin, and a glass for each of us. The housekeeper and a maid were placing large plates of food on each table.

The girls were talking and helping themselves to whatever they wanted and to as much as they wanted. Irene, sitting next to me, took two servings of meat! Was that allowed? I had never experienced anything like it in my life.

"Don't you want to eat?" Irene asked and shoved the plate with the spaghetti towards me. "Take this and then put the sauce and meatballs on top." Soon I was munching like everybody else until my stomach refused.

Was it time for a bath and bed? Not yet, this first day did not want to end. "Come, let's get the ice cream money." Irene waved me along to our housefather. He gave each of us some coins.

"Do you hear the jingle? That's the ice cream man with his cart. He comes by every evening." Irene nudged me along the sidewalk. Following her example, I gave my coins to the man and made my very first purchase. He filled a cone with chocolate and vanilla ice cream and handed it to me. Never in my life had I tasted anything so soft, creamy, and cold. It was delicious!

Life was never boring at the Jewish Children's Home. For the first time in my life, I was allowed to go to school. I learned to read and write in English and also had other subjects like earth science, biology, history and math. I liked them all, especially after my English got better. To help me with it, I received special one-on-one tutoring at night.

When we were not busy with school or homework, we skipped over to the park across the street and played. We never had to do any chores. Even our beds were made and our rooms tidied up by one of our helpers. A cook prepared our meals, and the housekeeper had our laundry done. The cleaning woman kept the whole house neat and clean at all times. Both the house-mother and the housefather were always ready to listen to us and give us hugs.

Volunteers like Miss Miriam took us to special events like a show or movie. To get ready, we would shower and shampoo our hair. I loved how the white foam covered my head and how fluffy and silky my hair felt after-wards. Before, I had always washed my hair with soap. Shampoo was one of the marvelous new things I had never known about.

Other outings were frequently planned for us on weekends, or we did more shopping—always a favorite activity of mine. I believe we were all happy to be in the orphanage. I can't remember us fighting about anything, and when the boys roughhoused or wrestled on the floor, they did it for the fun of it.

Many children stayed for only a short time before being placed in a foster home or being adopted. New children took their place. I stayed two full years and loved it. These years were the highlight of my childhood and provided me with a smooth transition into adolescence.

⤿

I was 14 years old when my dear caseworker called me into her office. "Nadia, I found a good foster home for you. You no longer have to live in an orphanage."

She gave me a suitcase to pack my things in, and the next day we went to Ohio where my foster parents lived on a large farm not far from Cincinnati. They had four children close to my age, and, because the summer vacation had started, we worked in the fields and helped with the cows, pigs and chickens.

I must admit it took me some time to get accustomed to my new surroundings. The farmhouse seemed small and crowded compared with the spacious rooms at the orphanage. My foster siblings were friendly but always busy. Everybody had to do a lot of farm work.

My foster mother taught me how to milk a cow, and soon I had to milk several cows twice a day. That was one of my nicer jobs. Like all of us, I also had to clean the manure out of the cow barn using a pitchfork. It was stinky and extremely difficult for me because of my weak right leg and my poor balance. I worked carefully, trying not to fall and land in the mess. Working in the field was also not easy for me, as I had trouble walking on uneven ground with my orthopedic shoe.

I was not sad when school started and we didn't have to do as much farm work. In the morning, I walked to the road with my new siblings and waited for the school bus. The first time the bus driver helped me climb up the big steps onto the bus. Thereafter, I was pleased that I could do it on my own.

One morning I left the house late and missed the bus. Walking back to the farmhouse, I wondered if my foster parents would drive me to school or if it would be ok to miss it just once. Nothing had prepared me for what happened next. Angry at my dawdling, my foster parents spanked me hard. I was stunned, hurt, and outraged all at once. Never ever in my life had anyone ever hit me—not in the hospitals, camps, or orphanage. Everyone had always been nice to me. And why did my foster parents hit me, but never any of their own children?

The following Sunday I drove with the family to Cincinnati, where we often visited their relatives. On our way we passed a big multi-story house standing by itself.

"What kind of house is that?" I asked.

"It's the orphanage," my foster mother explained.

"See, if we hadn't taken you in, that is where you would be living. Aren't you glad to be with us?"

I had a different opinion and remained silent.

That night I got up, secretly dressed, and sneaked very, very quietly down the stairs and out of the house. Slowly and carefully, I walked down the lane to the road. I waved a white rag I had taken along, and the approaching car stopped.

"I ran away from the orphanage. Would you please take me back?" I asked.

The responsible driver took me straight to the entrance and waited in his car until the front door opened and I had stepped into the orphanage.

I had left all my things at the farmhouse, reasoning that I could not escape unnoticed with a suitcase. I knew that the orphanage would give me all I needed. And they did. After the night nurse got over her surprise, she helped me as well as she could. I gave her the name of my caseworker and the Jewish orphanage in the Bronx.

A few days later my caseworker arrived by train from New York.

"Nadia, what happened?" she wanted to know.

I told her what had occurred and ended with, "I never want to go to another foster home. Can I go back to the orphanage?"

The answer was no. The Jewish orphanage was only for newly arriving children. However, after many phone calls, my caseworker had a new place for me.

The next day we traveled by train to Cleveland, Ohio, and went to the Jones Home for Children, an orphanage and foster-care home. It would become my home for the coming years. Like the other older girls in the home, I attended the local high school and later graduated.

⌇

When I was fifteen, I went to one of my orthopedic appointments at the Cleveland University Hospital. Dr. H asked me:

"Nadia, what do you wish for your sixteenth birthday?"

"I would like to wear high heels," was my answer.

"Well, that is a big wish," Dr. H. mused. "You know, Nadia, your left leg has grown nicely but your right one has not. Your legs are of unequal length. That's a problem that interferes with your gait and balance. To make your legs equal or at least almost equal in length, I have to shorten your good leg. This requires surgery and lots of rehabilitation with much work from you. If all goes well, you will no longer have to wear the orthopedic shoes with the big platform sole on your right foot. You will be able to wear sneakers or sandals and, who knows, maybe even high heels."

I absolutely hated surgeries. I had had so many. But this time was different. This time I was deciding to have surgery, not having the decision made for me by some strange physician. The prospect of no longer having to wear a cumbersome, ugly orthopedic shoe gave me all the motivation I needed. I knew Dr. H. was a good orthopedist who cared about me. I trusted him.

The surgery went as planned, as did the six months of rehabilitation at Cleveland Rainbow Hospital. When I went back to Jones Home, I was wearing tennis shoes and walked with more ease than before. Was I able to wear heels? Not yet, but after I bought a pair of high heels with my babysitting money, I practiced until I could walk with my fancy shoes. I wore my heels for Dr. H, who got a kick out of it.

After high school, I went to college for two years. I then moved into an apartment with a friend and got a good and interesting job with the local TV station. I met my prince, my husband, Jack, and we married.

Jack got to know a visiting professor from Russia, and he told him my story. The professor offered to give my name, address, and phone number to the Russian Red Cross. Jack gave him the address and phone number of his parents as we did not yet have a permanent home.

Searching for the Lost Child

Nikolai was already retired, even though he had not yet reached the "Golden Years." He felt well, and was full of vigor most of the time. But there were days when all his joints ached, and it was hard to get out of bed in the morning. Nikolai had cancer.

When the nuclear disaster of Chernobyl occurred, his military unit was sent to assist with the evacuation of the surrounding villages. During the assignment he and his comrades were exposed to high levels of radiation. Years later during a routine health assessment, cancerous tissue was detected, and treatment began. The spread of cancer had been stopped, yet he still had to undergo radiation at regular intervals. He retired from the

Soviet military and received a nice pension. Life was not bad, but he missed work. His opinion was, "without a challenge, life is boring."

In 2006 Nikolai received his new challenge. On Memorial Day in the Ukraine, Nikolai decided to visit his home village of Krekhaev and the grave of his father Ivan. Nikolai had been raised by his mother and had met his father only once. While standing at the grave of his father, an old woman approached him.

"Who are you and why are you standing at this grave?" the woman asked.

"My name is Nikolai P. and this is my father's grave."

"Then I must be your aunt since Ivan is my brother." She went on to explain that her brother Ivan had another child out of wedlock, named Nadia, who was lost in Berlin during the war.

Nikolai was intrigued by this news and decided to find out everything possible about this mysterious half-sister. He could once again use his detective skills, as he had been trained as a detective by the military.

The next day he went door to door in this village of about 900 houses. He hadn't been home for many years and enjoyed meeting old friends as well as neighbors he had never known. He asked everyone he talked to about Nadia B., his lost half-sister. Several old women remembered Nadia and knew her mother Katarina, or Katya as they called her, quite well. He took careful notes during each interview and photographed the friends or relatives of Katya and Nadia.

Slowly Nikolai pieced together the story. Maria, Katya's best friend, who had experienced the tragic events of the war with her, was still alive. Bedridden, but alert, she filled in details:

"Your father was drafted into the Russian Army like all the other young men of our village. While they were away, the Nazis came to our village in the summer of 1943 looking for partisans. They drove us out of our houses and then burned them. Oh, Nikolai, it was a terrible fire. Nadia was four years old and she screamed and screamed.

All of the women and children were made to march with the Nazis. For days we would walk until we came to a railroad station where we were loaded onto a freight train that took us to Berlin, Germany. There we entered a forced labor camp for people from Eastern Europe.

Early in the morning each day, we were taken to a railroad station where we worked all day. The children were left behind in the camp by themselves until we returned in the evening. How lonely they must have been all day long without anyone caring for them.

Nadia, right, with her friend in the forced labor camp

Nadia became very weak and one morning she could no longer walk. Katya convinced the German camp officer to help her get Nadia admitted to the hospital.

The doctor diagnosed bone tuberculosis, and she was admitted to the Oskar-Helene-Heim, the best orthopedic children's hospital in Berlin. According to the law at that time, children of forced laborers from Eastern Europe were not to be treated in German hospitals, but were to be treated in separate, and inferior, facilities. In Nadia's case, the physician subverted the law at his peril.

Katya was allowed to visit Nadia once a week. The camp officer loaned her a bicycle to travel to the hospital. The law did not allow East Europeans to own a bike or to leave the camp unaccompanied. The camp officer did not follow the law.

Then Berlin experienced a very destructive bombing attack, and when Katya came to the hospital, it was mostly rubble. The part still standing was empty.

"Where are the children?"

"Where is my Nadia?" she called out.

No one could give her an answer. She went several times but no one knew anything.

The war ended. The Russian soldiers came and opened our camp. We were free. It did not mean much because Berlin was just rubble, and we could not find anything to eat. The children never returned to the hospital.

Finally, the Russians transported us back to our village. Oh, what a sad sight it was—the houses burned and the fields destroyed! What a terrible war it had been. Nikolai, be glad that you were not yet born!"

⤚⤳

Katya died in 1989, but her son Stepan still lived in the house she had rebuilt after the war on the same spot where she had lived with Nadia. Katya had married Stepan's father after the war. Stepan was Nadia's half-brother. Nikolai went to visit him.

"Isn't it amazing! We never knew each other, and now we find out that we have the same half-sister!" Nikolai exclaimed and gave Stepan a big bear hug.

Next Nikolai contacted the Ukrainian Red Cross. Their search was unsuccessful. Nicolai decided to try his luck with the Russian Red Cross.

After two years of searching, Nikolai got lucky in December of 2007, when the phone rang at the house of Jack's parents. They had passed away, but Jack's sister, Maureen, lived there. Maureen answered the phone.

"This is the Red Cross in New York. We have a request from the Russian Red Cross for Nadeschda B. Is she available?"

"Sorry, she is not reachable at this number. Nadia B. is the maiden name of my sister-in-law. I can give you her number."

So it was that Nadia was found.

Nadia Visits her Native Village

Picking up the phone that day in 2007, a member of the Red Cross asked me: "We have a request from a gentleman in the Ukraine who wants to talk to you. He says he is your half-brother. Would you allow us to give him your telephone number?"

"I have to talk to my husband first," was my tentative answer. My first reaction was, "This is a prank."

I had lived all my life without knowing about my early childhood, my parents, or relatives, and I was doing just fine. I had my own family—my husband, my children, their spouses, and my grandchildren. Why should I talk to some half-brother who was not even from Russia, my probable home country?

My husband Jack thought that the Red Cross would process only legitimate requests. He encouraged me: "Nadia, why don't you talk to him? Maybe he knows something about your parents and where you were born."

The call was arranged.

Nikolai had found a translation service to assist with our conversation. As we talked, I learned for the first time in sixty-nine years that I was born on the 26th of October, 1938 in Krekhaev, a village about twenty miles north of Kiev in the Ukraine, and that I had been baptized in the Russian Orthodox Church.

My parents had married other spouses after the war and were no longer alive. I had two half-brothers. Nikolai was the son of my father and his wife, and Stepan was the son of my mother and her husband.

More information was exchanged by email with the help of my daughter Debbie, and Nikolai's son, Dimitry, who did most of the work.

Dimitry sent a picture of me as a small child. I thought the girl looked strange, but Jack and Debbie saw a resemblance to me.

Nikolai asked if we would like to come for a visit. I hesitated. "My home is here. Why should I go to this strange country?"

"Mom, you know you have an accent. All my life I've wondered where it came from. All my life I've wondered about the country you lived in as a small child. I can't wait to go there," Debbie asserted.

Jack supported her. He, too, thought it would be good to visit.

⤸

On the morning of May 5, 2008, the national Ukrainian holiday commemorating the deaths of loved ones and of fallen soldiers, Nikolai greeted each of us with a long emotional embrace.

"Nadia, my sister! Jack, my brother-in-law! Debbie, my niece!" he exclaimed. "I found you!" he rejoiced and hugged us again.

He had planned the whole day for us. He had hired a nice man, who would translate all conversation into English for us. Everyone in the village knew that Nadia, the lost child, was coming. Even the local TV station had been notified, and they came to document the reunion.

First, we went to my family home, the house my mother had rebuilt after the war, on the very spot I had spent my first years of life. Many relatives had gathered in the front yard awaiting our arrival. Tanya, a niece of my half-brother Stepan, offered me bread and salt—the traditional Ukrainian welcome. One by one everyone greeted us and talked to us with hugs, kisses, and tears. Stepan had lunch ready for all of us.

Nikolai had us stop and look at a portrait hanging on the living room wall.

"My dearest Nadia, do you see the girl in the picture? It's you, my lost sister," and he gave me another one of his emotional embraces.

Stepan stepped to my side. Looking at me and then at the painting, he haltingly recollected what our mother had shared with him. "Nadia, when our dear mother Katya came home after the war without you, she had only one photo of you, standing next to your friend. She found an artist who used this photo to draw a picture of you, and here it has been hanging ever since for sixty years." Tears were streaming down his face when he added: "My dear Nadia, our mother talked about you everyday."

My eyes were wet as he embraced me. Debbie cried and hugged her uncle. When she looked up, she noticed that everyone had tears in their eyes, even the cameraman.

⤸

After lunch, we walked to the cemetery where we were greeted by more relatives and friends, talking about things they remembered. We proceeded to visit my mother's grave and my father's grave.

Many people were at the cemetery to honor their loved ones. Again and again, people came over and greeted us. One of the old women, wearing the traditional colorful scarf, remembered how I had liked to work with her in her garden. Another recalled how my mother had searched for me in vain.

An older man, who had been a small child like me when the Nazis came, recollected the march to the train station and recalled the camp in Berlin.

"Each time he talked about these horrible events, he started to cry, and we cried with him," said Debbie. "It was so emotional."

After visiting the cemetery, we went to the home of my mother's best friend Maria, who was bedridden. Her sister Yelena, who was blind in one eye and walked with two canes, guided us there slowly but gladly. As I stepped close to Maria, she patted my hands and stroked my face. "My Nadia, no one knew you were alive. It's a miracle; it's magical that you are standing here. God blessed you, my child."

⌒

At the end of the long emotional day Nikolai said: "It was good, Nadia, that you did not return after the war. In our village you might have died from tuberculosis. Many people died after the war. Everyone told us how they were starving at that time."

"All my life, I was taught to hate the Germans and hate the Americans, but now I know it was the Germans and the Americans who saved my sister's life."

Aftereffect

Asked about how the experiences of her childhood have affected her life, Nadia responded:

"I am grateful for all I got. I am strong and resilient. I am a hard worker. Since I was sixteen I always had a job. I never call in sick and I do a good job. I am bored at home."

"I never watch war movies or violent shows. I dislike fireworks. I am sure this is because I had been exposed to war and bombings."

"My childhood was deprived in many ways. My children were astonished when I told them that as a child I never got a Christmas present. My
husband Jack gave me my first Christmas gift."

"I never forgot my first enchanting visit to Macy's in New York. I love
shopping. Even if I don't buy anything, I enjoy browsing through Macy's
or any other big fancy store. If I am sad or bored, I go there and feel happy.
Quite a few sales ladies know me and are pleased to see me. Sometimes I
shop for other people and find the item they had been looking for in vain."

The Lost Children of World War II

How many children were lost during the end of WW II? The International
Tracing Service (ITS) registered almost 350,000 missing children.[2] The German Red Cross received over 300,000 requests to trace missing children.
This indicates that over half a million children were separated from their
families during the war.

The task of accounting for the total number is made difficult by the
fact that initially several organizations searched independently and tried to
reunite families after the war.

The Central Tracing Bureau of the British Red Cross together with
the United Nations Relief and Rehabilitation Administration (UNRRA)
searched and cared for non-German lost children of the war. German children were considered enemy nationals and as such not the responsibility of
the UNRRA.

In 1945 the need for family unification was extraordinary in Germany.
Almost every family was missing one or more members. About 14 million
German or German-speaking persons, among them 1.5 million children,
fled or were expelled from the eastern German provinces and from Eastern
Europe. Responding to the pressing need, several separate Red Cross search
services became active in the occupied zones of Germany, which later became centralized and eventually connected to the International Red Cross.

Finding lost children in Germany was especially difficult because many
of the children lost during the refugee treks had been very young and their
names and other identifying information could not be established. Anyone
who found or rescued a child was asked to give detailed descriptions about
the location and the condition of the child. For instance, the finders were
asked to describe the clothing the child wore, birthmarks or injuries, and
provide any other identifying information.

---

2. See Zahra, *The Lost Children*, 3.

Parents and relatives usually did not limit their search to the Red Cross services. One could see search notices and photos of missing children at any public place like train stations, public shelters, advertisement boards, or news columns. As soon as newspapers and magazines were published again in Germany, they, too, had sections with photos and search notices of missing children.

As in Nadia's case, searches continued for decades. The International Red Cross reports on its website about the unification of two Ukrainian sisters in September of 2008, four months after Nadia's trip to her village.

Paralleling Nadia's fate, one of the sisters had been transported from her home to a forced labor farm in Germany and was later helped to emigrate to the US.

Forced Labor in Germany during World War II

Nadia's story tells that the women of her village were forced to work at a Berlin railroad station. Similarly, other civilians from occupied eastern territories were transported to and forced to work in Germany. Initially the government used propaganda to induce civilians to voluntarily work in Germany. As the numbers of volunteers dwindled, the occupied local government was asked to provide workers for Germany. It also happened that German troops rounded up civilians at public places and forcibly transported them to Germany to work there.

By 1944, 7.6 million forced laborers, including prisoners of war and concentration camp inmates, worked in the "Greater German Territory." They replaced a full quarter of the German work force, which had been drafted into the war.

Voluntary foreign workers and forced laborers from western countries had better work conditions and received better treatment than those of eastern nationality. "East Workers", as they were called, faced many restrictions. For instance, East Workers:

Could only leave the camp as a supervised group

Needed a written permit to leave camp on their own

Could not use public transportation

Were not allowed to own a bicycle or a camera

Could not go to any public place or event frequented by Germans

Had to attend separate church services

Could only use a certain restaurant during certain hours

Received less pay than western workers

Western foreign laborers were supposed to earn as much as a German worker in the same position.

The working conditions and nutrition of the forced laborers placed in small German towns must have been superior to those of large prisoner of war or concentration camps. For instance, the death rate of the 2,229 forced laborers working in Langenfeld, Rheinland, Germany was about 0.8, which includes death by war activities, such as bombardment.[3]

The darkest and most shameful part of the treatment of the civilian forced laborers concerns the children born to East Workers. A pregnant woman did not receive any work protection. She was forced to give birth in a separate and inferior hospital and had to resume work shortly thereafter. Her infant would be placed in separate and inferior orphanages, which had a high death rate, and which were hidden from view of the German civilian population. Due to strict gender separations and severe penalties for German perpetrators, relatively few pregnancies occurred.

∽

A German Forced Labor Compensation Program was established in 2000. Over 4.37 billion Euros was paid out to about 1.7 million of then still living former forced laborers. The recipients received a one-time payment of 2,500 to 7,500 euros.

3. Stadt Langenfeld. *Forced Laborer in Langenfeld*, 118–385

Ildiko, left, with her family

Chapter 13

We Lived in a Military Hospital Train

Ildiko, born February 1934 in Budapest, Hungary

ILDIKO'S HAPPY FIRST CHILDHOOD remembrances begin in Nagysurany, (Šurang in Slovak) a small town with an important train crossing at the border of Hungary and Slovakia.

In 1939, after the region had been annexed to Hungary, Ildiko's father was sent to Nagysurany to be its postmaster. Having previously lived in the big city of Budapest, Ildiko's family enjoyed life in the small town and its surrounding lovely, fertile countryside.

Ildiko narrates:

I remember being outside roughhousing with my father. "He holds me with his big hand on my tummy and raises me high up into the air. With my arms and legs stretched out, I fly like a bird and love it.

Today I like to fly in airplanes. Does flying remind me of the happy playtime with my father?"

In 1940, when I was six years old, I entered first grade. I proudly went to school with my eight-year-old sister Stefania and nine-year-old brother Jozsef. World War II had begun, but we were neither afraid of bombs nor of foreign troops. Hungary was allied with Germany, which appeared advantageous at the time. In 1941, when Germany declared war on Russia, Hungarian troops fought under Hungarian command with the Germans.

Young men were enlisted, but my father did not have to serve, because he was older and had an essential work assignment. For several years, we lived as if it were peacetime without any shortages. Nevertheless, the war had seeped into our consciousness. When my playmates and I played with our dolls, our husbands were fighting in the war, and we were waiting for them to come home.

In the spring of 1944, a Hungarian hospital train rolled into our town, and German troops followed shortly thereafter. The war was bursting into Nagysurany. Two German officers were assigned to room in our house. One of them was a pharmacist from Berlin, Germany. When he heard, that my mother was afraid the Russian Army would reach our town, he recommended, "Why don't you go to Berlin? There you will be safe from the Russians." He seemed convinced that the Red Army would never conquer the capital city of Germany. Little did he know what would happen . . .

In April and May of 1944, Hungary was attacked for the first time by the Allied airplanes. Until then, our country had been spared, because we had been out of range of the English and American bombers. Now their new technically advanced planes targeted us.

When the air raid sirens sounded, we ran to our basement and waited until we heard the all-clear signal. I remember an enormous air attack. The Americans bombed a German ammunition train standing about eleven miles down the train tracks. The resulting explosion was indescribable. "The heavens were trembling!"

Then a great tragedy befell us. Unexpectedly, our father died of a heart attack in July of 1944. Now, just now, as we endured terrible bombing raids, were threatened by the advancing Red Army, and had strangers living in our house, we lost the protection of our dear father. Our calm, big, strong father, who had been our pillar of support, was no more. Our dear Édesanyám (sweet mother in Hungarian) was all we had now. With no time to grieve, she had to act and care for us.

Life went on; more changes occurred and none for the better. The personnel of the military hospital were sent to live with various local families. A family of six persons was assigned to room with us, and we had to share our kitchen with them. Just one room remained ours. Here Jozsef, Stefania, and I sat and waited for hours for our Édesanyám, feeling utterly alone and lost.

Within a few weeks our life had changed dramatically. Before, our parents had always been there for us. All of a sudden, traumatized by our father's untimely death, and surrounded by strangers, we had to fend for ourselves. Feeling overwhelmed by our bad fortune, we huddled together. Luckily, our mother was able to cope. To support us, she took a job at the military hospital; she left early in the morning and returned in the evening.

The news from the war zone was not good. The Red Army was marching towards Hungary. The commander of the military hospital decided to move it to a safer area. Everything was loaded onto the train.

The front section of the hospital train contained the hospital beds for the sick or wounded soldiers, and was equipped with an operating room and a pharmacy. Next came the living and sleeping quarters for the physicians, nurses and orderlies. Towards the end were the wagons, which housed the kitchen, the laundry and the sleeping quarters for the non-medical staff. To accommodate non-essential staff and some of their family members, a couple of boxcars were added at the end of the train. We were allowed to travel in one of those.

Traveling with the Hospital Train

Mother packed several suitcases with essentials and added three oil paintings she loved. She took them out of their frames, rolled them up, and placed them carefully among our clothes. I was allowed to take along my special album with handwritten notes and poems from my friends. We never lost these keepsakes on our long journey. Now, over 70 years later, they are treasured mementos from our homeland.

As soon as we were packed, we rushed to our boxcar and soon thereafter, the long train left the station. It all happened so quickly, that I never said goodbye to my best friend. Even today it makes me sad, whenever I remember her.

The boxcar we traveled in had straw sacks spread on the floor for us to sit or sleep on; one for each of the twenty-seven passengers. Besides hospital workers like my mother and related adults, there were also several children on board. I was the youngest.

We left in the middle of December. A wooden stove, sitting in the middle of the car, was our only source of warmth. Every time the train stopped or started, the stove rattled menacingly, but luckily it never fell over.

Where was the train going? During normal times the destination would have been prearranged. But these were not normal times. For now, we were on our way to Austria.

The train traveled very slowly. Again and again the conductor would call: "Everyone get off the train! The tracks are destroyed." Then we climbed out and walked until the train had changed to a different track. If no other options were available, the train stopped until the tracks were repaired, and our journey could continue.

In Austria, our chief officer was unable to find a place for our hospital. On Christmas Eve, the train sat in a desolate spot outside a rural train station.

My mother got off the train to check out the environment. When she discovered a huge pine tree, she broke off a large branch. The branch was stuck into a straw sack so that it stood up, and became our Christmas tree. After having travelled many hours, many days, and nights together, we had gotten to know each other well and now celebrated Christmas together like a large family.

Next our journey took us to Czechoslovakia. In the Sudetenland, a mostly German speaking part of the country, the Cloister of Hirschberg agreed to house our hospital, and its personnel were sent to live with local people. We were assigned to stay with a very nice German woman. It was in the middle of January 1945 and we were incredibly thankful to live in a house instead of a metal boxcar. It was heavenly to sleep in a real bed. The adults too were glad to work again in the hospital, instead of sitting around with nothing to do.

Jozsef, Stefania, and I were on our own, and we ventured into Hirschberg. At times we would do errands for our mother. Buying groceries turned out to be complicated. To do so, one needed food coupons, something we were not used to, and we had to know the word for the item either in Czech or in German. Once when my mother wanted honey, we had no inkling what to call it. Pointing to the sugar coupon, we spread our arms wide and fluttered humming around the store until the sales lady guessed what we wanted. I think we were pretty proud handing our Édesanyám our purchase.

Around the middle of February our "luxury life" came to an abrupt end. Again we heard: "The Red Army is approaching!" Again the train was loaded. Before we left, I had our hostess write a verse into my poetry album. I still enjoy reading her goodbye wishes.

This time our destination was Germany. When our train pulled into the railroad station in Bamberg, Germany we were greeted by screeching air raid sirens. Every one scrambled off the train. The twenty-seven people of our boxcar family found shelter in a bunker. After the all-clear, the friendly German warden allowed us to stay and spend the night there.

According to plan, our train was to leave at eight the next morning. We were there at eight o'clock, but our train was not. It was gone! "Oh no, all we have is gone with the train!" We could not believe it. Here we were in the middle of a war, in a strange country with nothing except the clothes on our back.

"Take the next train to Nürnberg," recommended the stationmaster. "There you will catch up with your train." Following his advice, twenty-seven

Hungarians squeezed into the already totally full train to Nürnberg. When we arrived, our train was nowhere to be found.

What should we do?

At the information office we were told: "Yes, there was an Hungarian hospital train here. It left for Hirschberg in Bavaria, Germany. "

We were relieved, but not very long. The wailing of the air raid siren made us rush to the nearby bunker. It was already full and we were turned away. We ran to another. It too was full, as was the third one.

Huddled outside around our mother, we experienced the incredible loud bombardment. It was as if a thousand thunderstorms were raging all at once. I believed we all would perish. Fortunately, no bomb detonated in our immediate vicinity and no flying shrapnel hit us, or anyone of our travel family.

After two or three days of exhausting travel, we arrived thirsty and hungry, unwashed, and unkempt at the Hungarian military hospital train and . . . ? Extremely disappointed, we realized it was not our train. Apparently, two Hungarian hospital trains were roaming through Germany.

Our countrymen were sympathetic to our plight and took care of us as well as possible. They shared their meager provisions with us, put mattresses on the floor for us to sleep on, and let us use their bathroom facilities.

At night my mother took our clothes and washed them in a sink with toothpaste—no soap was available—and hung them up. The next morning we would wear them again, even when they were not all dry. This was the way we stayed clean.

After several weeks, we finally got word about our train. Instead of south, it had traveled north and was stationed in Lautenthal, close to Goslar, Lower Saxony, Germany. How could we get there? It was March 1945. The American troops had advanced to the left bank of the Rhine River. Their low-flying planes flew daily missions over all parts of Germany shooting at anything and everything that moved, especially trains. To be safe from them, we would only travel at night.

Our south to north train travel through war-torn Germany became a harrowing experience. Determined to face the danger together, we never lost sight of each other, regardless of how dark it was, how often we had to change trains, or how long we had to sit and wait for a train to arrive. At times it was an advantage that we did not have any luggage.

Once, when we sat in a waiting train in a large train station, Hungarian sounds waffled through our open window. We opened it all the way and started a conversation with a Hungarian woman.

After a few pleasant words the woman's raw feelings surfaced. This is what she told us:

"Yesterday our train stopped suddenly. 'Get off! Get off!' 'Low flying planes are approaching!' Everyone panicked, and we got out as fast as we could. I held my little Carl firmly by the hand and we ran up the embankment away from the train. We dropped face down, close together into the grass. The planes were already over us. I felt two thuds very close by . . . " With a toneless voice the woman continued: "the third hit my little Carl. He . . . died instantly . . ."

The stark image of the deadly bullet killing the child terrified me. Dread and fright swelled inside me. I no longer felt hunger or thirst. When we continued our journey that night, our train came to a stop in the middle of nowhere. Bombardment during the day had destroyed the tracks. We got off and walked through the night along the tracks in search of the next train station.

I remember how dark it was and how tired my legs felt. We walked past a small town where bombs had hit the houses along the street. As we picked our way through the rubble, we heard from somewhere: "Hilfe! Hilfe!"[1] Was someone hurt, buried or pinned in rubble? Not knowing the location and too tired, scared, and worried about our own fate, we walked on. Eventually, we came to a train station and our journey continued.

At last we reached Lautenthal. Joyous and relieved, we spotted our hospital train. We had been missed; the people on the train had worried about us and were happy to see us. We were sent to stay with local families. Thankfully, we slept on a mattress, instead of a bench in a train station.

We had just two days to recuperate. More alarming news was coming our way: "The American troops are advancing towards Lautenthal. There will be battles with German troops stationed in the area!" The hospital orderlies and nurses rolled our patients on gurneys into an abandoned salt mine shaft to protect them from the fighting. Then we and all the hospital personnel and townspeople gathered there too. The battle raged all day.

By the next morning the town was occupied by the Americans. As we came out of hiding, they asked us to line up in two rows—the Germans on one side and we Hungarians on the other side. Each one of us was searched for weapons. The soldiers pulled the shoulder boards and rank insignia off the uniforms of our medical officers. They took watches and jewelry from us. Then an American officer talked to us, but we understood not a word. When some soldiers threw chewing gum at us, we guessed: "The investigation is over; we can go home."

Early in the morning on the third day of occupation, the American soldiers came to town, gathered all Hungarian men, and marched them away. Our hospital commander was pulled from his sleeping quarters in

---

1. "Help! Help!"

his pajamas. Our patients were transferred to a nearby hospital. Only the women and we children stayed behind.

What was going to happen to us? What was happening to our men?

We waited. Slowly one day after the other passed. After one month all the men returned unharmed. What a relief!

The Americans ordered our hospital train to proceed to Osterode in the Harz Mountains of Germany. We were joining Camp Osterode, a Hungarian military hospital. It had been a German military hospital, which had been turned over to the Hungarian army several months prior.

Camp Osterode

The camp had two large entrance gates with a two story main building between them. Then came two rows of barracks that housed the hospital and living quarters. At the far end of the camp were several buildings, one of them was the school. We were assigned to a barrack, which we shared with other people of our travel family.

Soon our mother would go to work in the hospital. Again we were left without her, but we never felt lost and alone at Camp Osterode. We were surrounded by people we knew well, who, if needed, would care for us as one of their own. The children we had traveled with were our friends and soon other children joined our group. Slowly Camp Osterode became our new home in a foreign land. We would live there for six years, even though we did not know it yet.

In 1947 an official Hungarian delegation came to our camp to transport the hospital back to Hungary. The few remaining patients were transferred to other hospitals and the hospital equipment was shipped to Hungary. We too were asked to return to our homeland. Anyone refusing to be repatriated would lose his or her Hungarian citizenship.

From friends and family back home we knew much about everyday life and the political situation in Hungary. It was occupied by the USSR and had a communist government. My mother and many of her friends despised both.

We were Hungarians and longed to return to our homeland. The adults discussed our options for several days and long into the evenings. We children, too, took part in the debate. The day of the final decision arrived. About a fourth of the hospital personnel returned with the transport to Hungary. We, our friends, and several hundred other persons decided to stay.

From this day forward Camp Osterode was no longer a hospital, but a refugee camp managed by the British Military Authority. Officially, we were stateless Displaced Persons (DPs), signifying that we did not live in the country of our origin due to the events of World War II. As such we were under the care of the UNRRA, the United Nations Relief and Rehabilitation Administration.

Our basic daily routine continued as before. Our three meals a day were cooked in the camp kitchen and we ate them together in the big dining room. The food provided was sufficient but very, very simple and lacked variety.

In summer we improved our diet on our own. Like our German neighbors, we would gather berries wherever we could find them—at the edge of roads, by railroad tracks, in meadows, or the edge of woods. In fall, we looked for mushrooms and nuts in the nearby forest.

Even though a high fence surrounded our camp, no rules required us to stay in the camp. Anytime, day or night, we were free to come and go as we pleased. We would walk to the next town for errands and travel by train to another destination if we had the funds. Of course, we were bound by travel restrictions that applied to every person in occupied Germany after the war.

The quality of camp life steadily improved due to various initiatives of the adults. Our mother remarried. She and my good stepfather made our education and personal development their main goal. Together with other interested inmates, they opened a Hungarian High School for us and the other children in the camp.

No more loafing for us. We attended school everyday except for Sundays. The subjects taught and the lesson plans mirrored that of a Hungarian high school. As in my home country, high school started at fifth grade and finished at the end of the thirteenth grade with a tough exam.

I think school started out easy for Jozsef, Stefania, and me. Yet, as our parents managed to get more Hungarian textbooks for us, and the variety of our classes expanded, the school improved. Our teachers were well qualified. Our school principal had been a language professor. He taught us Hungarian, German, and French. Our priest instructed us in Latin, an engineer in math, and a former hospital physician in the required sciences. After a couple of years our school gained official certification and those who passed the final exams were qualified to enter a university.

The adults also organized many fun activities for us. We had a soccer club to which my brother belonged. Stefania enjoyed and was good at track and field events. I belonged to the Girl Scouts. Other girls belonged to a ballet club. They organized recitals we all attended. Adults with special talents contributed in various ways. We had piano concerts, poetry readings, and special events at Easter and Christmas.

I remember our years at camp Osterode as being filled with fun, friendship, goodwill, and the security a large family provides. A German canon says: "Not much is needed to be happy." We experienced this kind of happiness despite the deprivations.

These are some of them:

- Every morning for six years we ate nothing but oatmeal cooked in skim milk for breakfast. At dinner our vegetable was often beets. To-day pigs eat them.

- All food items were in short supply. Everything was rationed: bread, margarine, jam, if available, milk, fruit—everything. We never were free to eat as we pleased.

- Meat, eggs, and many other things were rare. Only on holidays we might have a little bit of candy or chocolate.

- Heating material and electricity were rationed. At 10 PM all lights went out in camp.

Books were rare and much in demand. One of the teenage boys was very good at reading out loud. In the evening while we girls knitted or crocheted, he would read us the newest fiction. And then just when the plot got juicy, the lights went out. "Oh no, now we have to wait until tomorrow to hear if Robert married Susan," we may have called out.

Of course not everything was good. To us the worst part about camp, were the insects we had to deal with. For a while we were all infected with lice. Fortunately, we could get rid of them. The other plight we suffered from was bed bugs. They lived in the cracks of the barracks' plywood walls. What-ever we did, we could never got rid of them completely. One summer, all the barracks were smoked with a poison, while we lived and slept outside for two days. When we moved back in, we slept undisturbed for a while, and then the vermin tortured us again.

It was the goal of the refugee organization to close all camps as soon as possible. They encouraged and organized our immigration to countries that had agreed to take refugees. Belgium, Venezuela, Australia, and Canada were the first counties offering to take us. When immigration to the USA was possible, we applied.

⌒

In 1951, we received permission to immigrate to the USA. A Hungarian couple in Cleveland, Ohio vouched for my newly wed sister Stefania and her husband. Half a year later they did the same for my parents, Jozsef, and me. Because the immigration center on Ellis Island had been closed, we were processed at Camp Weindorf in Hamburg, Germany before we departed by boat to New York. We were happily reunited in Cleveland.

Soon we were all employed.

Aftereffect

"How did the events during and after the war affect your life?"

"My best friend from the camp lives in California. Whenever we talk on the phone, our conversation unfailingly touches on shared memories of Osterode. We are in agreement that in spite of bedbugs and shortages, we were happy there and acquired important life lessons."

"We learned to make do with little, to appreciate small pleasures, and to enjoy nature. We acquired sound judgment, were able to make good decisions, and find our way regardless of obstacles."

"It was a disadvantage for me that we left Osterode before I had finished high school. In the US it was important that I take a job quickly. Consequently, I never completed my secondary education."

"There was nothing good to remember about our long train journeys during the last months of this terrible war. It was a string of anxiety-filled hours, days, weeks, months—unimaginable for a person who has not experienced it. Our last journey through Germany was an especially horrifying and traumatic event. I don't wish for anyone to have to experience it ever."

"How difficult it must have been for our mother to be responsible for three children in the middle of this chaos. She never complained, cried, screamed, or despaired. Her caring, steadiness, calm, and confidence made it possible for us to survive this man-made madness without suffering permanent harm. Jozsef, Stefania, and I are forever thankful to our mother and remain so after her death."

Displaced Persons after World War II

The term Displaced Person (DP) was coined by the Allied Nations after World War II. It referred to civilians, who lived outside their home country, and needed help to return, or had to be resettled. When the military of the USA, Britain, France, and Russia occupied Germany in the spring 1945, about 6.5 to 7 million Displaced Persons lived in the country. They had been concentration camp inmates, forced laborers, or civilians from Eastern Europe, who came to Germany for fear of the Red Army.

Initially the United Nations Relief and Rehabilitation Administration (UNRRA) took care of the Displaced Persons. Later the UN Refugee Agency

(UNHCR) was founded and assumed the responsibility for all homeless Europeans. It was estimated that in all of Europe 12 million people were displaced as a consequence of the war.

It had been the goal of the Allied Nations and the UN organizations to assist Displaced Persons to return to their country of origin as soon as possible. For DPs from Northern, Western, or Southern Europe the repatriation happened without delay. The transfer of the forced laborers from Eastern Europe to their home country proved to be challenging. At the conference in Yalta February 1945, the Allied Powers had agreed that all citizens from the Soviet Union would return home, yet many Russian forced laborers were afraid to do so, as they feared reprisals for their work done in Germany. Their apprehension was well founded. About 157, 000 repatriated Russians were sentenced to death for collaboration with the Germans.

Until the Displaced Persons could be returned to their country of origin or resettled in another country, they lived in camps that previously had been army barracks, prisoner-of war-camps, forced labor camps, or concentration camps. By the end of 1946, almost one million DPs were still living in camps in Germany. One may assume that the living conditions in most DP camps were worse than at Osterode.

Beginning in 1947, DPs who could not return to their country of origin or who refused to be repatriated were resettled in other countries. Belgium, Great Britain, Canada, and Australia were the first countries that offered to take Displaced Persons. Venezuela, Brazil, and Argentina also participated in the resettlement program. Starting in 1948, the USA accepted more DPs than any other country. The resettlement program had been a huge undertaking. It ended successfully in 1959, fourteen years after the war, when the last DP camp in Germany was closed.

Military Hospital Trains

Ildiko lived several months on a Hungarian military hospital train. She tells us that two such trains existed and most likely even more hospital trains were used by the Hungarian military.

Germany operated eighty military hospital trains during World War II. The primary function of the trains was to take insured or sick soldiers from the front line of battle to military hospitals in safe areas or to the homeland. It functioned like an emergency hospital on wheels.

A military medical officer, a physician, was in charge of the hospital train. He oversaw a medical staff of doctors, nurses, and orderlies, as well as the non-medical staff needed to run the hospital. The trains usually had thirty-seven cars with the capacity to take care of up to 300 patients. Besides patient beds, the train had an operating room, a pharmacy, a medical supply room, a kitchen, and a laundry. Additional train cars housed the administration office and the sleeping/living quarters of the medical and non-medical staff.

Several freight cars were added to the military hospital train Ildiko traveled on, when it left Hungary at the end of the war. The freight cars provided primitive, temporary housing for non-essential staff and their families who wanted to flee from the advancing Soviet army.

Heinz, right, with his sister Renate and brother Peter

Chapter 14

I Was Ten Years Old
and Took Care of my Family

Heinz, born July 1934 in Gumbinnen,[1]
East Prussia, Germany

HEINZ'S ANCESTORS EMIGRATED IN the seventeenth century to East Prussia from Austria and southwest Germany. They settled in Gumbinnen, which is close to the border of Lithuania about sixty miles from Königsberg,[2] the capital of East Prussia, Germany. Some buildings in town recalled the Austrian heritage. For instance, the main church was the impressive Salzburger Kirche.

In 1922, Heinz's father, Richard, traveled to the USA in search of Ida, his hometown sweetheart. Her parents had sent her from Gumbinnen to Chicago to prevent her from marrying him. Happily reunited, away from meddling parents, Richard and Ida married and settled in Chicago, where their son Helmut was born in 1924.

Years later, Richard's fathers business improved, and he urged him to return. "Richard, you are my oldest son and my heir. Do come and see to it that our business continues to flourish. I am getting older and need your

1. Today Gusev, Russia.
2. Today Kaliningrad, Russia.

153

help." So after living in Chicago for ten years, Richard and Ida returned to their hometown in 1932. Two years later in 1934, their second son Heinz was born.

                                                 ~

Heinz has resided in the USA for over fifty years. When asked about his childhood during World War II, he writes about some of his experiences in English. Others he relates in either English or German—depending upon how he remembers them best:

My first recollections begin in the early summer of 1939 when we lived in Gumbinnen, a provincial town of 24,000 inhabitants. My father was the manager of a beautiful apartment building, called Villa Maria that belonged to my grandfather. It was located on Heeres Straße, close to the center of town. Villa Maria was three stories tall, had many apartments, a dental office, and a saddlery.

We lived in the spacious second floor apartment over the entranceway. Our balcony overlooked Heeres Straße, and from our windows in the back we could see the Pissa[3], the river that flowed through our town.

Heeres Straße (Army Street) was the main street of Gumbinnen and at that time, an important East-West crossroad. Its name highlights the fact that Napoleon's Grand Armée marched along Heeres Straße, on its way to Moscow. Upon their sad return some of the starving, freezing, and sick soldiers died here and were buried in the sandy hills not far from where we lived.

Some boys told me, "There you can find old bones from the French soldiers that glow in the dark." "Really!" I never actually saw the bones, but it always puzzled me, why they would glow. Much later, I read that the French covered the corpses with a chemical to speed their disintegration, and that caused the glow.

During this last summer of peacetime, my mother took me to visit my aunt Lieschen in Stolp,[4] the third largest town in West-Pomerania, Germany. We took a train to Königsberg and from there we went by express train to Stolp. The train crossed without stopping though the western part of Poland, the Polish Corridor, and three hours later we arrived in Stolp.

Aunt Lieschen was happy to see us and our stay was as pleasant as could be. We did not know it then, but at a later time, we would stay at Aunt Lieschen's apartment under very different circumstances.

My father was drafted when the war started in late summer. He was born in 1899, had already served in WWI and now had to do so again. For

3. Today called Pisa.
4. Today Słupsk, Poland.

several years he was employed in France, where he served as a cook for the officers' corps. In 1941, after my brother Helmut had turned seventeen, he joined the Navy and served on a minesweeper in Norway.

Now my mother and I were by ourselves in our large apartment. Life in Gumbinnen continued to be peaceful. Only when a radio program was interrupted and an official announced, "This is a special message from the War Ministry . . . " were we reminded that our country was at war.

Life was good. During the summer my mother and I went swimming every day in the new public swimming pool. Then Mutti would read, while I tried to teach myself to swim. Instead of swimming in the shallow water, I jumped into the deep end of the pool. I usually was able to grasp the edge of the pool, and climb out only to jump back in again. Once, when I didn't grasp the side of the pool in time, a man noticed me struggling and gasping for air and pulled me out of the water. I do not think that my mother realized that I didn't know how to swim at all. Engrossed in her book, she didn't mind me splashing around in the deep end.

I enjoyed a little bit of danger. In early winter, when the Pissa was covered with the first thin ice, I had to try it out by running a quick half circle over it while the softly frozen surface wobbled under my feet. After many days of freezing temperatures, the solid ice became a popular playground for all children. In spring, the thick ice would break into big pieces. I would jump from ice floe to floe and ride them downstream to the next bridge where the ice was still solid, and climb back to shore.

I enjoyed my freedom and unsupervised playtime. It was wonderful. However, knowing that school was going to start put a damper on my fun.

I was already seven years old when Mutti took me to school on my first day. When she started to leave without me, I fell apart.

"You want to get rid of me!" I screamed.

"No, no, you can't leave me here all alone!" I hollered.

Why did I panic? Was it the experience that my Papa and Helmut had gone away and left me? Did it seem to me that now I would lose Mutti too?

Fortunately, my mother stayed calm. She simply took me home. "My little Heinz will calm down," she must have thought. And so it was. The next day when she left me at school, I did not protest. Very soon I liked school. Learning to read was easy for me. In third grade, my last year of school for a long time, I read everything that interested me—on billboards, in the newspaper, and in books.

Our family got bigger. In 1941 my brother Peter and in 1942 my sister Renate were born. While Mutti was busy with the little ones, I was free to do as I pleased. One of our favorite spots was the park along the Pissa, where army sleds were parked, ready to be used in winter.

Another adventure was my boat ride down the Pissa. At a boat rental upstream I rented a rowboat for fifty German Pfennig (approximately fifty cents) an hour. "You may use it for three hours," the friendly rental agent said. Off I paddled. When I passed our house, little Peter spotted me wanting to come along, but the steep berm made stopping unsafe. Quickly I paddled out of his sight. Even for me, still unable to swim, the boat ride had been dangerous.

In July 1944, I turned ten years old and became eligible to join the Hitlerjugend — Hitler's Club for Boys. Most of my peers joined, but I did not care to, and Mutti never suggested it. One of the local party bosses lived in Villa Maria. Once, when we were standing on the bank of the Pissa, he asked me:

"How old are you, Heinz?"

"I turned ten in July."

"Why aren't you in the Hitlerjugend?" he wanted to know.

"Oh, I have been sick," I pretended. "But now I am feeling better. Soon my mother will go with me and have me enrolled."

My little white lie satisfied him. He never asked me again or gave us any trouble.

During the war, my father had been at home on leave several times. I remember best his last visit home. It was in the fall of 1944, when his unit was pulled out of France and ordered to go to Russia. On his way there, he came home for a few days. My parents celebrated his visit home with many friends.

"Heinz, go get us tickets for the next show at the movie theater," my mother said and gave me the money. I enjoyed doing the errand.

I was walking down Heeres Straße at about 6 PM with the movie tickets in my pocket. Suddenly, the whole sky lit up as if a giant Christmas tree came floating down from heaven. I heard bombs exploding. Never before had something like this happened in Gumbinnen. I started running home as fast as I could. My wooden sandals fell off my feet. I did not mind and ran faster without them. Even the pieces of glass, raining down from broken windows, didn't slow me down.

When I burst into our apartment, the party was still going strong. The loud music blasting from the record player had drowned out the bombing.

"Bombs! We are being bombed!" I screamed.

We all ran to the basement. It had extra thick, sturdy walls and would protect us, if our house were hit. Soon the whole neighborhood seemed to congregate in our large basement; many women were praying.

There was a little basement window looking out to Heeres Straße with a low wall protecting it on the outside. I crawled through the window and pulled myself up on the wall, so I could look down the street. What I saw stopped my breath. The tower of our stately Salzburger Kirche was engulfed in flames. It collapsed before my eyes.

No one in our basement was hurt. Fortunately, the Villa Maria had not been hit. But the windows were blown out by the air pressure, caused by the enormous explosions. The electric power was out, too. Later, we learned that on this day October 16, 1944, over 200 Russian bombers had returned from an unsuccessful mission and dropped their load on our small town.

This was the beginning of the end of East Prussia as our home.

My father left for Russia, and soon the war came closer to us every day.

We heard cannons firing and the detonation of explosives. First the noise was muffled as it came from far away. Then, with each passing day, it became louder and more threatening.

Mutti decided: "*It's time to go!*"

She did not wait for the official evacuation order. Resolutely, she packed our most important items in a suitcase and into large bags, without worrying about all the nice things, we would leave behind. Earlier, in Chicago, Mutti and my dad had started out with nothing. If needed, they would do so again.

The next morning, my mother sat Renate into the baby carriage and placed a large bag at her feet. Mutti and I carried the rest and little Peter scampered between us. This was the way we went to the train station.

For now the trains were still running regularly. Mutti bought our tickets to Stolp. The train ride wasn't as fast as the last time we visited Aunt Lieschen. On our way there, we were detained in a refugee camp for three days before continuing on.

Stolp

Our first apartment in Stolp was built into the old city wall not far from the Town Museum. I remember it as an interesting place. From our front windows, we saw the houses of Stolp and in the back, deep down below, flowed the Stolpe River. Instead of paddling on the Pissa, I now played on the Stolpe.

One morning I noticed that the door of the museum had been broken open. Of course, I had to take a look. I sneaked inside and in the semi-darkness I saw a sparkling saber lying among many interesting things. I took it home.

Soon thereafter, Aunt Lieschen left for Berlin and let us use her apartment. We moved to Otto Straße 5, which was close to the center of town. Here we celebrated Christmas with pea soup for dinner. Food had become scarce. When Mutti sent me to get groceries, the items on her list were frequently not available. Potatoes were the only item I could always buy.

We celebrated Christmas alone, without knowing the whereabouts of Papa, Helmut, or my grandparents. We found out later that a few days after we left Gumbinnen, an extended battle between the Russian and the German armies had been fought on the outskirts of the town. When the Russian troops conquered Gumbinnen in January 1945, most civilians fled or perished. We never saw our grandpa or grandma again or knew their fate.

On a day in early March 1945, Mutti sent me to the small grocery store at the near-by street corner.

"Heinz, get us some Kunsthonig (a honey substitute)," she said.

When I arrived, the door was broken down. Astonished, I looked around, but no one was in sight. On my way back, I saw something big and brown at the side of the street not far from our house. It was a dead horse, lying there looking kind of peacefull.

"What was going on?" I puzzled and raced home.

"The Russians are here," was Mutti's explanation, after I told her what I had seen.

"Was there anything left to eat in the store?" she asked.

"Yes, there was."

"Heinz, go back and get what we can use," Mutti instructed me.

I went back to the store and got as much as I could.

This was the beginning of a new job for me—getting enough food for four people to live on, any way I could.

⌣

The little corner store was soon totally empty. All other stores stayed closed. On March 8, 1945, the Russian troops conquered Stolp without any German resistance. They burned buildings, broke down doors, and fired into windows.

After things calmed down, I ventured out into the empty streets to see what had happened. A window of the bank was broken. I wiggled through it and landed in a mountain of money. Next to it lay a dead man. Was he a bank employee? We had enough German marks. I was looking for food and climbed out.

An injured man was lying on the lawn next to the National Socialist Workers Party of Germany or Nazi Party Headquarters.

"Water, Water," he groaned.

I hurried home, but Mutti did not want me to return with my glass of water.

"Look, Heinz, two Russian soldiers with machineguns are standing beside the building. What will they do, if you bring the water to the man?"

I obeyed Mutti. All the Germans were hiding during those first days of occupation. So far, nobody had noticed a thin ten-year-old. It was better not to draw attention to myself.

Instead, I checked out the warehouse bordering our yard. I found an unlocked door and opened it quietly. Wow, what did I see in there? Hundred pound sacks of sugar! For many months Mutti had been happy, whenever she could buy fifty grams of sugar at the store. And here were one-hundred-pound sacks of sugar sitting around. I decided I had to take a sack home immediately. But how? I did not weigh much more than fifty pounds myself.

I pushed and jerked a sack to the door and pulled it outside. Did I roll it, kick, or drag it? I don't know how, but I successfully got the heavy sack home. I was glad to have acted so quickly. As soon as the Russians knew about the sugar, they loaded it onto a big truck and drove off.

The sugar became our treasure. It was worth more than silver or gold. When the bakery across the street opened again, Mutti sent me with a little bag of sugar, and I got a loaf of bread for it. She also let me walk to the next village to barter food for sugar.

I had fun looking at the other items stored in the warehouse by wealthy townspeople before they left for the West. My favorite was a trunk with little jewelry cases, which held all types of coins. I found old Prussian Thaler, small gold coins, and even old Roman coins with the head of Caesar engraved on them. I marveled at them all, and then put them back in the trunk.

Less valuable, yet even more interesting to me, were the many books. I perused them and took home whatever seemed fun or exciting to read. Soon, I knew more about many subjects than other children my age.

Yet, during the coming months my primary business was not reading, but getting food for my family. Not much was available in the newly reopened stores. Additional sources of food were needed.

Ahead of the Russian occupation, many people had fled Stolp and their houses were standing empty. "Heinz, maybe you can find some food in there," Mutti suggested. I started searching.

"Mutti, look what I found," I proudly called, coming home with my booty.

The fleeing homeowners usually did not take their canned goods, but left them in their basement. I was happy, whenever I found something good, and so was Mutti.

Roaming through the streets of Stolp, I was not afraid of the Russian soldiers. But for the women in town, the occupation forces were a constant threat. Frequently, a group of Russians would party in our attic at night. Besides doing other things, they would smoke. Once this caused a fire and damaged the roof. From then on, water dripped into our apartment when it rained.

The Russians admired the Americans, who had been their partners against Germany. When the officers found out that my mother had lived in Chicago, they respected her. We were their friends and sometimes they would visit us.

Once my mother allowed some young soldiers to make vodka in our kitchen. Hardly older than I—maybe fifteen or sixteen years old—they were very nice to me. Happily they explained to me how alcohol is distilled. I already knew some Russian words and learned a few more right then. They offered me some of their home-brew. I did not want to appear like a small-town boy and took a sip. I never drank again for years to come. It tasted that bad.

The word got out quickly that the Russians were friendly to us. Often we had eight to twelve women sleeping at night in our apartment. I did not really know what was going on, but realized, that we were helping them, and that they were thankful to my mother. Until most of the soldiers were pulled out, our place was a sanctuary for women.

The resumption of some civic order did not alleviate the food shortages. It continued to be my job to supply us with something to eat. For a while, I had a little horse and a wagon. Together with a friend who was two years older, I traveled though the countryside looking for food. One day we hit the jackpot: a cheese factory producing a local Camembert called "Stolper Jungchen." There were shelves and shelves full of ripening cheese. They were not quite ripe, but we did not care. We loaded them in our wagon and had cheese for weeks. Even if we did not have bread, the Jungchen tasted really good without it.

In the evening, I put my pony to pasture on the lawn behind our house. I wanted very much to ride my pony, but it did not like that at all. Each time I tried to mount it, it threw me off and even tried to kick me when I was on the ground. How treacherous!

I did not have my little horse for long. On one of our trips, several Russian soldiers waved machineguns at us, meaning: "Get off the wagon. We want the horse and buggy!"

I missed my pony. But there was nothing I could do about it. My next food search was again on foot. In a basement I found huge pieces of meat curing in salt brine. Proud and happy I brought them home. Sadly, we never could get rid of the strong salt taste and could not eat them.

Another time I found a large bag of flour. My mother wanted to make pancakes with it, but did not have any fat. Instead she poured a little sewing machine oil into the pan. Swoosh, it caused a fire as it got hot. Later she sprinkled a little salt into the pan before spooning in the batter. That worked. The pancakes fried with salt were quite tasty.

⌒

In July 1945 Stolp and all of Pomerania became part of Poland, as agreed upon by the Allied Nations, the new Polish government was phased in. Polish stores opened and the previously German owned stores were handed over one by one to Polish merchants.

Mutti had enough German Reich Marks, the legal German money until 1948, but they became useless in Stolp. The Polish shopkeepers accepted only Zlotys, the Polish currency. We had none. At the same time my food search had become difficult. Polish people from the eastern part of Poland were being resettled, and they moved into vacant houses and apartments.

What to do?

There was a very attractive young woman living down the street from us, who was a favorite of the Russian officers. They showered her with delicate gifts, such as silk stockings and intimate apparel.

"She got the most expensive stuff!" was rumored.

"Is this really true?" I wondered.

I went to resale clothing stores. Indeed, silk stockings were very expensive and the other frilly things were too. I made a plan. I was barely 11 years old, but good at planning and execution.

First, I watched at what time the fancy lady usually left her apartment. Once I knew this, I sneaked in and found out where she kept her valuable clothes. The next day I took along bags, which I loaded with what I thought was really expensive.

Safe at home with my loot, I became very worried. The Russian friends of the young lady would soon hear about the theft and search our neighborhood for the missing items. What would happen to us, if they found them here?

We had a tile stove in our bedroom. Its exhaust pipe had a vent with a cover. I removed it, stuffed my bags into the pipe and carefully replaced the cover.

Indeed, the following day the Russian officers, with machineguns hanging over their shoulders, stormed into our apartment and searched it. I held my breath pretending to be engrossed in my book. My skin prickled when they rummaged through our bedroom. I was still frozen in place when they passed through the hallway. Only when they had closed our door behind them, did I jump up with relief. They had not found my hiding place.

Early, really early the next morning, I sprinted with my soot stained bags through town to the resale store. I sold all for 700 Zlotys.

Wow, now we were rich! On my way home I stopped and bought ten grams of real coffee for my mother, knowing how much she loved it; and for each of us I got a little cake.

My little sister Renate had boils on her skin from malnutrition. They were so bad that Mutti asked a gypsy woman to heal her with magic spells and prayers. Renate did get better. I was sure that my cake had at least partially contributed to her recovery.

Sometime later the Polish Government gave us the choice of either staying in Słupsk, as Stolp was now called, or leaving for West Germany.

In October 1945, we left Słupsk, again, with only as much as Mutti and I could carry. In a refugee camp by Stettin, we were registered by the American occupation administration. We got a medical exam and were treated for lice, even though we did not have any.

We learned that we would be sent to Hochfeld, a village close to Wilster in the West German state of Schleswig-Holstein. Before our departure, Mutti gave our address to the Red Cross.

In the West

We went to Wilster by train. From there a farmer took us by horse carriage to Hochfeld, a little village with the wrong name. Instead of being on a high field, as the German name implied, it was situated two meters below sea level and surrounded by swampy fields.

We arrived at eleven o'clock at night at our designated place, a room in a traditional Lower-Saxony Farmhouse. It was a tiny chamber furnished with one bed and a table. Mutti slept in the bed and I slept beside it. My little brother Peter and sister Renate slept under the table.

Next morning, we noticed that the large farmhouse had only three sparse rooms. The rest of the farmhouse was livestock stables and barn. People, animals, straw, and hay were all united under one huge thatched roof, which reached almost to the ground. The farmer and his family, who shared their limited space with us, spoke a Low German dialect that we could not understand.

I learned the dialect quickly and soon talked like the locals. Later in the US, it helped me with English because to me Low German is a mixture of German and English. On this first day in Hochfeld, I learned nothing; instead I became very sick.

I was taken to a hospital in Glückstadt, about forty miles away, where I stayed for a month. During the first week I was blind and lost consciousness periodically. The doctors did not know what caused it and suspected typhoid fever. Slowly I got better and recuperated fully.

During my last days in the hospital, I helped the kitchen staff. With a little wagon I went to the railroad station and picked up a delivery of butter, cheese, and other food items. As a reward I got a little butter and cheese to eat.

A big surprise was awaiting me when I arrived home from the hospital—Helmut was there! We hadn't seen each other for a long time. I was so happy he was home!

The Russians had captured Helmut. Somewhere in Hungary he jumped off the prisoner train and managed to escape without being shot or recaptured. With the help of the Red Cross, he got our address and found us. During the war Helmut had injured a leg, one knee was stiff for the rest of his life.

⤳

Across from us was the one room village school.

"Heinz, it is time that you go to school again," stated Mutti. According to my age I would start in sixth grade.

"Sixth grade!" I cried. I had had no instructions since the third grade.

"Will I be able to do sixth grade work?" I worried.

Soon I noticed, that I was not behind, but ahead of my classmates. This was due to all the reading I had done.

The people in the village were not unfriendly to us, and no soldier with a machine gun threatened us. Nevertheless, we suffered in Hochfeld. We were always hungry. We received food ration coupons. They provided us with meager "hunger portions" of basic food items. We owned nothing to barter for food. The farmers living around us were also very poor. They hardly had enough to eat themselves. The poor soil of the swampy fields yielded meager harvests.

Of course, I tried to improve our diet. Sometimes I would bring one or two eggs to Mutti, which I had gathered in the high grass by the creek. The hens had laid them there instead of in their nests. By carefully observing the chickens, I knew their habits better then the farmer's wife.

Many sparrows fluttered and hopped around the farmyards. "They may provide us with some meat," I thought. Indeed, I was able to catch a few sparrows with a mousetrap. The result was disappointing. The small birds had very little meat on their bones. It was not worth the trouble.

Mutti's efforts yielded better results. She wrote a long letter to our relatives in Chicago describing our dire circumstances. The packages they sent to us were lifesavers. How would we have survived without them?

Helmut tried to find a job, but there simply was no work to be had in Hochfeld. His goal was to go to the US as soon as possible. After all, he had American citizenship. Even this took time. Luckily, his special status helped us to get better living quarters in the town of Wilster. Here we roomed in the large house of a physician. Besides us, other Displaced Persons (DPs) lived there. I remember meeting a magician from Hungary.

During all this time, we had not heard from my father. After the war, he was taken prisoner by the Russians and imprisoned in a work camp. There he contracted malaria. Since he was no longer able to work, he was released. By some good fortune he survived the illness. After contacting the Red Cross, he found us in Wilster. Finally, after many years apart, our family was reunited and remained together until Helmut left for the USA a year later.

The school in Wilster was better than the village school in Hochfeld. Even though I was a DP, I was accepted by the local teens. I learned not to show how smart I was, instead to be good in sports and to be a good friend

At the end of my last year in school, the two top students received a prize. It went to a girl in my class and to me. It was a big prize. I got eight hundred Marks! An enormous sum if one considers that my father got twenty Marks a week in government support. My prize money flowed into the family coffer and my mother bought a used watch for me.

"Why didn't my parents let me keep some of the money?" I wondered then and still do today.

The small town of Wilster had 4,000 inhabitants after the war. Half of them were refugees. Consequently, unemployment was a big problem.

Neither Helmut nor my father ever found employment. When I finished school, there was no job or training program available for me. After a long search, I was accepted into a three-year-long apprenticeship in mechanical engineering in the locomotive factory of Glückstadt. In order to be at work on time, I had to catch a train at 4:45 AM; I did not return to Wilster until late in the evening. It was tough, really tough, but I persevered.

After finishing two years of my apprenticeship, my father and I emigrated to the USA. My mother had left a year earlier with Peter and Renate.

My training in Glückstadt turned out to be very helpful for my job search and employment in the US.

Aftereffect

Asked how his childhood during the war affected his later life, Heinz responded:

"Due to my experiences during wartime, I became independent and self-assured at an early age. I learned to size up a new situation quickly and make good decisions."

"I enjoy what I have, when I have it. The first ten years of my life my family was well-to-do and well respected. The next ten years we were very poor refugees. You never forget this."

"My early experience of independent reading and learning later helped me at work and in life."

"I never have problems with people in authority—at work, in public, or with the police. If a conflict arises, I will turn probing questions into personal conversations and soon all tension evaporates."

The Evacuation of East Prussia

After World War II, East Prussia was annexed by the Soviet Union. The other parts of Germany east of the Oder-Neisse Line became part of Poland. The people who had lived there either fled as the Red Army advanced or were later expelled.

The ethnic Germans, who had been living, often for many centuries, in Russia and other eastern or middle-European countries, shared the same fate. They too were expelled. Altogether 12 to 14 million German-speaking civilians lost their homes and homeland.

Probably the saddest story of this period was the flight of the people from East Prussia in the winter of 1945. It happened under the most unfavorable circumstances: freezing temperatures, part of the trek over ice, and in close vicinity to intense fighting. Adding to the challenge was the unique geographical location.

East Prussia was separated from the rest of Germany by a strip of land belonging to Poland, called the Polish Corridor. During peacetime and during the war years when Germany occupied Poland, this had not caused a problem. But when in January 23, 1945 the Soviet Union advanced to the area, East Prussia became cut off by land from Germany. The only remaining escape route was over the frozen Vistula Lagoon.

Heinz and his family belonged to the lucky few who had left East Prussia by train without much difficulty when it was still possible. Gumbinnen, due to its location close to the border, experienced combat operations already in October 1944 about three months earlier than other places in East Prussia. Because of this and the foresight of Heinz's mother, his family left early and did not share the disastrous fate of their countrymen. At the time of their departure most civilians of East Prussia were still hoping that the German army would repel the Russians. In fact, the few who advocated leaving the province early, were punished as traitors.

When in January of 1945, the official evacuation orders were given to towns and villages in East Prussia, the daytime temperature had plunged to as low as -4 degrees Fahrenheit and icy winds made it feel even colder. The Red army was advancing fast and the evacuating German troops were crowding the escape routes. As civilians had no cars—these had been confiscated by the military long before—they travelled in large treks of horse drawn-wagons or walked.

One witness describes the helter-skelter evacuation out of Hirschberg,[5] East Prussia on January 20, 1945 as follows:[6]

> " . . . *The nights were long and the road was covered with a sheet of ice. Snow drifted over the fields. To keep the wide main road open for military vehicle traffic, the trek was detoured to side roads where the east wind howled. From afar we heard the thundering of the artillery and saw the glow of burning villages. On the overloaded horse-drawn wagons many people were crowded between bedding and clothes. Others were walking on foot pulling a loaded handcart or pushing bicycles. Babies cried in the middle of the turmoil. German chain-driven vehicles rattled by. Women begged for a ride on the hopelessly overloaded wagons. The horses could not pull forward on the slippery icy road, fell down, or moved sideways. Wagons crashed into ditches . . ."*

The witness reports that the Russian Army overtook the trek soon thereafter.

᠅

Other wagon trains managed to flee from the fighting and against all odds succeeded in reaching West Germany. The most dangerous part of their long journey was crossing over the frozen Vistula Lagoon. This was especially true if the weather had changed by the time the wagon team reached the large body of water.

---

5. Today Jedzbark, Russia.

6. Zmijewska, "Kriegsende in Ostpreußen," para. 7

The witness Helga describes her family's flight from their estate in Vollmarstein[7] , Sensburg County, East Prussia beginning on January 25, 1945. This excerpt describes the crossing over the frozen Lagoon:[8]

"The ice was covered with water and a wide strip along the shore had also melted. Luck had it that during the night it froze again and the soldiers were able to build a bridge over the open water at the shore. Men were not allowed to leave East Prussia; they were pulled out of the wagons, as happened also to the father of the family we were taking along. At dawn the anxiously waiting people drove their teams onto the Lagoon keeping a distance of 55 yards between them. Upon stepping on the ice the skittish horses spooked. My sister and I walked. The wagon wheels swirled up the melted ice. Even our freshly marked route over the ice was pockmarked by bombs from low-flying planes and damaged by wagon teams who had crashed through the ice. Again and again there were delays; but the wide spacing between wagons had to be maintained due to the danger of breaking through the ice. This five-mile-long stretch took many hours. Often we had to pause because a wagon had broken through the ice, was unable to move on and was left lying. Then we would detour around the fresh break, but sometimes our set route would lead us over loaded wagons and horse corpses frozen into the ice. A carpet would cover the horses' remains. Then we would lead our rearing horses over it with great effort overcoming our disgust. The low-flying Russian planes had an easy job with us. The dark wagons on the bright ice sheet made us easy targets for their machine guns on board. Luckily they were poor marksmen, rarely hitting their targets, but the fear of being shot at was always present as was our worry about our even heavier loaded wagon. We walked behind it trying to keep it from skidding on the wet slippery ice.

When we had to wait for a long time, the ice floe our team stood on slowly sank. Frightened to death we starred at the crack in front of our feet. My sister later told me: "At that time I made a bargain with my God: If we would survive this journey, I would never ever complain about anything in my life, regardless whatever happens. I would work hard, in spite of what was required and be content with everything." And then finally, after half of eternity had passed, the horses pulled hard, and stepped onto the higher solid sheet of ice. With a terrifying jolt our wagon, too, got onto the solid ice and we carried on. When we reached the Vistula

7. Today Nowe Nadawki, Russia

8. Lion, *Unsere Flucht aus Vollmarstein in Ostpreußen*, para. 16–18.

*Spit — a forty-five-mile long narrow peninsular stretch of land,
which separates the Vistula Lagoon from the Gdansk Bay — we
had to drive along it until we came to the bridge the soldiers had
built across the open water to the shore. The soldiers helped us get
up the steep sandy bank. Leaning into the spokes of the wheels
they pushed our wagon and the horses up the embankment. We
had survived the drive over the Vistula Lagoon and were on safe
ground."*

Facing more danger Helga and her family continued their
difficult trek to the West. It took them seven weeks. The family
they had taken in, traveled with them to Pomerania, where they
were able to board a train.

Starting on January 21, a large German military operation brought up
to 900,000 refugees to safety by boat from the ports of Gdansk and Pillau
(now named Baltiysk). This good news is diminished by the fact that tor-
pedoes from Russian submarines hit several passenger ships. The greatest
disaster happened when the large passenger ship Wilhelm Gustloff sank and
up to 9,000 —the exact number is unknown—refugees, mostly women and
children, drowned.

Annelies, left, with her friend and cousin

Chapter 15

We Had to Leave in Fifteen Minutes

Annelies, born July 1936 in
Oberlautensdorf,[1] Czechoslovakia

ANNELIES AND HER HUSBAND Algy have lived in the Midwest of the US for almost fifty years. Here they raised their children and worked with local organizations to improve the neighborhood. Karl, Annelies's older brother, emigrated with his wife to Australia where he managed a vineyard. Her cousin Roland founded a successful roofing company in Windhuk, Namibia. Her parents lived until their death in Forchheim, Germany and her dearest cousin, Ingrid, lives near Darmstadt, Germany.

Annelies's close family is scattered over four continents —America, Australia, Africa, and Europe. That was not always the case. Once upon a time the parents lived with their two children Karl and Annelies, their grand-parents, uncles, aunts, nephews, nieces, cousins, and in-laws in or near the city of Oberleutensdorf in the Sudetenland, a border area of Czechoslovakia that had been the home of ethnic Germans for many centuries.

1. Today Litvinov, Slovakia.

Oberleutensdorf was a coal-mining town. The coal was used in a hydrogenation plant for the production of synthetic gasoline. Annelies's father, a mining manager and materials controller, occupied an important position at the coalmine. They lived in one of the stately multifamily houses on Schiller Street. Her maternal grandparents ran a grocery store nearby in the Bergesgrün section of town. Annelies's paternal grandparents had a farm and hauling business in Unterleutensdorf.

As a prelude to World War II, Hitler annexed the Sudetenland. This meant that ethnic Germans had to contribute to the war effort and could be drafted by the German military.

～

This is Annelies' story:

During the first years of the war, our life was hardly affected. My father was not drafted as a soldier because his work was considered essential to the war effort. Food rationing did not interfere with our lifestyle. We always had enough to eat. What we couldn't get with food stamps, we got from our grandparents. But the bombs, they were bad.

I was eight years old in 1944 when the Allies expanded their aerial warfare to include our area. Our air-raid shelter was the old vault cellar in our apartment building. My father built a cot for my mother and me to rest on during the air raids. He and Karl would sit on benches. Many a night the air-raid sirens would wake us up and we would rush down into the cellar for safety. In the evening, I laid my clothing next to my bed so I could dress quickly when the sirens blared.

At that time, I was in second grade. Our teacher encouraged us to collect bomb fragments and to give them to the school so that the metal could be reused. We also collected bones; they were needed to make soap. Sometimes the sirens went off during the day while I was in school. When this happened, we crouched in the hall with our hands folded behind our neck and our head supported on our knees—a very inadequate protective measure.

At the beginning of 1945, my father was drafted into the army. He was sent to the front without military training or adequate equipment. His brief military service earned him 4 1/2 years in a Russian prisoner of war camp! For the longest time we heard nothing from him.

As the air war intensified, our mother had to care for us alone. The bombers came nearly every night. Instead of running to the cellar, we went to a shaft that the men had dug into the side of a hill. It was a very secure shelter during the bombardments, but it was cold and damp. We had to stand because the ground was wet. I was horrified to stand crowded close together with the other people while the bombs exploded. Each time the all-clear signal sounded, and we were allowed to leave the shaft, a rush of relief overcame me.

Once, when standing in the shaft, we heard a strong, heavy bombardment in the distance. It lasted a long time. Dresden, located about forty miles on the other side of the mountain, was totally destroyed that night.

In April of 1945, the Russians marched toward our city. My mother packed all our essential things into our little wagon and we tried to flee from the advancing troops. She had heard how much young women suffered under Russian occupation. We walked through fields and meadows and met German soldiers who were also fleeing.

One of the soldiers noticed that I was struggling to keep up with Mutti and Karl. "Come little girl, we will give you a ride." After a nod and a thank you from my mother, he lifted me up onto the tank. There I sat, high above the road, resting my tired little legs. Awesome! In spite of the terrifying flight, I remember it as a great adventure.

The Russians, however, caught up with us on the same day and, unobserved, we returned home by hidden paths. That night and for many nights to follow, the residents of our apartment building barricaded the old, heavy front door with thick beams. We were able to prevent any drunken soldiers from breaking into our building.

Nevertheless, our life was now harder than before. Not only the Russians, but also the Czechs sought revenge for what the German soldiers and the Nazi government had done to them during the war. The watchword was to collectively punish all Germans.

Our German school was closed. All adults had to wear a white armband, and there was no police protection for us. German men and young people were rounded up and put in a camp. The Russians had freed the miserable inmates of a large concentration camp. It was now used by the Czechs to imprison Germans. Even thirteen-year-old boys of Karl's age were forced to work in the coal mine. Fortunately, Mutti through some connections secured a place for Karl as a farmhand on a large farm. There the work was less strenuous and he would not go hungry. My mother and other women had to clean the concentration camp barracks.

⌒

It was July 26, 1945, the name day of my mother's mother, when armed Czech soldiers banged on our door at 6 o'clock in the morning. Mutti was already dressed, as her work began early. But I was still in bed.

"You have fifteen minutes to pack your things together," they ordered us. "Then you have to get out of here!"

While the soldiers with their weapons hanging over their shoulders watched, my mother packed two knapsacks, one for me and one for her, as fast as she could.

Our eighty-five-year-old great uncle lived in the same building. The previous evening, he had received a notification that he had to move out of his apartment the next day. Feeling sorry for him, Mutti had helped him pack and had prepared travel provisions for him. Now we too were kicked out and had only fifteen minutes to pack!

The soldiers marched us with many others to a place outside of town where still more soldiers stood around. They grabbed our knapsacks, dumped everything out, and took what they liked. They let us gather what was left—from then on that was the entirety of our worldly possessions.

Additional people were taken to the area. A neighbor with her adult daughter and our two old aunts were fellow sufferers. We had to stay at this location for the entire day without anything to eat or drink. We thought of our grandmother. We had promised to visit her after Mutti returned from work to celebrate her name day with her. Surely she was waiting for us and was worried. A good acquaintance saw us and told grandmother what had happened; but we didn't know that.

Late in the day the soldiers ordered us to climb into a waiting truck. We were driven over the border to Germany. Here the truck stopped abruptly. Two soldiers got out of the driver's cab, let down the tailgate, and gestured with their arms. " . . . Out! Out!" Whoever was too slow got a shove with the gun butt. We were driven to the side of the road like wild cattle. The soldiers closed the tailgate and jumped into the truck. The motor revved, and the truck backed up. We scattered aside frightened. The truck made a sharp turn, the tires squealed, and it roared away.

Our pathetic little group stood forsaken on the side of the road. We watched the truck until the clouds of dust that it left behind disappeared on the horizon. It drove back to our homeland . . . and we? We stood in a strange land on a deserted road. What were we to do? I remember sleeping with others in the dusty, warm attic of a farmhouse that night.

The next day, together with our two aunts, the neighbors, and our eighty-five-year-old uncle we traveled a short distance by train to Freital, a town near Dresden, where relatives could care for our uncle. In spite of the short distance, the trip took forever. We had to get out of the train twice, and walk part of the way, because the railroad tracks had been destroyed.

The relatives took in our old uncle, but there were no accommodations for the rest of us. The small city was overflowing with refugees from the ashes of Dresden. Together with our aunts and neighbors we walked through the land like vagabonds. It was difficult, but my mother was never discouraged. She always found a way out of a difficult situation.

One time when we were very hungry, she said to me, "Go to the bakeries and ask for a piece of bread. You are a child. They will give you something."

And so it was. Proudly I came back with some bread for us.

Another time my mother secretly and quickly broke off a ripe cucumber in a stranger's garden. We sat down in the grass by the side of the road and slowly ate it.

Our fate turned for the better, when the neighbor woman in our group got to know a farmer from Großjena and we decided to go there.

Großjena is a small village with a population of about 600 located north of Naumburg on the Unstrut River. Here we found temporary shelter with an innkeeper who let us sleep in his dance hall.

It turned out not to be a safe place, because at night several Russians broke in looking for young women. Luckily, my mother and the young neighbor noticed the intruders in time, ran out through the back door, and hid in the vineyards.

"Nix Frau"[2] the old aunts assured the Russians.

They didn't believe it. Pointing at me as evidence they demanded: "Frau!"

Angrily looking through everything without finding the objects of their desire, the soldiers finally left frustrated.

That night Mutti slept in the vineyard. Today when I see an ad for the popular Rotkäppchen[3] champagne, I think about how its grapevines once protected my mother.

The housing office assigned our group to a wooden shack on the banks of the Saale River. It was a weekend cottage without heat or a toilet, but it was furnished with bunk beds, and it was safer at night than the dance floor.

My mother was confident that we could live in Großjena and decided to retrieve my brother. This was a difficult and dangerous undertaking. First she had to travel by train as far as the border. There she blackened her face, took an old basket, and dressed as an old woman looking for mushrooms. She slipped over the (at that time) unguarded border and went to the building where her parents lived. There she hid in the cellar.

An old neighbor saw her and helped by telling my grandparents where she was. They secretly came to her at night. After hugging and kissing each other, they exchanged the news of the past months and made plans for Karl

2. No woman.
3. Little Red Riding Hood.

to flee with Mutti to Germany. Since he had a free weekend, he had come to his grandparents from the farm where he worked. With good provisions Mutti and Karl were careful to depart at a safe time, so they would not be seen or robbed when crossing the border.

"Won't you flee with us?" my mother had asked her parents. Although the Czech authorities had closed their store, her parents hoped to be able to continue living in their house. "Oberleutensdorf is our home. We are too old to go to a strange land."

What's more, they were not alone. My mother's two younger sisters lived with them. Since Aunt Irma's husband had been drafted, she and her young daughter had moved back home. Aunt Else, who had lived with her Czech husband near Prague, had returned to her parents with her five-year-old son to escape the anti-German threats from which her husband and his family could not or would not protect her.

I had remained with my great aunts in Großjena and I was worried. I knew how dangerous it was to smuggle oneself across the border. What would happen to Mutti? Would the soldiers catch her? When would she come back? Would she come back at all? Long hours and days I anxiously waited for her. Finally, she arrived and Karl was with her. I laughed and cried with joy and relief. How happy we were to be together again.

Besides the good news from my grandparents, Mutti told us the tragic story of her oldest sister. Three days after our deportation, Czech soldiers came to her house when she was alone with her three children. They demanded that she show them where in the yard her husband had buried their valuables. She didn't know anything about this. The soldiers didn't believe her and tried to force a confession from her. Even her nine-year old son was questioned harshly. The swearing and cursing of the soldiers caused her six- and four-year-old girls to cry piteously. As the soldiers left, they threatened to return.

No one knew what drove my aunt to take the next step. Fear? Panic? Despair? In a fury, she lunged at the children with a kitchen knife and slit their throats and wrists, and grabbed a rope to hang herself. This was how my uncle found her when he came home early from work. Her wild look and traces of blood all over led him to suspect the worst. She didn't want to let him in. He pushed her roughly aside and found his children lying in their blood. They were still alive. His shouts for help brought neighbors who helped him staunch the bleeding and carry the children at a run to the hospital. All three were saved, though there was no saving my aunt. As her children were taken to the hospital, she went to the attic and hanged herself. My uncle found her dead.

My mother was very different from her sister; she faced challenges head on. In spite of our difficult situation, she radiated infectious confidence and overcame each new demand. She found work for my brother with a farmer in Großjena and arranged for all of us to live there. The farmer agreed to rent us a room furnished with two beds for twenty marks a month. One bed was for my mother and me and the other one for Karl. Our toilet was an outhouse by the manure pile, and we carried water from the pump in the farmyard. The stove in our room served for heating and cooking. We lived this way for the next three years.

Employment was not all that Karl needed. He was fourteen years old and Mutti decided he should learn a trade. She went to the agricultural office in Naumburg and accomplished that Karl's employer and his farm became a recognized teaching operation and Karl would do an apprenticeship of farm management right there.

Mutti found work sewing for people in the neighborhood. She earned four marks a day—fifty pfennigs per hour. It was very low pay considering the cost of living. Usually, my mother took me with her, and I played with the children of the families she sewed for or with the friends I had made on my own.

Mutti enrolled me in the local elementary school. The small school in the village had two classes, one for the first through fourth grades and the other for the fifth through eight grades. I liked our teacher. He was an older gentleman, who had been hired again after the war. Through his effort, his students learned what they had missed in the last years of the war. I gladly went to school, and the teacher was satisfied with me even though I didn't do my homework as carefully as he wished.

When my mother did not have sewing work in the summer, she went with me to the "stubble fields," fields that had been harvested, to glean leftover shafts of grain. In autumn we searched for potatoes or beets, overlooked in the harvested fields. She was pleased to have my help, but when I began to complain of how hot and tired I was, she said, "Annelies, sit on the edge of the field and rest." She continued to work tirelessly. She knew how important each potato she collected was for us in winter when there was little to eat. We weren't starving as we had been during the expulsion, but food was still scarce and our meals small.

Against the strong prohibition by the military government, the Russian occupation troops came to the farm during the night, stole a cow, secretly slaughtered it, and buried the remains. Karl would find this spot the next morning, quickly dig up the skeleton, and bring what was still usable to my mother. She washed it thoroughly at the pump and cooked it. We ate it in the evening with vegetables or potatoes. Many of the pieces exuded fat, which we used for frying.

For cooking and frying, we needed fuel, so on her free days Mutti often went with me to the woods. We collected dry pinecones as fire starters and thick branches as firewood. We also gathered berries and, with time, we knew where and when to find the best blackberries, wild strawberries, and blueberries.

Everything we had was re-used. If I had outgrown a dress, Mutti made a skirt out of it for me. If the skirt was too short, she let out the hem. If it still wasn't long enough, she added a cloth strip. Since there was little fabric to purchase, every remnant was used or repurposed. Mutti made me two red rompers from a swastika flag.

After milking, the farmers stretched round, white muslin cloths over the milk cans and secured them with muslin ties before they poured the fresh milk into the cans. Mutti sewed the soft white ties together and made me a pretty embroidered summer dress with them. From the round cloths, she sewed underpants for me. I unraveled a sweater that had become too small for me and used the yarn to knit myself woolen socks.

Mutti sometimes received sugar or flour from her customers, and when we had enough, we traded them on the black market for socks, underwear, or whatever else we badly needed. Shoes were the most difficult to get. Sometimes one could buy poorly made wooden sandals. They hurt my feet and fell apart after a short period. I went barefoot the entire summer, even to school. It didn't bother me because nearly all of my classmates went barefoot. The clothing of the local children was similar to mine.

Only when the farm children ate their ham sandwiches during recess and my bread slices were thinly spread with margarine, did I feel poor and underprivileged. The same sad feeling welled up in me before the holidays, when the farmwomen went with their big baking sheets to the community baking oven in the village, which smelled so deliciously of freshly baked goods. I knew there would be no cake for us. We were refugees. It was especially hurtful, when days later, spoiled cake landed in the manure pile. Why hadn't they given us some of what was too much for them?

In retrospect, the lack of tasty food during the day was a minor nuisance compared to my plight at night. Then the anguish and fears of the last months of the war and the time thereafter revisited me. Defuse nightmares made me scream out loud and woke me up. Mutti would take me into her arms and walk with me around until I calmed down. I don't remember any details about my dreams. Fortunately, they never bothered me at any later time.

Through contacts with relatives, former neighbors, and family friends, my mother heard of the expulsion of her parents in the fall of 1945. Everything that they had accumulated over sixty years stayed behind. They too, had to start all over.

Compared with our deportation, theirs was more orderly. After receiving notice twenty-four hours in advance of the forced departure, they traveled by train together with my aunts and their children to Germany. They were sent to Dornburg-Camburg, a picturesque town with a 1,500-year-old history, not far from Großjena.

Outside of town they were assigned two rooms in the manor house on an estate that had been subdivided among small farmers. The larger of the rooms was used as a bedroom for the women and children, and the smaller room served as their kitchen and living room. My grandfather slept on a cot in the kitchen and when I visited I slept in a deck chair.

Although Dornburg-Camburg was only twelve miles from Großjena, it took forever for us to travel there. Early Sunday morning we would catch the small train along the Unstrut River to Naumburg and transfer to the train to Dornburg-Camburg. Today Google Maps indicates that the train reaches the town after two stops and fourteen minutes of travel time. When we made the trip after the war, just the waiting time in Naumburg could be over an hour. The train was always very full, and it often stopped in the middle of the route continuing after a long pause. When we arrived in Dornburg-Camburg, we still had to walk two miles to the estate where my grandparents and aunts lived.

After I had made the trip several times with my mother, I was allowed to travel alone. Usually I traveled without a problem but not always. Once, when the train stopped short of the platform at Dornburg-Camburg, I remained on the train waiting for it to pull up to the proper stop. But as the train started up again, it clattered through the station and stopped at the next village.

Oh, my goodness, now I had to take the train back to Camburg and had no ticket to do it! After a long wait, I bravely got on the train going in the opposite direction. During the endlessly long trip of about five minutes, I watched the compartment door and hoped fervently that no conductor would appear and discover me traveling without a ticket. I was in luck, although not very much, because in the meantime, it had become dark, und I was very afraid to walk the two miles alone to the estate.

I knew that my Aunt Irma had found an apartment in town when my uncle returned from the prisoner-of-war camp. I knocked at her door. She was home but her daughter Ingrid had the measles and she was afraid I would be infected. In spite of this, I stayed with her and, luckily, did not become sick.

Another time I missed the connection with the last train to Großjena on my return trip home. Now I had to walk one and a half miles from Naunburg to Großjena in the dark carrying my bag. I must confess, that I was very afraid on the way home. What's more, my mother was worried, when I didn't return at the expected time. Neither we nor my grandparents had a telephone. The only thing for us to do was to hope that, in spite of me being late, I would arrive home safely, which I did.

Mutti heard from the husband of her deceased sister that he had been expelled from Czechoslovakia to the French-occupied zone of western Germany. He lived with his three children in Eggolsheim, which is between Bamberg and Forchheim. We had absolutely no news from our father.

Finally, Mutti learned through the Red Cross that Vati was in a Russian prisoner-of-war camp. We obtained the camp address and were allowed to exchange letters with him once a month. Because my mother knew that the conditions in the West were better than those in the East, where we lived, she advised my father to seek released from the prison camp to the West and to apply for a permit for us to join him there.

Following her advice, when he was released in 1949 after 4 ½ years of imprisonment, Vati went to his brother-in-law in Eggolsheim, West Germany. He tried in vain to find a place for all of us to stay there, to find work for himself, or to get an entry permit for us. He wrote my mother that he was sick and tired of talking to clerks. He missed us very much and after over four years he yearned to be with his wife and children again. As soon as he could, he would come to Großjena.

My mother didn't want that.

"Once Vati is here, we will never get away from this place," she said.

Instead, she decided to flee with us immediately to the West. This was not easy because the border between East and West Germany was closed and no one could cross without a permit. But as always, my mother solved this problem her own way.

⟿

She packed a large suitcase with all of the important things we owned. The next day Mutti and I took the train to the nearby border town, and Karl, who was now eighteen years old, would find his way alone to the West.

At the border, my mother put me and the suitcase on a bus to Göttingen. "Don't worry, Annelies," she assured me. "Children are not asked for permits." She had explained our situation to a woman at the bus station, and the woman promised to claim me as her child. Mutti would have a smuggler take her over the border at night. "When you arrive in Göttingen, go to the railway mission in the evening. I will come there and pick you up when I have made it over the border," she told me. "Have a good trip, Annelies!"

No, I didn't have a good trip. Apprehensively I sat with my large suitcase beside the strange woman. I choked up when the border police came on the bus and checked us. It usually annoyed me that I was always treated like a child because I was small, even though I was thirteen years old. But this time, I was very glad that the official didn't check me, just as he didn't check the other children on the bus.

After a short ride, we arrived in Göttingen. All of the passengers got off and went on their way. My "bus mother" helped me lift my suitcase off the bus and then she left as well. I stood alone in the strange city. What should I do? With effort, I heaved my suitcase onto the sidewalk, sat down on it, and thought about my plight. The suitcase was too heavy to walk around with in the city. I had six marks of West German money and decided not to spend it. Perhaps someone would become aware that I had just crossed the border illegally and would send me back. Even though I was hungry and thirsty, I didn't dare to buy something for myself.

Toward evening I went with my suitcase to the train station and looked for the railway mission. Alarmed, I discovered that it was on the first platform. In order to get there, I would need a platform ticket. "Oh no, I have to buy a platform ticket!" "With West German money?" I was afraid to ask. Undecided, I stood in the train station.

It became darker. "I have to go to the railway mission," I explained to the clerk at the counter. "A platform ticket, please," I said and put a mark in the tray. The clerk took it and shoved the ticket and some change towards me. Flabbergasted, I took it. It had been so simple!

Now it was necessary to get the suitcase down a flight of stairs and then up the steps to the platform. I managed to do that as well. The railway mission teemed with people. "Perhaps I will wait first in the Red Cross station," I thought. It was at the other end of the platform. To my great disappointment, it was also totally full. Disheartened, I walked back in the dark and became aware of how alone and abandoned I was. An indescribably feeling of sadness overcame me. Loud sobbing and tears welled up and could no longer be held back. They burst out releasing the anxiety and tension that had built up in me.

A man came out of the mission and heard me. He asked about my anguish and waited patiently until I could tell him everything. He went with me to the mission and explained my situation to the friendly assistant. She found a place for me to sit and watched over me. When her shift ended, and my mother had not yet arrived, she asked me to come with her. Together we walked to her apartment, which was close by. She made me a liverwurst sandwich that never tasted so good before or ever after.

"You can sleep in my sister's bed. She passed away. Tomorrow morning at six o'clock, we will go back to the mission, and I am sure your mother will be there waiting for you."

The next morning we heard that a woman had come to the mission during the night, looking for her child. She left a message that she would return early, and she did.

Before we traveled further to Eggolsheim, my mother bought a smoked herring for us, and it was delicious. When we finally arrived where my father was staying, my brother was already there. What a joy to be united again!

It took a long time for us to feel at ease with each other and at home in our new homeland. My father and I had to establish a new relationship. He treated me like the nine-year-old child he remembered. However, I was now a teenager and had learned to think and act independently. So his well-intentioned guidance was not well received by me. It took years and patience on the part of my father to establish a warm relationship with one another again.

Life was not easy for my father. The four and a half years of imprisonment had left scars. For some time afterwards he suffered from nightmares. Like me, he awoke at night screaming and sweating. Then my mother would walk with him until he calmed down and was able to fall back to sleep again.

The difficulty of finding work and a place to live was another problem. After waiting for six months, we were assigned two rooms to sublet in a farmhouse. The farmer had his own idea about the arrangement. He stood with his axe before the front door and wouldn't let us in. The official at the housing office was called and with his help we were able to move in. It was not until 1960 that we got our own apartment and I had my own room. By that time I was twenty-four years old and worked as chief secretary at an up-and-coming company.

Very soon Karl found a responsible position at a private estate. Since his agricultural training was interrupted by our flight to the West, his hourly wage was no more than that of an untrained laborer, and he saw no possibility to improve his situation. Karl had married young; he and his wife decided to emigrate to Australia. Shortly after that, our cousin Roland emigrated to South Africa. I met my future husband during a visit with a friend in the U.S. and emigrated in 1967.

Aftereffect

"Did the war and the expulsion have a lasting influence on your life?"

"Oh yes," confirmed Annelies. "After I had to give up everything several times, I don't put much store in possessions. I am glad for the things in our house, in the garden and our newly remodeled bedroom. However, I know that I could give it all up at any time, as long as I can call one room my own.

My experience in East Germany between the ages of nine and thirteen certainly influenced me in many respects. While Mutti and Karl worked, I had many hours every day during which I could do whatever I wanted freely and unobserved. I learned to form good friendships and to take care of myself. I lived in nature, and enjoyed the security and freedom of a village child. In summer I splashed with my friends in the Unstrut and taught myself to swim. In winter when I returned in the afternoon to our cold, empty room, I learned to start a fire in our stove without ever burning myself. When I played in the snow I ignored my freezing fingers and feet. I knew they would thaw when I returned home.

I also learned something that always dampened my easygoing cheerfulness. I experienced very early how it feels to be a more or less despised minority. If something unpleasant happened, the first thing said was, "Certainly, a refugee must have done that." If the farmer's wife found less fruit than expected, she knew, "The refugees have secretly picked my cherries!" She didn't consider that a lot of stripped cherry pits might mean that sparrows were the cherry thieves. If a stone hit a stall window, a refugee kid had thrown it. If the rake wasn't in the usual place, the refugee had mislaid it. And when the farmer realized later that he himself had left it on the wagon after work, he didn't correct his unwarranted suspicion. "Oh well, this time I was mistaken, but I know for sure that at such and such a time, they have done this or that.

I learned not to expect anything positive from strangers—no friendliness and, above all, no help. I have little empathy for people who think help and support are their due. That is not how the world works. I learned in early childhood that I have to work hard for everything and, in the end, I am responsible for myself."

The Expulsion of Germans from Czechoslovakia after World War II

Czechs, Slovaks, and Germans lived together for over 700 years in Bohemia and Moravia, the area from which Czechoslovakia was created in 1918. Historical records show that in 1204 the king of Bohemia called upon German farmers, craftsmen, and merchants to settle and develop the mountainous borderland of his kingdom. Later the Kingdom of Bohemia belonged to the Habsburg monarchy (1526-1918).

After the loss of the First World War, Czechoslovakia was created from Bohemia, Moravia, and the mainly German Sudetenland. At the time, German representatives requested that the Sudetenland be annexed to Austria, but the victorious powers rejected the petition.

In 1938, Czechoslovakia had a 23.4 percent ethnic German minority. Sudetenland, where the majority of Germans lived, was an economically important area of the country. It had coal mining, ironworks, a glass industry, hardware, and machinery industries. Hitler needed this area for his war plans, and used the supposed cruel suppression of the Germans by the Czechs as a pretext to occupy Sudetenland. The controversial Munich Agreement of 1938 did not prevent it. Hitler's occupation of Czechoslovakia three months later was the prelude to the Second World War.

During the war, the Czechs suffered from the brutal measures implemented by the German administration and the excesses of the German occupation soldiers. Examples of this include the complete destruction and extermination of the villages of Lidice and Lezaky as collective punishment in retaliation for the assassination of the Nazi leader Reinhard Hydrick, as well as the bloody suppression of the Prague uprising in May 1945. Understandably, this led to a strong anti-German atmosphere.

Upon returning from exile, President Edvard Benes declared on May 12 and May 16 that the removal of the German populace from Czechoslovakia was absolutely necessary. The pent-up hate of the Czech citizens led to brutal rioting and mob action against the Germans. The "wild expulsions," which include the so-called death march of 27,000 ethnic Germans from Brünn/ Brno on May 30-31, 1945, were examples of rampant collective punishment.

At the Potsdam Conference of the victorious powers on July 17, 1945, the Czech government was allowed to remove the ethnic German population from their land by humane means. The official removal of the Sudeten Germans began in January 1946. During this year, around 2,246,000 ethnic Germans were expelled, mainly to Germany, and to a small extent to Austria. No compensation was provided for lost property. Approximately 250,000 Germans were allowed to remain in Czechoslovakia with limited citizenship.

It is astounding how much the discrimination and expulsion measures the Czech government used against the German-speaking population resembled those used against the Jews by the Nazi government. A ban on education and career; a ban on marriage between Germans and Czechs, dispossession of German businesses, land, and houses; house searches; abductions from homes; concentration camps; forced labor; the use of freight trains or trucks for the transport of people.

Of all of the brutal measures enacted by the Nazi government, I felt the use of yellow armbands to identify a despised people was particularly mean and malicious. It is sad that the Czech government adopted this damnation. They only changed the color. Instead of yellow, every Sudeten German had to wear a white armband.

Vaclav Havel became the first democratically elected President of Czechoslovakia from 1989 to 1992 and the first President of the Czech Republic from 1993 to 2000.

On March 15, 1990, when the German President Richard von Weizsacker visited Prague, President Havel in his address at the state dinner spoke about the violent history of their two counties:[4]

> *"Even after everything that has happened, there is still fear of Germans and a greater Germany. There are people still living who have experienced the war, lost their loved ones, suffered in concentration camps, hid from the Gestapo. Their mistrust is understandable, and it is completely natural that it has been transferred to others.*
>
> *It follows that our task is to overcome this fear. We have to understand that it was not the German nation that caused our agony, but particular human individuals. . . . To speak abusively about Germans in general, about Vietnamese, or about members of any other nation, is to condemn them merely for their nationality."*

Two years later on February 27, 1992 in an address at a state dinner in honor of a visit by German Chancellor Helmut Kohl President Havel said:

> *"The disease of violence and evil spread by Nazism ultimately afflicted even its victims . . . . We accepted the principle of collective guilt and instead of punishing individuals, opted for collective revenge. For decades, we were not allowed to admit this, and even now we do so with great reluctance. But just as the Germans have been able to reflect upon the dark side of their history, so must we."*

---

4. Havel in Albright, *Prague Winter,* 339–340.

Irmgard

Chapter 16

Shots Went off Around Us

Irmgard, born November 1939 in Düsseldorf, Germany

"EVEN THOUGH I WAS very young at the time, I vividly remember the war," Irmgard tells me. "My first memories, when I was three years old, are like pictures stored in my mind:

"I am sitting at the edge of our street close to the railroad tracks. It is around midnight, yet it is not dark. A huge fire has turned the night into day. "Stay here! Don't move!" I hear my mother's urgent voice. I sit beside her sewing machine and stare at our house. Flames are shooting from its roof.

We live on the first floor. Mutti runs to get more of our belongings.

"Mrs. Trautmann, don't go in!"

A loud, shrill cry of warning comes from our neighbor. As my mother hesitates, I hear a terrible thunder. The staircase crashes down and buries everything under burning wooden steps. The fire leaps into the rooms where we had lived and slept an hour ago. I scream and cry.

As small as I was, I must have comprehended the danger and was gripped by mortal fear. Even when my mother re-appeared and held me in her arms, I continued to cry for a long time. Mutti had been very lucky. The warning from the neighbor woman had made her pause long enough that the burning debris and rubble had landed in front instead of on top of her.

That night everything we possessed went up in flames, but we, my mother, my brother Herbert, two years older, and I had survived along with the sewing machine. Mama grabbed it, when we fled the house. She was a good seamstress and the sewing machine was her prized procession. My mother would make good use of it in the years to come.

We found refuge in a nearby school building together with other families made homeless that night. After receiving some emergency supplies, we were evacuated to Thuringia. A local family in the village of Windeberg by Mühlhausen had been directed to take us in. Since we had lost everything, we had to ask our host family to share whatever they could spare. It must not have been easy for my mother to be dependent on the kindness of total strangers.

My brother Herbert and I had no problem. We enjoyed exploring our new environment and playing with the village children. Close by was a handsome, large farm. Soon Herbert became friends with the farmer's son Rudi, who was his age.

Once when Rudi was called in for dinner, Herbert played by himself in the farmyard. He climbed on a carriage that was sitting in front of the barn. Pretending to take a ride in it, he accidentally released the brake. Slowly the carriage rolled down the sloping yard and ran into the large wooden gate.

Upset and crying, Herbert ran home to Mutti and told her what had happened. Immediately she returned with him to the farm to apologize for the accident and the damages Herbert had caused. Fortunately, Rudi's mother not only accepted the apology, but she also engaged in a lively conversation with Mutti. The two women immediately liked each other. So the pitiful accident led to a surprisingly good outcome: Rudi's mother invited us to live on the farm.

The resulting move improved our life immensely. My mother would sew for the farm family and they shared with us their meals of homemade sausages, garden-fresh vegetables, milk, and eggs. We children enjoyed playing in the farmyard, fields, and countryside. The war and what we had experienced—waking up at night to howling sirens, bombs dropping from the sky, and the terrifying fire—were all but forgotten.

Herbert and I still remember the farm well. From the street you stepped through the large gate into the yard; to the left stood two stately houses; across were the stables; to the right were the barn and a low long building that was occupied by several evacuated families. We did not live there; we instead had a room in the main house.

At the end of March 1945, the Americans came to Windeberg. I remember the two soldiers who patrolled the entrance to the village. They walked up and down, and up and down I walked with them. They gave us gum, candy, and chocolates. How relieved our parents must have been by their friendly treatment of us.

Unfortunately, the nice American soldiers moved on. My mother heard that the Soviet troops would come to our area. Rumors, as well as eyewitness accounts of Russian brutalities, were circulating in the village. Mutti decided to flee, and together with other evacuated women and children, we started out on foot in the evening. Each one of us had a backpack and in addition Mutti and Herbert carried a handbag.

"Herbert, don't ever let go of Irmchen,[1]" urged Mutti sternly and held me by my other hand. Through the night, we walked to the Mühlhausen train station, where we all boarded a train.

We were hardly underway, when we realized that the train was not traveling west but east toward Russia. What a terrifying mistake! When obstacles on the tracks caused the train to stop, we immediately scampered off and hastened back. We had not walked far when Russian soldiers stopped us. They ordered us into their station and took all we had. Since we did not have much, it was not a big loss for us. My mother had sewn her watch, the only item of value, into her bra, where the soldiers did not find it. After a short time, they dismissed us and the other mothers with children. They kept several young single women. How awful!

Scared and shaken we moved on. Afraid to be recaptured, the mothers decided to leave the train tracks and find their way west through the woods. It was getting late and it soon became dark. Herbert remembers how we stumbled on in the pitch darkness—running into trees, tripping over roots, being whipped by branches. The cracking and creaking noises of the forest canopy scared him.

Then more dangerous noises erupted. Unwittingly, we had entered the battle zone between Russian and German troops. We huddled together hidden in dense vegetation. From far away and close by shots rang out; rapid firing erupted; cannons shelled and tanks rattled. Even today I can recall the fear and fright that gripped me that night when I was five years old.

We walked on the next day. Along the way, we saw a man holding up a cardboard sign. "Amis," it said. We had reached the area occupied by the Americans. Hallelujah! That night we spent in an American refugee camp.

We returned to the railroad station and waited for the train that would take us West—back home to the Rhineland. Mutti pushed Herbert ahead of

---

1. Diminutive of Irmgard.

us onto the crowded train. When she tried to get in with me, not an inch of room was left. An impenetrable wall of people blocked the entrance. No one made room for us.

The worst fear of all mothers seized Mutti: to be separated from her child. We had to get on the train or would lose Herbert. The conductor signaled that the train was about to leave. With the will of sheer desperation, Mutti forced her way in. "Never again will I let someone get ahead of me!" I remember her swearing.

⌐

We traveled to Paderborn to my grandmother and aunt Lehnchen, my mother's mother and her youngest sister. Herbert and I felt safe and secure with them and stayed there while my mother traveled to Düsseldorf. She got two rooms for us close to uncle Johann, my father's brother, and his wife aunt Zilli in Himmelgeist, which at that time was a mostly rural settlement south of Düsseldorf. Located at the edge of the floodplain of the Rhine River, Himmelgeist was safer then the city and since it was close to her brother–in-law, Mama felt secure. Our father was still at war.

It must have been during the first days of April, the Americans would not reach Düsseldorf for another two weeks that we moved to Himmel-geist. The two rooms that the housing office had assigned to us were ut-terly primitive. They were on the first floor of a crudely built two-story workshop that was an addition to a house. There was an iron stove, a range, and a faucet without a sink or drain. Our toilet was the outhouse in the yard. For bathing my mother heated water on the stove and poured it into a zinc tub. A bomb must have shaken the house so badly that mortar had dropped from the ceiling, exposing its beams and making a hole that connected us with the rooms above.

The next evening Mutti went to visit aunt Zilli, leaving us by ourselves. Suddenly, the air raid sirens began to wail. Great fear gripped Herbert and me. We were alone; our mother was gone. "Maybe a bomb will kill Mutti and we will not see her again ever!" we thought. Our heartrending sobs and cries were heard through the hole in the ceiling by our neighbor above. "Please, children, calm down," she called down to us. "Your mother will be home soon. It was a false alarm. The planes have already passed over us."

During the last days of the war, more tragedy occurred. We traveled with Mama to visit her oldest sister Aunt Grete, in Düsseldorf-Oberbilk, a densely populated working class neighborhood. When we turned into the courtyard, where my aunt, uncle, and twenty-year-old cousin lived, their big apartment building was gone. We stared at a heap of black, smoldering rubble. A man lay dead at the side of the courtyard. It was eerily quiet. A neighbor told us that a bomb had hit the building the previous night. My uncle and cousin had perished.

Aunt Grete survived, because she had traveled to visit our grandma in Paderborn and had stayed overnight. The death of her loved ones was devastating for my aunt. I do not believe her grief ever faded.

                        ~

Finally, the war ended for Düsseldorf. We hardly noticed, when the Americans took the city. What we did notice was that the sirens went silent and no bombs were dropped.

After a short time, school started again in Himmelgeist. The little schoolhouse had not been damaged, and the old teacher lived as before with her sister in the apartment over the classrooms. In April 1945, I started first grade. On my first day of school, I didn't get the traditional cone with sweets as Herbert had. I believed this was very unfair, even though I knew that one could not buy candy anywhere. Our school had two classes; one for the first to fourth grade and the other for the fifth to eighth grade. I do not think that we learned much.

Severe food shortages marked the first three years after the war. Stores were closed or empty. When a bakery had bread for sale, long lines formed outside before it opened. As had been the case during the war, rationing coupons were needed to buy anything whether it was food, clothing, or household items. If you had expended your allotment of food coupons, the only way to sustain yourself was to barter or to buy food on the black market for extremely high prices that we could not afford.

Mutti worked hard to assure that we would not go hungry. From Henkel, a company producing soap and detergent, the former employer of my father, we received a package every month with detergent and cleaning products. For days my mother would walk from farm to farm to barter soap for food. She would sew or alter clothes in the evening until late at night to earn money or receive food in exchange for her work.

Once she was given delicious fresh cream. Of course, I wanted to taste it. As I was about to do so, Herbert sternly warned me: "Don't eat it! It is tractor grease!" Disgusted, I took the cream away from my lips. I had been a finicky eater all through my childhood. My brother's teasing was all it took. I never liked cream thereafter.

Another time, we visited grandma and Aunt Lehnchen asked me to accompany her to her job. She worked in the mess hall of US barracks. I remember well all the good food I was allowed to eat. Before we left, the cook gave me a bar of Cadbury chocolate. Happily I opened it in grandma's kitchen. As I tried to break off a piece, Herbert called out:

"Don't eat it! It is . . ."

"Stop it, Herbert," Aunt Lehnchen reprimanded him. Turning to me she said: "Irmchen, break the bar in the middle and both of you will have one half." The chocolate was delicious.

⤳

Many men returned from prisoner-of war-camps, but my father did not. Before the war he had worked as a fireman for Henkel. Because he did not join the National Socialist Workers Party (NSDAP or Nazi Party) he had been drafted into the army early, had had few privileges and had rarely been home. I did not remember him.

My mother told me the following story: Her brother Franz had come home from the front for a visit with our grandma and we went to see him. At the end of the day, Uncle Franz traveled with us by train to Düsseldorf. He looked nice in his clean uniform. I looked at him again and again and asked my mother: "Mutti, he is not my Papa; he is my Uncle Franz, right?" The other travelers would smile. But isn't it indescribably sad to witness a small child trying to make sense of her world at war, where all men look like soldiers, and she no longer remembers her father?

In the spring of 1947, my brother and I walked after school to Aunt Zilli's for lunch, as we frequently did. To our great surprise, the whole family was assembled including my mother. A stranger sat next to her. It was a family feast of red cabbage, potatoes and meat to celebrate the man's return from a prisoner-of-war camp. The strange man at the table was my father. I heard that he initially had been in a French prisoner-of-war camp and was then transferred to a Russian camp, where he had to work hard without much to eat. Now, after two years he had been released.

During the meal I looked at him again and again. "He is my father," I said to myself, almost doubtful. I poked around in my food. Everyone enjoyed the good home cooked meal, yet I liked neither the red cabbage nor the meat.

"Irmgard, eat your food!" These were the first words my father spoke to me, followed by: "Irmgard, you may not get up from the table until you clean your plate!"

I stayed at the table as ordered, but did not eat. An hour passed. The food was cold and more unappetizing. My father's order was firm and so was my resolve not to eat. "Why didn't you stay away!" I thought to myself, knowing this was a very mean idea. Around four pm while still sitting in front of my lunch, I finally devised a solution. Rapidly, I shoved the disgusting food into my mouth until my cheeks were round like apples and I was hardly able to close my mouth. Off to the bathroom I sprinted, and spit it all into the toilet. When my father saw me at my empty plate, he was relieved. Approvingly, he said: "See, you did it."

Herbert and I had our first communion on April 18, 1948. It was an important family event, requiring lots of preparation. My mother's wedding dress had survived the war in grandma's closet. Mutti undid the seams and from the fabric pieces sewed a beautiful white dress for me to wear to church that day. She made a matching wreath that I wore like a crown. Neighbors and friends gave her supplies, which she used to bake several cakes for the celebration to which our relatives were invited.

She arranged for the cobbler to put new soles on our shoes. It was my father's job to pick up the shoes. He zoomed off on his used, newly acquired, light motorcycle. The cobbler had our shoes ready. Papa paid for them and clamped the package on the bike rack. On his way home, he made a short stop at a store. When he came out of the shop, the package with our shoes was gone!

These were the only shoes Herbert and I owned. Shoes were extremely scarce and no new ones could be bought. I can't remember what Herbert and I wore on our feet to church the next day. Perhaps, that day I thought, "Something like this could only happen to my father. My mother would have taken care that our shoes would not be stolen."

My father remained a stranger to me, even though I felt he liked me. When he cried on my wedding day, I knew he loved me.

Aftereffect

"Did your experiences during the war affect your life?" I ask Irmgard.

"As a child I was always extremely frightened during storms. Loud thunder was incredible scary to me. Even today I am unnerved by thunder. It fills me with an ominous foreboding. I believe that the enormous, close-range bomb explosions, I experienced as a small child, caused this."

The End of World War II in Düsseldorf

On the 2nd of March 1945, the 83rd U.S. Infantry Division conquered the Rhineland west of the Rhine and with it the suburban towns across the river from Düsseldorf. From that day forward the old town, the city center, and the harbor of Düsseldorf were within shelling range of the US military. It seemed to be only a matter of time before the city would fall.

The regional party boss, F.K. Florian decided that the people of Düsseldorf and the surrounding area had to be evacuated and the city defended by German troops. The evacuation order included Himmelgeist, where Irmgard and her family lived and Langenfeld, the hometown of Wolfgang and Gerhild (the principles of the story: We waited for our Father to come home). For once, the local government including the local Nazi party did not follow the order. Furthermore, the German military didn't have the means and the troops needed to implement the plan.

Consequently, K. F. Florian withdrew the order and issued a new one. This time, he ordered the complete evacuation of the people, and the subsequent destruction of all services—water, gas, electric, and telephone lines, railways, and bridges. His goal was to leave nothing for the Americans, but scorched earth. Predictably, the local government and party liked the revised plan even less. Instead, the decision was made to defend Düsseldorf against the Americans using the police and civilian defense corps. Even this plan would cost lives and create more destruction.

Lieutenant police chief and Nazi party official F. Jürgens, believed that at this point, only complete surrender would make sense, saving further pain and blood. He conspired with two longtime underground resistance fighters and provided them with official papers. On April 16 he sent them to negotiate the peaceful surrender of Düsseldorf.

The peace delegation reached the Americans troops, who were approaching from the south and east. They were able to negotiate with the US commander averting at the last minute a 1,000-bomber air strike that had been planned ahead of the invasion. The next day the US military took the city without a shot being fired.

Tragically, Franz Jürgens and four co-conspirators did not survive to see the peaceful surrender. Shortly after the negotiators had left, the conspiracy was discovered. The men were court-martialed and shot hours before the Americans arrived.

Gerhild and Wolfgang, right, with Heide and Helgi, left, and nanni Anneliese
holding baby Reinhold, 1945

Chapter 17

We Waited for Our Father to Come Home

Wolfgang, born 1934 in Remscheid-Lennep and Sieglinde,
called Gerhild, born August 1940 in
Langenfeld, North Rhine-Westphalia, Germany

WOLFGANG AND GERHILD ARE the first and fourth of five siblings who grew up in Langenfeld, a community consisting of mostly rural villages about three miles east of the Rhine, located between Cologne and Düsseldorf, Germany. The rail line and the main highway B 8[1] that connect the two cities runs through Langenfeld.

Even though Wolfgang and Gerhild grew up together, they responded to the stresses of war in their own unique way due to their age difference.

During the War

Wolfgang remembers:

Father opened the window in our bedroom, rested both hands on the windowsill, and leaned forward. I did the same. We had a wide view over our tree nursery, the fields beyond, the next village, and the train tracks

---

1. The road exists since Roman times. In 1944 it was called Reichsstraße 8 and later Bundesstraße 8 (B 8).

running north as far as we could see. Highway B 8 and the houses of Langenfeld were to the right. To the left were the Knipprather Woods and hidden by the woods the Rhine River beckoned. Together we looked over the wide-open flat plain.

Father turned to me:

"Wolfgang, I have to go back to the front line. Now it is your duty to protect your mother." His voice was calm and serious. He hesitated a moment and then pulled a pistol out of his coat pocket.

"Wolfgang, I will leave this pistol here for your mother." The gun rested on his palm like a precious stone. Pointing to its parts and handling it lightly, he explained to me how to aim at a target. Without letting me touch the gun, he slipped it back into his pocket.

"Wolfgang, a pistol is not a toy but a dangerous weapon. I showed it to you, because I trust that you will keep this in mind. It can only be used in a dire emergency."

It was in May of 1944 when Father said this. We had frequently talked during his nine-day furlough, but never so seriously. I had just turned ten years old and was as happy-go-lucky, reckless, and full of energy as boys that age can be. Father's words made me pause and reflect. He had talked to me like a man. I swore to myself that I would never, ever disappoint him. From this day forward it was my responsibility to protect my mother.

I was convinced I had the best father in the world, and my friend Päule thought so too. Last summer, Father had played Indian games with Päule and me in the Knipprather Woods. Back then he had been carefree and exuberant like us. We had sneaked through bushes, crawled commando style through tall weeds, and jumped up with a victory cry surprising each other. We stumbled about, rolling in the grass and laughing.

When Father was home, life was never boring. Every day was a holiday. Father would take me swimming, and he showed me how to do the "dead man's" float by keeping my back straight and breathing easy. He was confident that I could climb to the top of the tallest tree. He patiently waited as I came back down and praised me. Of course, Father also paid attention to my siblings, Heide (8 y.), Helgi (7 y.), and Gerhild (3 y.), but he spent the most time with me. Sadly, he was never home very long.

In 1940, Father had been drafted to serve in the German military. At first, he had been a common soldier, but was now the officer in charge of a bridge building and repair unit in Russia. Even though he wasn't home much, he took part in our life from afar. He wrote almost daily to Mutti. They would talk about us in their letters and make most decisions about us jointly. For instance, during the coming summer they would discuss at length what school they wanted me to attend at the end of fourth grade—an important decision for German parents.

For our birthday or for Christmas, Father would send us a card. Last time he had made a funny poem for Heide. He would correspond with his father, our grandfather, or Opa, as we called him, about plantings in the tree nursery. This year they had decided to set aside a portion of our land for farming.

After our grandmother had died, we had moved into our grandfather's house at the tree nursery. I loved to live here. When I came home from school and passed the railroad crossing, I saw the nursery before me. A tall, lush, green hornbeam hedge surrounded it. From afar it already promised: freedom, fun, and adventure. All the things I missed in school.

When I entered through the wooden gate, our two-storied house was on the right; to the left was the ranch style office building. The gravel drive went straight ahead, past the nursery plantings, and then curved left to the nursery buildings. "Back-there," as we called it, was the gardeners' workroom, a small stable for our horse, Freya, a toolshed with the wagons, and a barn.

Something interesting was always going on back-there. As soon as lunch was over, I checked it out. Usually, the gardeners worked somewhere on the nursery grounds, and the three French prisoners of war that Opa had hired would be by the barn. They did the farm work and took care of our cow, a few sheep, and Freya. Hopefully, André would put Freya in front of the wagon and make a delivery. Almost daily he did deliveries and I loved to go along.

"Please, pretty please, may I hold the reins?" I begged André once again. He gave in. Proudly I sat on the bench next to André holding the reins in my hands. I clucked with my tongue just like André would do. Freya responded by trotting along the straight path to the road leading to Monheim, a village on the Rhine, that was our destination. My plan was to slow down before the intersection, stop and make sure that the streetcar, which traveled along the road, was gone, and then turn to the right towards Monheim.

That was my plan, but Freya had a different one in mind. She saw the horse pasture that Opa had rented for her across the road and sped ahead disregarding my commands.

What happened next was a matter of seconds. The streetcar rang its bell, its brakes screeched; André tore the reins out of my hands and with all his might pulled Freya sharply to the right barely avoiding a head-on collision with the streetcar. There was a crashing noise. The drawbar of our wagon hit the outside handle bar of the streetcar and tore it off. That was the end of my career as coachman.

Although I had caused an accident, André did not hold a grudge against me. As before, he allowed me to ride Freya from the pasture to her stable each evening. Holding onto her black mane, I would gallop bareback like an Indian. It was the highlight of my day.

The French prisoners of war came to work early in the morning before the gardeners. They lived in a camp not far from us. First they would take care of their own three sheep and rabbits, which they were allowed to keep in the nursery.

I believe they did not get enough to eat at the camp. Once when I played in the barn, I found their cachet of apples, potatoes, and some other vegetables. "Don't tell anyone," they urged and I didn't. It's possible Opa wouldn't have minded anyway. "I am glad we have the three Frenchmen to do the farm work," he had written in a letter to Father.

In the summer of 1944, the air war expanded to the small communities along the Rhine. Cologne and Düsseldorf had endured extensive bombardments for several years, but not the villages or small towns. Now bombers targeted our train station and the factories around it not far from our tree nursery.

Even worse were the low-flying Allied fighter planes prowling over the countryside. Walking home from school, we would hear the approaching planes or the warning sirens. When this happened, I knew what to do. In a flash we would jump to the side of the road and throw ourselves into the weeds and tall grass. "Don't move! Then the pilot will not notice us," I ordered and took care that Heide and Helgi lay still.

Next our school was closed. One of the teachers came to a neighboring farm and taught us there. The three of us and a few neighborhood children gathered in the comfortable living room of the farmer. We scribbled in our workbooks, and Helgi scratched on his slate while the teacher watched over us drinking homemade cider. Wonderful! I no longer had to worry about my grades and the scheduled examination at the end of fourth grade. During recess or after class, we were allowed to play in the farm's huge barn.

I was almost sad when our farm school closed. The teacher said that his trip to our neighborhood had become too dangerous for him.

The low-flying planes were a constant threat. I remember looking out of an upstairs window when a plane roared directly towards our house. I was sure it would attack us. In panic, I raced all the way down to the basement. Sitting on the last stone step, I listened. I heard rapid firing but nothing hit our house. I remained in the basement for a while, recuperating from my fright.

When all was quiet, I ventured out. The plane had targeted an empty train sitting on a sidetrack in front of the cross guard station. Of course, I had to run over and investigate. As I looked at the many bullet holes that had pierced the train car, the signalman limped with his stiff leg that he had injured in the war, over the track to join me. Like old buddies who had survived grave danger, we assessed the damage. He told me that he had crawled under his table during the attack. I was amazed—he was a grown man and had been a soldier.

⌒

Every day the war came closer to us. American and German troops were fighting on the west side of the Rhine. Supposedly the front line was still far away, but at night we sometimes heard faint war noises in the distance. We no longer slept in our rooms, but in the basement. To the side of the stone steps was a fourteen by fifteen foot room with three small windows. Here we put my grandfather's drawing table, which he had used to make his landscape plans, and covered it with mattresses. It became a bed for Heide, Helgi, me, and my fourteen-year-old cousin Paul. Gerhild slept in a crib. Mutti and Paul's mother, our aunt Liesel, had their beds to the side, and Opa's bed stood in the hallway.

It was interesting to sleep in the basement, however, what was going on in the tree nursery was more exciting. A German anti-aircraft unit moved into our nursery. At the western end, the soldiers stationed several big guns under tall trees to hide them from airplanes. They dug several bunkers for them to live in and covered them with beams, straw, and twigs. Next they dug a network of trenches crisscrossing the nursery. The soldiers used them to move about without being seen. The unit's two officers stayed in the up-stairs rooms we had vacated.

My friend Päule, Helgi, and I observed everything. I believed it was very good that the soldiers had come to us. Remembering my responsibility for Mutti, I was sure the soldiers would protect her and all of us. I regarded the two officers with respect and admiration.

I liked the first lieutenant best. I showed him my secret—the pistol Father had left behind as a protection for Mutti. I wanted to know how to use it and begged him to show me. After some pleading, the lieutenant went with me to a spot far away on the nursery. He put the gun in my hands. "Bend your elbows slightly and focus," he instructed me.

Alf, Opa's hunting dog, impatiently moved about. I aimed and pulled the trigger. *Bang*. With a sharp bark, Alf dashed away. Spooked, I lowered the gun and looked around. Had I shot Alf? No, he made a wide circle, came back and jumped high in the air with excitement. Alf assumed we were going hunting and couldn't wait. Disappointed, he tagged behind us as we headed home. "Wolfgang, now put the pistol back in its hiding place," the officer ordered and I did as I was told.

Our grandfather assumed the soldiers endangered us, and he had good reasons for believing this. His concern for our safety must have pained him greatly. Most likely, because of the severe stress he experienced, he fell ill with rheumatic fever, which became so bad that he lay in bed "stiff as a board." He was unable to move a joint and became totally helpless. At night he had to be carried to his bed in the basement.

His physician no longer made house calls. To receive the prescribed three injections per week, Opa had to be loaded on the wagon and driven to his physician, who at the time lived in the forester's house in the Knipprather Woods. In his diary, Opa described how shells had pockmarked the meadow and the garden around the forestry. Every time he was happy to have returned home without incident.

His illness was frustrating for our grandfather, who had been active until now. It must have been even worse for my mother, who had lost his support, had to nurse him, had four small children and was pregnant with her fifth child. Our sixteen-year-old domestic help and our twenty-year-old nanny helped her with her daily chores. Aunt Liesel would have assisted but couldn't because she suffered from chronic rheumatoid arthritis.

Even during normal times, my mother's plate would have been loaded to the brim. How had she been able to manage her personal stress and the environment at the same time? How was she able to stay calm and thoughtful? She never cried; she never yelled; she never lost her temper. Every day she planned and cooked the main meal for many people. Our secretary and perhaps a gardener would eat with us. She made the Christmas preparations and we celebrated the holiday as usual with a decorated tree, small gifts, and cookies.

In January and February of 1945, the danger from the advancing American military increased. At night when we slept in the basement, we might hear shelling. The Rhenania-Ossag oil refinery on the Rhine in Monheim, just three miles away from our house was carpet bombed by the British Air Force. Päule, Helgi, and I would later find deep bomb craters in the Knipprather Wood. Fortunately, no bomb had landed in our vicinity. The anti-aircraft unit stationed on our nursery had not fired and therefore hadn't been noticed by the bombers.

Did this frighten my mother? I don't believe so. She seemed to know no fear. Instead of sleeping with us in the basement, she put her bed in our living room—the nicely furnished room we only used on holidays. Solid wooden shutters protected the windows. Nevertheless, the first floor was not as safe as the basement. Perhaps it was more important to Mutti to get a good night's rest unbothered by us than to be safe.

On the other hand, my little sister Gerhild was more nervous than all of us together. Every night she kept us up with her wiggling and climbing. She tells it best herself:

For a long time I had complained that the baby crib was too small for me. Finally, I was allowed to sleep on the big table with my sister and brothers.

The table was high for a 4-year old. To get up, I first had to climb into the crib and then pull myself onto the table. It took some time until we were all settled in, Mutti had kissed us good night, and turned off the light.

Hardly five minutes later, I felt the urge to pee. So I climbed— now in the dark—over my siblings, slid down into the crib, down to the floor, and ran tip-tap with my little bare feet over the cold cement floor, and plink, plink did a few drops into the potty. Then tip-tap, climb-climb, wiggle-wiggle back under the cover. I repeated this two or three times until I finally fell asleep and had annoyed my brothers enormously.

Today I am surprised that I was not afraid to do such a difficult activity in the dark. I must have been very fearful of the noises, the bombs, the planes, and the cannons even though I don't remember it. My nightly problem never re-occurred after the war was over.

My mother's due date was approaching. Her midwife lived in Düsseldorf and would not be able to arrive in time when the labor pains began. Therefore, she came early and lived with us for several weeks, impatiently waiting for the birth.

On the 23rd of February in 1945, my little brother was born by candle light in our living room accompanied by muffled, distant artillery bombardment. He was named Reinhold after our father and grandfather. He was a healthy baby. We marveled at him and were happy that all was well. Mutti wrote the good news to Father.

Soon Mutti was up and about again. Unfortunately, she did not have enough milk for Reinhold. He needed additional baby formula, which he did not tolerate. As a consequence, he developed severe diarrhea and lost weight. Mutti took him to the University of Düsseldorf children's hospital, which had been evacuated from its regular location to the state hospital 1.5 miles from our house.

Baby Reinhold was admitted to the hospital and twice a day Mutti rode there by bike to continue to nurse him as much as she was able to. Mutti believed that the clinic saved Reinhold's life. Slowly he recuperated. In the photo taken in September of 1945 we see a thin baby with alert eyes and a big head.

My mother's ride to and from the hospital was dangerous. A week after Reinhold's birth, on the 1st of March, the American troops had reached the Rhine. They set up their artillery across from Monheim along the west bank of the river. By air the enemy line was about 3.2 miles away from our house. All of Langenfeld was in shooting range of enemy artillery for the next seven weeks.

That was a long siege; a long time of waiting and uncertainty for the adults. Random shelling occurred at all hours. The military jargon was that the troops were "softening enemy territory" prior to the invasion. Invasions should have started within days, except there was a big problem. The Americans could not walk over the Rhine, because the bridges up and down the river had been destroyed either by allied bombing or by the German troops.

I remember when several grenades grazed our house and ripped deep pits into the cow pasture right behind it. Helgi and I, seven- and ten-year-olds, would investigate the holes like seasoned experts and assess the damage that would or could have occurred if the explosives had fallen short of their flight path.

These excerpts from our grandfather's letter to Father reflect the situation as an adult experienced it:[2]

> *Langenfeld, March 15, 1945*
>
> *Dear Reinhold!*
>
> *The war continues on. We are here close to the front. We already experienced grenade fire several times from the opposition. An anti-aircraft unit with bunkers and all is stationed here on the western border of the tree nursery. Wolfgang said: "Grandfather, you will not recognize how it looks back-there." Artilleries are stationed even in the surrounding area. If the artillery is heavily used one can assume that it results in heavy enemy fire. Even if the gunners tell me, "during artillery fire you will be totally safe in your basement," it is possible and probable that our house will be destroyed. . . .*
>
> *Yet if the Allied military plans to cross the Rhine in our area, one has to assume that the British will carpet bomb Langenfeld. Then most likely not much will remain of our house. . . .*
>
> *It may happen that I will die during all these events. It may also happen that all of us will be killed by a large bomb.*
>
> (He continues to writes about his testament and care for us in case we become orphans.)

---

2. Translated from German by Sieglinde Martin

I bid you farewell and thank you for all you have done for me.
I have loved you very much even if I did not show it much. You
have been my friend and my pride.

Your wife is well and all the children too. They laugh, have
fun, and enjoy life and do not know of the danger that threatens
them. May they live on for you and you for them.

Farewell,

Your Father

At the time our grandfather wrote the letter it had been dangerous to be outside. We lived mostly from our own provisions. A portion of our basement had a dirt floor. In fall we had stored potatoes, carrots, beets, turnips, apples, and jars of canned vegetables and fruit. A sack of wheat was hanging in the hallway. I would weigh it in my hand and notice it becoming lighter. We were a big family and several additional persons ate dinner with us every day. Regardless of how well Mutti parceled out the food, our supplies were getting low. I noticed that she worried about it and consoled her: "Mutti, don't worry, soon the rhubarb will grow."

Aunt Liesel had different worries. She was upset because Paul, her only child, had been called to the Volkssturm, the civilian defense corp. "Isn't the war lost?" she asked.

I did not believe it. I knew the German soldiers always win. But then it happened, at the end of March that the second lieutenant disappeared. We heard he had deserted. Päule, Helgi, and I could hardly believe it.

"What a coward, what a dodger," we ranted with disgust. I was especially enraged because the deserter had taken the pistol that Father had left behind for Mutti's protection.

It got even worse. A few days later, the artillery unit withdrew from our tree nursery. The first lieutenant explained that they had to leave because the enemy may surround them.

"They withdraw, and we?" "Who will protect us now?" I called out. Opa seemed relieved that the troops had departed. Why didn't he share my worry? I didn't understand my grandfather. With all my heart I wished Father would come home to us.

⤺

The soldiers had left in a hurry, leaving the bunkers and the trenches in place. Päule and I had wanted to see them up close since they had been built.

Now they were all ours. There was no one to bother us or shoo us away while we investigated them.

Fantastic! We were the brave soldiers who raced through the trenches and stormed the bunker. How well it was built! We sat on the earthen benches along its walls and found them comfortable. We looked at everything and tried to take in all the details.

"Päule, some day we have to build a bunker like this, what do you say?" Päule agreed.

We looked around some more and found a fat, unexploded grenade. Wow! What a find! We opened the grenade carefully. Rows of ammunition sticks were neatly lined up inside. "Wolfgang, why don't we take them out?" Päule suggested. "See, they come out easily." They did. Together we had a "great idea." We lined the sticks up in a long row in the trenches. I found several yards of sturdy string with the gardeners' supply. We carefully rolled the string around the last stick and ran the string a few yards out of the trench. We opened a remaining stick and sprinkled the gunpowder on the string. I snuck matches from the house and we were ready.

Swoosh! What a te*rrific firework!* The flames were shooting high out of the trench. So high, they singed the leaves of nearby trees. We were overwhelmed and satisfied by our success. And then we thought about the blackened twigs and wondered what kind of punishment we had earned this time, so we stole away.

I don't remember if Mutti had seen the fire. Usually, I would wait until bedtime to confess my sins of the day. At that time Mutti typically took whatever had happened in stride. This time too?

During these last days before the invasion, the adults had their own worries. Opa had his hunting rifles wrapped in oilcloth and buried in a deep pit next to the office. Mutti had white sheets ready to hang out of the windows. They signaled, "We surrender" and hopefully prevented a house search by the invading troops. I believe the adults were waiting for the terrible war to end.

The remaining German troops in the eastern part of Langenfeld prepared for a last battle. The Volkssturm dug out a pit across our road, east of the railroad tracks, as a barrier for enemy tanks. Nothing prevented them from passing our tree nursery and that was a good thing, even though I did not understand it then.

On the evening before the invasion, the military commander in our town had the good sense to dissolve the Volkssturm. My cousin Paul came home. He did not have to fight the well-trained, well-armed US soldiers. He would not be killed, injured, or put in a prisoner-of-war camp. Some of the Volkssturm members decided to stay and fight.

The History Work Group of Langenfeld describes how the American troops marched into our town on April 16, 1945, a warm sunny spring day. They came from three directions. From the south they marched along highway B 8:[3]

> "*The first wave of American soldiers marched in two rows . . . through the center of Langenfeld. The distance between them was sixteen feet. Each soldier tightly held an unlocked machinegun in front of his chest.*"

The western column came from the Rhine and moved along the gravel road about fifty yards north of the tree nursery. No military unit advanced along the street in front of our house.

Helgi remembers: "*When the Americans came we were not in the basement. We only slept there at night. It was a nice day. We could see the column of soldiers and tanks from the window, from our yard, and from our back patio. We had a white sheet hanging from a northern window of the second floor.*"

Meanwhile I was in our attic and I looked with Opa's hunting binoculars out of the attic window. From there I had a wide view of the surrounding countryside. First I looked at the column passing north of us. Next I focused the field glasses on the soldiers marching along highway B 8. I concentrated on the details I saw. *Peng!* Instantly I dove down from the window. Something— a bullet?—had hit the window frame. *Peng!* Another one hit the wall above the window. Alarmed and gripped by fear, I flew down the stairs and jointed my family.

After a few hours it was all over. We did not see or hear the American troops anymore. Most likely, they were marching north towards Düsseldorf or east towards neighboring towns.

I wanted to talk to Päule, and find out if he had some news. His family lived close to highway B 8 at the end of our street. At the intersection I saw something unknown to me. A dead man lay at the side of the road. His eyes were open, starring into nowhere. I recognized his uniform. He had been a member of the Volkssturm. A strange creepy, feeling grabbed me.

When I got up the next morning, I knew the war was over but didn't understand what it meant. As long as I could remember there had been war. What was now? "We will win at the end of the war, because German soldiers always win." I had never heard anything different. But yesterday, the Americans had taken our town. Yesterday, a dead German soldier had been lying by the road. It did not make any sense to me.

---

3. VHS Arbeitskreis Geschichte. *Langenfeld 1945–1949 Berichte und Erinnerungen*, 13.

I walked back-there to find out what our gardeners had to say about this turn of events. Several workers were standing in the barn. An older man, who had never talked much before, pointed to the barn's ceiling beam and said: "That's where one should hang Hitler!" I looked at him speechless. Never in my life had I heard words like this.

(Note: Of course, I had not heard it before. Years, months, weeks, or even a day earlier the speaker would have been arrested and either shot or sent to a concentration camp.)

Puzzled I walked back to our house.

Our maid had arrived and told us about a sad incident that had happened yesterday. Our neighbor Mr. Jakobi had been standing on the water tower next to his greenhouses and had looked with his binoculars at the soldiers marching on highway B 8. The lenses of the binoculars had reflected the sun's rays like a metal object would do. An American military sharpshooter must have assumed that Mr. Jakobi was pointing his gun at the soldiers and shot him from a great distance.

I thought about what I had heard. I had pointed my binoculars southeast towards the soldiers in the same way as Mr. Jakobi. Had the sharp shooter tried to kill me as well? The very thought made me shudder.

After the War

Gerhild remembers:

During the morning hours, the US troops marched through the western part of Langenfeld. We saw them from afar. The soldiers did not enter our or anyone else's house. No civilian had been wounded or killed beside Mr. Jakobi. No woman had been endangered or assaulted. The next day the troops marched to Düsseldorf.

The war noises disappeared with them. No artillery shelled, no grenades flew over our house, and no warplanes threatened us. The war and the long siege were finally over. We had survived a long, dark winter.

I was allowed to run and play with my brothers and sister, after they were told to keep an eye on me so I wouldn't fall into a trench. I remember standing at the edge of one and looking deep down. It must have made a lasting impression on me.

For many years afterwards, I sometimes experienced this nightmare: I was alone in a wet, muddy field and came to a deep hole in the ground. I stepped away from it, only to notice that another deep crack was opening in the ground. It would happen in every direction. I did not like the dream. It made me nervous.

Unfortunately, the brief peace after the war gave way soon to new dangers. The US military disarmed our police and/or discharged them. They opened the doors of the forced labor camps.

Wolfgang noticed that the rabbits and sheep of our prisoners of war had disappeared. The Frenchmen had butchered them and were on their way home. It was not possible for the Polish and Russian workers to walk home. Some of them found leftover guns and ammunition and because no police could stop them, they took revenge on the Germans or enriched themselves.

Houses like ours, that were located outside of town, away from other dwellings, became the primary target of robbers. Our nanny lived with her parents in an isolated house. One morning she came to us very upset and told us that they had been burglarized that night. The burglars had herded them into a room and held them captive, while they stole whatever they wanted. She and her parents had not defended themselves and the bandits had not used their guns. It was known that people had been shot during robberies.

We took measures to prevent possible break-ins. Every evening we closed the wooden shutters and hooked them tight. We locked our sturdy doors and barricaded them. We kept Alf's cage door open during the night, so he would bark and attack intruders.

Alf did what a good guard dog does. One night we heard his loud menacing bark. Some hoodlums tried to get into our house. Shots rang out, Alf howled and something hit our house. Fortunately, the men left after a while. The next morning we found an unexploded hand grenade in the gutter, and our Alf lay wounded in the yard. Poor Alf, he had protected us. We nursed him and he slowly recuperated.

When our young gardeners returned from the war, they put up tripwires each night. It helped. Never again did robbers try to get into our house. Nevertheless, the danger was always present. A farmer in our neighborhood experienced eight break-ins. Once he was injured and had to be hospitalized for four weeks.

Another time when we all sat at the dinner table, two men in American uniforms arrived by car. One came into the room where we were eating, grabbed Opa's large radio and was gone with it before we realized what was happening. The other man broke our office window and took the typewriter from the secretary's desk. Off they zoomed.

What was going on? Had this been a brazen burglary or what?

The History Work Group of Langenfeld writes:[4]

---

4. VHS Arbeitskreis Geschichte. *Langenfeld 1945–1949 Berichte und Erinnerungen*, 26.

"The number of military confiscations was endless. Several private homes, schools, and the indoor swimming pool had been confiscated shortly after the occupation forces arrived. Our district manager asked the town mayors in a letter of August 2, 1945 to confiscate musical instruments, radios, and typewriters for the military government."

It is possible that confiscations were done without any explanation or written document. But Opa believed the brazen robbers were wearing stolen US uniforms.

⤳

Wolfgang worried about our well-being. The war had ended. Why wasn't Father coming home? From the bottom of his heart he hoped he would return soon.

When Father had come home on furlough, he usually arrived during the night. It would probably be the same way now. Often Wolfgang would listen at night for his steps. One stormy night, he heard the gate creak and ran out full of happy anticipation. No one was there. The wind had swung the gate open.

Father's last letter was dated February 28, 1945. It had been sent from Latvia, where Father's unit had been stationed. Thereafter, the Soviets had retaken the country and disrupted all communications to Germany.

Many men returned from captivity at the end of 1945, during 1946 or in 1947. But our father did not return. We were all waiting for him. At night before I fell asleep, I would often think of my father. During his last visit, I had been three years old and did not remember him. What did he look like?

I had seen his pictures. In one of the photos he had this big, cheerful smile, which convinced me that he was a wonderful father. I wished he were home. I believed he would scold Wolfgang when he teased me, and encourage Heide and her friend to include me in their play.

I knew that Father was needed to manage the tree nursery. Our secretary and Aunt Liesel would say so again and again. Opa was ill and too old to run the business and Mutti had too much to do as it was. Father would take care of everything. He would protect us from new danger and Mutti would not have to worry as much.

Maybe it is hard to believe that a five-year-old child would come up with my idea. Not just once, but several times I thought about my plan:

I would talk to Stalin. I would say to him:

"Please, let my father go free. Please, let him go home. He is needed on the tree nursery. We all wish very much for our father to be with us."

Half awake and half dreaming I was convinced that I would get Stalin to listen to me, and he would release Father right then.

During the day I knew it was a fantasy, and I was too embarrassed to tell anyone about my secret plan. I don't believe I missed my father during the day. I was too busy playing, helping Mutti, and visiting with the many people who came to the nursery.

During those same years the people and many children in the Rhineland suffered from the consequences of the war: hunger due to food shortages, homelessness due to destroyed houses, suffering from the cold due to lack of clothing and heating material. Yet for us children on the tree nursery, life was filled with freedom and adventure. We thank our mother for it.

Even though Mutti had grown up in a city house with a tiny garden, she developed the skills needed to run a small farm and improve what our father and grandfather had started.

Refugees from the lost eastern territories streamed to the West including Langenfeld. Mutti let it be known that we needed a farmer and soon a young farmer and his wife applied. Mr. and Mrs. Zimmermann had fled from East Prussia over the frozen Vistula Lagoon. They were in need of work and a place to stay.

The job Mutti offered was ideal for them and the available room acceptable. The next day they moved into the annex that had been an office. The room was rather small, but had a separate entrance, running water, a table, chairs, large bed, and a wood-burning stove. It became a home for them.

Mr. Zimmermann made our ravaged land productive. Instead of trenches, we soon had small fields of oats, potatoes, beets, and vegetables. He grew what we and our animals needed and a few tobacco plants for his pipe. Besides chickens, we had geese, sheep, a goat, a cow, pigs and a beehive.

Later the parents of Mrs. Zimmermann would join them and they too contributed to our household. The old mother cleaned, combed, and spun the wool from our sheep. With the yarn we knitted warm but itchy socks and sweaters. The old father cut roots in the woods and willow twigs along the Rhine meadows. With them he made handsome, sturdy baskets.

The Zimmermann's were raising their own pigs along with ours. All of them were butchered in late fall. Mrs. Zimmerman and her mother, assisted by Mutti and our household help, would prepare a variety of sausages and meats according to traditional East Prussian recipes.

All sorts of smells would drift from the kitchen through our house. I did not care for them, and was glad when instead the scents of Christmas replaced them. We all loved to help with the baking of Christmas cookies.

In summer and fall we had other chores. We picked berries from the plantings of current, raspberry, and black berry bushes. Our grandfather had planted a wide variety of fruit trees years ago as customer samples. By now they were fully-grown and bearing fruit. It seemed that each week, another variety was ripe and ready to be picked: sour cherries, half-sour cherries, sweet cherries, small yellow plums, large purple plums, prune plums, early pears or apples, sweet pears, and more and more apples. Added to this bounty, we harvested hazelnuts, walnuts, and chestnuts.

Most of our chores were fun, but others, like pitting cherries and shelling beans or peas, could become tedious. It was much more fun to hike to the woods and gather blackberries, mushrooms or beechnuts.

We enjoyed being part of what was going on in the tree nursery. School did not take much time out of our day during the years after the war. That was fine with us. I was almost seven years old when I started first grade together with fifty other children. Our school hours were from eight to ten AM, then school was over for the day.

Gerhild with her cousin

Besides school and chores, we had plenty of playtime. Visits from cousins made it more interesting. Relatives and friends visited us frequently. My mother especially enjoyed visits from one of her four sisters. Her youngest sister, our aunt Emmy had lost her husband in the war. She and her small son lived with us for many months.

In spite of the pleasant country living, we too experienced aftereffects from the war. One dangerous episode occurred during an otherwise fun filled day trip to a shallow bank of the Rhine. The water was clean and good for swimming because the polluting factories and oil refineries along the river had either been destroyed by the war or were not in operation due to the dysfunctional economy in 1946/47.

We enjoyed water play, swimming, and sunbathing. Little Reinhold played at the water's edge. Suddenly he disappeared as if a mermaid had pulled him under. He had slipped into a deep bomb crater hidden by shallow water. My mother, always vigilant, noticed it and being a good swimmer she immediately dived down and pulled him out.

Regardless of the abundance in summer and fall we too experienced food shortages in spring when our storage bins were empty or what was left was no longer edible, and we had to buy food. I remember bringing a sandwich of bitter cornbread and mushed old carrots to Opa. He looked at it disgustedly. We children ate this frequently and were used to it.

Sometimes we would hear gruesome war stories like the one Mrs. Zimmermann's parents told Mutti:

"The Russians had several of us villagers stand in line. One soldier raised his gun and started to shoot at us from left to right. Three shots—the first three people fell down dead. Then the fourth one, the fifth one . . . one more woman and we were next in line. I saw the soldier aim, pause, and lower his machinegun. He waved with his arm. We stood frozen at the edge of eternity. He angrily waved again. We understood he wanted us to disappear. "

I was five years old when I listened to the story and remember it as if I had experienced it myself. Mutti had not wanted me to be present when events from East Prussia were recounted, but I managed to stick around anyway. I liked to listen to adult conversations. If a story started with "before the war," what followed sounded like a fairytale to me. With longing, a visitor would talk about how "before the war" they had planned an addition to their house, and conclude with regret and sadness "and then the war started."

A stranger visited us and told us that he had been taken prisoner together with our father, who had shown him a compass he had hidden in a box. The compass would help him to return home when he escaped from the camp. Another visitor told us that he knew our father and had heard that many prisoners in his camp were dying from dysentery.

Whatever our father's "former buddies" told us it was not true. When West Germany had a government again, Mutti wrote to the wife of our first President, Dr. Heuss, and asked for help. I do not know if or what she answered. Our first chancellor Konrad Adenauer succeeded in having the remaining prisoners of war released from Russia in 1955. Our father was not among them. A year later, my mother received a letter from the Red Cross, confirming our father's death in a Russian prisoner of war camp.

Wolfgang found the full truth much later through the help of the German War Graves Commission. Translated Soviet records provided the following details:

Our father's military unit had voluntarily surrendered in May of 1945 at the end of the war and had been taken to a Russian prisoner of war camp. There his personal information had been documented, including father's statement that he had five children with the youngest being four month old. In November of 1945 our father was transferred to a different camp where he died three weeks later. The cause of death was starvation.

Wolfgang received the information in 2011 when our mother was 101 years old and was no longer interested, or able to comprehend it. Reinhold was sixty-six years old when he learned for the first time in his life that his father had known that he had been born.

It is estimated that 1.2 million German soldiers died in Russian prisoner of war camps

Aftereffect

We five siblings missed our father each in our own way. We blamed and still blame the criminal regime of Adolf Hitler and the war for our loss. It became second nature to us to reject war and all things military.

When in 1950, the West German parliament discussed rearmament even the then ten-year-old Gerhild listened to the debate on the radio. We siblings were in agreement that any re-militarization of Germany was wrong and in our words a "crazy stupidity."

Reinhold was the first male of our family to be drafted into the new German army. He tried to be recognized as a conscientious objector, which was astoundingly difficult so soon after the war. He had to pass a required test, for which the stern anti-war pastor of a neighboring town prepared him.

All of the grandsons and great-grandsons have followed Reinhold's example. Honoring our father, they too served as conscientious objectors. Opposition to military service and all wars became a family tradition.

Chapter 18

Arguments Against War

THE TOTAL NUMBER OF war deaths during World War II is estimated to be fifty-five million persons—approximately twenty-six million soldiers and twenty-nine million civilians. Hidden behind these staggering numbers are an even greater number of survivors, who experienced desperate and tragic events.

The suffering of the people and especially the children during times of war are enough of a reason to be against war. In spite of the suffering war causes, it continues to be a legitimate means of conflict resolution.

In addition to emotional reasons there are rational reasons to reject war. Some of them are discussed in this chapter.

War Undermines the Rule of Law

In our civil justice system, a person is innocent until proven guilty. The perpetrator is convicted and punished for his deeds. He is punished for the crimes he himself committed, not those committed by his father, brother, neighbor, or his fellow countrymen. This is the general rule of law in a civil society.

War undermines this fundamental law. In time of war, a person is punished not for what he or she did, but for a crime another committed or is suspected to have committed, or he may be collectively punished with other people for no crime whatsoever.

Depending upon the circumstances, these incidences are generally accepted as an unavoidable part of war. Especially heinous crimes may be designated war crimes or crimes against humanity.

The Nazis inflicted collective punishment upon civilians during World War II. There are documented incidents were German special forces burned an entire village and shot all its inhabitants. These unspeakable violent crimes of collective punishment were not done in secrecy, but openly committed for the purpose of terrorizing and subduing an occupied region or country into submission. After the war, these acts were called war crimes for good reason.

The German military leaders responsible for the war crimes and the holocaust, the worst of all crimes ever committed during war, were tried at the International Military Tribunal at Nurnberg, which had been set up by the Allied powers. Twelve defendants were sentenced to death and ten were hanged in October 1946. Nine additional defendants received prison terms.

The threat and the use of collective punishment have since occurred in international conflicts and civil wars. Madeleine Albright, the US Secretary of State from 1997 to 2001, writes in her book Prague Winter:[1]

> "As a diplomat, I sharply condemned ethnic cleaning in Central Africa and the Balkans and championed the creation of a war crimes tribunal to ensure that individual rather than collective responsibility would be assigned for humanitarian crimes. Collective punishments, such as forced expulsion, usually rationalized on the grounds of security but almost always fall most heavily on the defenseless and weak."

Madeleine Albright expresses the prevailing sentiment in the US and the international community concerning collective defamation, punishment, and expulsion of people. Functioning governments can and do control these crimes within their borders in peacetime. The question is: can they be prevented during war?

War is the violent conflict resolution between nations or large armed groups of people. It requires collective action and therefore promotes group thinking. Contempt, disdain, and hate towards the enemy are encouraged and desired. Hatred is fanned, because it will increase the soldiers' willingness to fight and kill the enemy. One may say that war as such is a form of collective punishment.

Collective revenge spreads in war like a virus. It escapes human control and cannot be contained within the military. History shows that rage and hate spill over to the civilian population. War undermines a person's moral self. Any empathy for the fate of an individual belonging to the opposing group or nation disappears. Our language allows us to regard the enemy as subhuman. They are "rats, coons, snakes, and so on" and as such must be eradicated.

No one, not even the sternest supporters of US military actions, wants our soldiers to commit any war crime. The question is: Can collective war

1. Albright, *Prague Winter,* 339.

crimes be prevented? Or is the only way to prevent war crimes is to prevent war itself?

Also, it does not help to minimize the effect of war on the minds of people involved in it, regardless if they are soldiers or civilians. The question is: Will the wars conducted by our government make our society more prone to violence? If yes, do we want this?

What Do Nations Gain from War?

Is waging war an effective means for a state to gain territory or political power? Research, which has addressed this question, answers in the negative, excluding a few rare exceptions. Usually, the warring parties do not gain more, but frequently gain less than what could have been negotiated before the outbreak of hostilities.

Does victory in war result in riches? It may have been true in the pre-industrial world, but today war does not pay. In our interconnected economy, the wellbeing of all people and nations are interdependent. Consequently, fighting a war, and the destruction it produces, economically harms the loser and the winner. Even if the winner does not experience any physical destruction through the war, its economy suffers from the economic uncertainty created and the loss of potential customers.

Most likely the following is true: Over time, the civilian populations of countries that abstain from war become more prosperous than the ones of comparable nations conducting wars.

Does the frequent engagement in war by the US Government impoverish us? Does it impoverish the middle class?

The Cost of War

The US Department of Defense base budget for 2015 is $495.6 billion dollars. The additional defense spending for international security assistance is $12 billion. Nuclear weapons and associated costs are $18 billion and overseas contingency operations (war) are $64 billion. This brings the total amount of our taxes dollars spent for war to $590 billion.

The total US discretionary spending for 2015 is $1.11 trillion. This means that Congress gives 54 percent—more than half of all discretionary money available—to the military. The percentage will be even higher if Veterans' benefits of $65.3 billion are included in defense spending. In comparison, spending for energy and the environment are $39.1 billion — 3 percent of the budget.

The US outpaces all other nations in military expenditure. Our military spending is roughly as much as the *combined spending* of the following countries: China, Russia, Saudi Arabia, France, United Kingdom, Germany, Japan, India, and South Korea.

How is it possible that we spend so much on our military? Why is this enormous expense needed to keep us safe when other countries spend so much less? Could our military do this more efficiently at a lower price?

One of the causes for our huge defense spending seems to be the price tag of our military equipment — foremost of all the fighter planes and aircraft carriers. For instance the cost of the F 22 Raptor Fighter mushroomed to $ 419 million per plane. The Air Force had bought 187 planes at the total cost of 67.3 billion when Defense Secretary Robert Gates terminated the program in 2009.[2]

Presently the Air Force is buying the F-35 Joint Striker Fighter, a single seat and single engine plane, at an estimated cost of $200 million each. For the fiscal year of 2016 Congress approved the purchase of fifty-seven planes. It is planned that the Defense Department will acquire 2,457 F-35 Joint Striker Fighters by 2035 at the projected *total cost of $ 1.4 trillion!*

Unfortunately, not only is the purchase price of these planes very high but also the fuel cost of flying military planes is extremely high. For instance the cost per flight hour for the following planes is:[3]

$ 45,986 for the AC-130 U Spooky Gunship
$ 57,807 for the B-113 Lancer Bomber
$ 68,362 for the F-22 A Raptor Fighter
$ 69,708 for the B-52 H Stratofortress
$ 78,817 for the C-5 B Galaxy Cargo Plane
$ 83,256 for the C-5 B Osprey Tilt-Rotor Helicopter
$ 163,485 for the E-4 B Flying Headquarter
$ 169,313 for the B-2A Spirit Stealth Bomber

According to Mark Thompson from Time, the numbers were supplied by the Defense Department in 2013.

The most costly military items are aircraft carriers. The US Navy has ten carriers in operation and purchased a new one, the Gerald R. Ford-class aircraft carrier, for 12.8 *billion* in 2015.

Even far more expensive is a new nuclear weapons program started in 2014 and supported by President Obama. It upgrades and converts old nuclear arms into small, stealthy and precise nuclear weapons, which

2. Sprey, "Member of the Fighter Mafia Passes," 7–9.
3. Thompson, "Costly Flight Hours."

potentially could be used. It includes a new air-launched nuclear-armed cruise missile. Military experts warn that this program is stimulating similar efforts by Russia and China and is pushing the world into a new nuclear arms race.[4] Its cost is projected to be $1 trillion of taxpayers' money!

The cost of ten years of war in Iraq from 2003 to 2013 was *$1,7 trillion, which is approximately $5,000 per second!* The cost per one American military person (soldier or support personnel) employed during the war amounted to $ 350,000. The benefits owed to war veterans are $490 billion. All the money was borrowed and is not yet paid for; consequently interest payments will increase the total outlay.[5] It would be good to remember these numbers before we agree to another war.

No Weapons of Mass Destruction were found in Iraq.

Environmental Damage Caused by War

The human toll and the destruction of man-made objects like buildings, bridges, streets, and other infrastructure systems are considered when the damages of a war are assessed for possible war reparations. So far, little attention has been paid to the environmental damage done by war.

The prevailing view has been that nature would heal itself at the end of a conflict. Grass will grow again, seedlings will become trees, flowers will bloom, and birds will sing again. That may or may not be true. The forest at the hill site may never regrow after the trees were burned and the soil washed away. Damaged fragile soil may never again produce a good crop, and polluted water may still be poisonous after decades. Potentially, war may change the climate of a region forever.

UN secretary general Ban Ki-moon called on nations to do more to protect the environment from the devastation of war:

> *"The environment has long been a silent casualty of war and armed conflict. From the contamination of land and the destruction of forests to the plunder of natural resources and the collapse of management systems, the environmental consequences of war are often widespread and devastating, . . . Let us reaffirm our commitment to protect the environment from the impacts of war, and to prevent future conflicts over natural resources."[6]*

4. Broad and Sanger, "Race for Latest class of Nuclear Arms Threatens to Revive Cold War."

5. Kelley and Ingersoll, "The Staggering Cost of the Last Decade's US War in Iraq."

6. Mathiesen, "What's the environmental impact of war?"

The use of herbicides by the US military in *Vietnam* to deprive the Vietcong of forest cover left the country with a poisonous legacy.

The spraying destroyed 14 percent of Vietnam's forests, diminished agricultural yields, and made seeds unfit for replanting. The military set fire to haystacks and soaked some land with aviation fuel to burn it. A total of 15,000 square kilometers of land was destroyed.

The application of Agent Orange was especially harmful to humans. It is carcinogenic and causes spontaneous abortions, congenital abnormalities, skin and lung cancer, lower intelligence, and emotional problems among children. An estimated half a million children were born with abnormalities due to the exposure of their mothers to Agent Orange, which continues to pollute water, soil, and vegetation in Vietnam.[7]

During the *Gulf war of 1991*, 751 oil wells burned in Kuwait. It took ten months to extinguish them. Approximately 100 million tons of CO_2 were released by the fires, which amounted to 1.8 percent of CO_2 released world wide per year. In addition, the fires sent 6 million tons of sulfur, 1 million ton of nitrogen and 1,000 tons of tar into the air. About 60 percent of Kuwait's desert was covered with tar and oil. Greenpeace reported that oil lakes formed that killed animals and plants, rendering a vast area unusable for the foreseeable future.

In Iraq the damage from the war and drought have reduced the harvests to a degree that the country can no longer feed its population and must rely on food imports. Another detrimental effect of the war is the pollution of drinking water. Because of the ongoing war with the Islamic State fighters, a full assessment of the war's environmental damage in Iraq is not possible at this time.

The *two wars in Afghanistan* have caused severe deforestation, leaving just 2 percent of the country with forest cover. The United Nations Environmental program reported that periodic droughts have increased the negative impact of the wars. The groundwater level has sunken, wetlands have dried up, and the productivity of arable land decreased. Within one generation the population has lost its agricultural base, the water to irrigate its fields, and trees as a source of fruit and fuel. Less than 12 percent of the people have access to clean drinking water. Due to food shortages, wild animals are hunted in remote areas. Endangered species like the snow leopards, wolves, and brown bears are in sharp decline.

War ordnance left behind after recent wars pose another environmental hazard. During the Falkland war between Great Britain and Argentina over the territorial control of the Falkland Islands, so many landmines were

---

7. Enzler, "Environmental Effects of Warfare."

placed and then left behind that the islands were rendered unusable by either country. By waging war, the two nations destroyed the object they desired.

After the Gulf war of 1991 approximately forty tons of depleted uranium continue to pollute the soil of Iraq. The carcinogenic radiation from the uranium may be the cause of the increased cancer and birth defect rate in Iraq. Unexploded ordnance poses another danger to the Iraq population.

Aged remnants from an Iraq chemical weapons program at the time of the Iran –Iraq war endangered American and American trained troops, as was reported in the New York Times on October 15, 2014.

Between 2004 and 2011 the troops found 5,000 chemical warheads, shells or aviation bombs. Twenty American troops were exposed to nerve or mustard gas in the process of removing the ordnance. These old weapons had been designed in the United States, manufactured in Europe and assembled in Iraq by Western firms.

〜

In the US, environmental pollution at *military installations* has endangered the health of service men and women.

From the 1950s through the 1980s, people living or working at the U.S. Marine Corps Base Camp Lejeune, North Carolina, were exposed to drinking water contaminated with industrial solvents, benzene, and other chemicals. These pollutants are known to cause various types of cancer and other serious conditions, for which those exposed will receive VA health benefits.[8]

The soil and groundwater of the former McClellan Air Force Base in California had been heavily contaminated by dioxins, furans, heavy metal, PCBs, volatile organic compounds, and other hazardous waste. It became an EPA superfund site in 1987. The cleanup work is ongoing and is projected to continue for up to ten more years.

〜

Military exercises pose another environmental risk. The Alaska Dispatch News reported on June 4, 2015 that Northern Edge 2015, the forty-two day long U.S. Navy exercise in Alaska, was strongly opposed by local fishermen and environmentalists for several reasons: interference with salmon migration; use of extremely strong underwater wide-scale live sonar that would endanger migrating whales and other marine mammals; and littering the area with 352,000 pounds of military waste, 2.9 percent of it being hazardous material like cyanide and heavy metal.

8. U.S. Department of Veterans Affairs, "Camp Lejeune: Past Water Contamination."

War and Climate Change

An important question must be raised, discussed, and included in all military decisions:

How much do the military and war contribute to climate change?

The United States Department of Defense (DoD) is the largest single consumer of energy in the world. It uses on average of 3,500,000,000 US gallons of fuel per year. This is as much fuel as a country like Sweden uses per year. The Department of Defense's energy consumption accounts for 80 percent of the federal government's usage.

The cost the Department of Defense pays for fuel is staggering. In 2013 the DoD was projected to spend about $17 billion for fuel. Sharon Burke, the Pentagon's director of operational energy plans and programs was quoted in the Department of Defense News:[9]

> "When the average American is paying $3 per gallon the price can soar to more than $20 per gallon in places like Helmand province, Afghanistan, when support costs are added in."

The human cost of the oil delivery in war areas is even more deplorable. By July 2012 more than 3,000 Americans had been killed protecting fuel convoys in Iraq and Afghanistan.

Military vehicles and planes use an enormous amount of fuel. An armored division of the Army can use as much as 600,000 gallons of fuel a day. The Abrams tank burns 250 gallons in one operating hour. Two thousand Abrams were employed in Iraq during the invasion. Ten thousand of these tanks have been produced.

The U.S. Air Force is the single largest consumer of jet fuel in the world:

The CV-22 Osprey Tilt–Rotor Helicopter uses about 350 gallons per hour.

The F-4 Phantom Fighter burns over 1,600 gallons jet fuel per hour and peaks at 14,400 gallons per hour at supersonic speeds.

The B-52 Stratocruiser burns 500 gallons per minute. In ten minutes the plane uses as much fuel as the average driver per year.

It is reported that when the F-15 Fighter blasts to supersonic speed it may burn four gallons a second!

In peacetime the gas guzzling vehicles, tanks, and planes are used predominantly during military exercises for training purposes, even though some military equipment, like airplane carriers are always in operation. Consequently, a standing army, especially a large one, uses a great amount of energy even in peacetime.

9. Daniel, "New Office Aims to Reduce Military's Fuel Usage."

During *a war* the energy required by the fighting force increases exponentially. The Watson Institute of Brown University calculated that in 2008 the U.S. military used at least as much energy as 1,210,000 million cars on the road that year. It has been calculated that the Iraq war added more greenhouse gases to the atmosphere than 60% of the world's nations!

The United States is not the only country to have a standing army that is engaged in warfare. China, Saudi Arabia, Russia, and Great Britain, the next four countries with big defense budgets — though far smaller than that of the US — also contribute to global warming. Saudi Arabia has been conducting a bombing campaign in Yemen for many months with dubious results. Saudi Arabia's advanced fighter planes have released untold quantities of greenhouse gas emissions during this air war.

Almost daily, we hear someone in the media mention climate change. We discuss its causes, wonder about its future effects, and think about solutions to the problem. Reducing emissions from cars, power plants, and commercial airlines have been already implemented or are planned. Isn't it surprising that military planes, tanks, trucks, and machinery are never part of the discussion? Not even the effect of the current wars on the increase of greenhouse gases is mentioned.

When the Kyoto Convention on Climate Change was negotiated, the U.S. delegation took care that the Department of Defense (DoD) was exempt from its requirements. During the climate talks in Paris 2015, military greenhouse gas emissions were again exempt from any requirements. While all countries report and monitor their greenhouse gas emissions, the DoD does not. Does our government know the number of DoD's emission per year? Do our representatives in Congress know it? Does the Department of Defense even calculate how much greenhouse gas it emits at all its word-wide facilities and by its operations?

Wouldn't it be helpful to know these numbers, in order to make informed decisions about reducing our energy consumption? Everyone wants to go green. We want to do the right thing to assure a bright future for our children and grandchildren. A person feels good about herself, when she reduces three weekly trips to the grocery store to just one. Of course, it is good, but it would be even better, if she would ask her congressman to reign in our military energy use as well.

How much would our greenhouse gas emission be reduced if a specific weapons programs were cut at home and then through negotiations worldwide? Why should civilians be expected to conserve energy, while a blank check is handed to the military?

When we become really serious about our carbon footprints, we will know the amount of greenhouse gases generated by each platoon sent to war, each bomb dropped, and each tank deployed.[10]

There will always be reasons to go to war. There may be even a good reason to go to war. If we know the price we will have to pay in human lives, in dollars, and in increased climate change that must be offset by civilian energy reduction, we can make an intelligent decision about war or peace.

10. Johansen, "Remember the carbon Footprint of War," 155.

Chapter 19

Never Again War

We, who experienced it as children, do not wish war for our children, grandchildren, or great grandchildren. "Never again war" is our motto.

Never again war—could this become reality? People asked may answer:

"It would be nice, but it's a dream."

"We always had wars, and we always will have them."

"Someone will make war. It's human nature."

"We don't learn from passed wars. We go to war again and again. It's insane."

"We need wars to fight evil in the world."

"People can't get along that's why we always have war."

"Maybe it is possible, but it will take a long time to achieve."

"We will have wars; too much money is in it."

Asked if we could do something to preserve peace, some answers are:

"People should live like the Bible tells us and love each other —then we will not fight wars."

"As long as we have a strong military, no one will attack us, and we will have peace at home."

"Being well educated and having a strong independent media will help us to avoid war."

"It's useless to talk about peace. It will never happen."

"We should teach our children to look at humanity as one."

∽

Most answers to the two questions are negative. People are resigned to the fact that war will always be with us. There is a resistance to talk about the issues. Raising questions about war and peace is not considered appropriate and polite conversation.

An exception to this social rule occurs if our government wants to go to war. Then the media will talk about war and expound the benefits of the planned military conflict. The general public is encouraged to discuss the pros and cons of war as well. Without fail, the war hawks will convince the majority of the people that they have the best answer. Is it futile to talk about peace at the start of a war? Perhaps we need to defy convention and talk about war and peace when we are not in a new war.

⌒

What is meant by "war"? What is meant by "peace"? War is the violent conflict between nations or large armed population groups. Here war is not used in a general way as in "war on drugs." Peace is the absence of war. In this conversation the word peace is not applied in its general meaning such as "peace of mind" or "peace within a family."

⌒

Are we predestined to have war? Is war an unavoidable human behavior or is it a man-made institution? President John F. Kennedy addressed the question in his 1963 commencement address to American University students:

> First: Let us examine our attitude towards peace itself. Too many of us think it is impossible. Too many think it is unreal. But that is a dangerous, defeatist belief. It leads to the conclusion that war is inevitable— that mankind is doomed—that we are gripped by forces we cannot control.
>
> We need not accept that view. Our problems are man-made—therefore, they can be solved by man. And man can be as big as he wants. No problem of human destiny is beyond human beings. Man's reason and spirit have often solved the seemingly unsolvable—and we believe they can do it again."[1]

It is significant that these words were spoken not by a dreaming coward but by a battle hardened war hero. Kennedy knew war and understood it. By his assessment war is a man-made problem and as such we can solve it, but as he indicated this won't be easy.

Just because something had always been customary, it does not follow that it will be with us forever. People change, societies evolve, and so do our

1. Kennedy, "Commencement Address at American University."

opinions about many human conventions. Let's feel free to openly discuss the usefulness of war in today's interconnected world.

In war, soldiers are called upon to kill other soldiers — to kill other human beings. In human history other forms of killings have been allowed, which lawful societies no longer tolerate. For instance, villagers would brand a woman as a witch and burn her publicly. In some regions, it was common for a man to revenge the murder of a family member by killing a member of the murder's family. It had been a tradition to dual with a rival and to shoot him. In the middle ages a noble and his knights would rob and perhaps kill a traveling merchant or attack the farmers of a village without being held accountable. These crimes and killings are no longer allowed, and the perpetrators are severely punished by law. A discussion of how these and other violent behaviors have been controlled are presented in Steven Pinker's book "The Better Angels of our Nature: Why Violence Has Declined."[2]

If it had been possible to prohibit these killings, why wouldn't it be possible to outlaw war as well?

Of course effectively outlawing war will not be easy and would not eliminate all wars—just as our criminal justice system does not prevent all murders—but it would reduce the scope and frequency of war.

We and all the other developed countries have been successful in reigning in murder and other crimes that once plagued society. Today we are much safer in our homes than people were 200 years ago. Break-ins and murder still happen but are far less frequent than in past times. Thanks to our good local and national laws, our well-trained police force, and our mostly fair justice system, we can peacefully sleep at night and enjoy our days.

Even in regard to war some progress occurred towards non-violent conflict resolution between nations or large population groups; but in many corners of the world people are not safe from invading armies and bombs dropping from the sky. While there is no threat of war occurring on American soil, our young people are asked to serve as soldiers, risking death or permanent injuries of war.

No, the people of the world are not at all safe from war and its destructive forces. As long as war is legitimate and as long as nations are allowed to pour unlimited resources into instruments of war, we will have war.

It certainly will take enormous effort to effectively outlaw war. To ban violent conflicts between two or several nations or large population groups requires supranational laws and law enforcement. We already have institutions for this purpose — the United Nations, the International Court of Justice, and the International Criminal Court. This is good, but they are still

---

2. Pinker, *The Better Angels of our Nature*, 1–188

ineffective for many reasons. One of them is the reluctance of the biggest war power of the world, the United States of America to support them. We, the people, as well as our elected leaders are ambivalent about the international institutions.

Some people believe war is needed. For instance, the political thinker, Ian Morris,[3] is convinced that war is necessary to bring order to our world. Each nation represents so many people and diverse interests that it is impossible to solve conflicts without war.

Is it true that war is the only solution to our problems? War is sanctioned violence. Isn't violence our biggest problem in the first place? We teach our children two wrongs do not make one right . . .

Without doubt, it is not easy to solve conflicts between powerful parties without resorting to violence. And yet it is possible to do so. Just look at the business world. A number of large business corporations have as much financial power and as complex organizational structures as small or medium size nations. Often these businesses are in sharp competition with each other. How do they solve their conflicts? Do they train soldiers? Do they arm themselves? Do they shoot at each other?

Corporations fight each other legally. For instance, a company may sue its competitor for violations of certain business rules. It also may happen that one corporation will buy another one. An expert may explain other possible negotiations, dealings, and strategies to solve business conflicts.

Whatever measure companies use, they do not shoot each other's employees or drop bombs onto their factories and office buildings. Though I wouldn't be surprised if a CEO confessed that sometimes she had wished for such a violent option. Yet, in business cool heads prevail. After all, firms want to make money, and with violent destruction it cannot be done. Even weapons producers only profit from the fighting of others.

Could business practices be a model for non-violent conflict resolutions between nations? I think so. Other people believe that businesses are the cause of wars and will never be a model for peace.

Is it true that businesses profit from war, are not interested in preventing it, but instead fan the flames of war? Even if it had been so at one time, it seems questionable today. Besides the producers of military hardware, who clearly benefit from war, what do the other small or big corporations in the US and other countries around the world gain from war? Don't they lose customers for their products due to war or armed conflict? Doesn't the turmoil in the Middle East result in an uncertain future, which Wall Street dislikes? Will not the failed states, which are the result of strive and war,

---

3. Morris, "*In the Long Run,* War Makes us Safer and Richer."

interfere with commerce? Doesn't war interfere with the free flow of goods and services? For instance, air traffic is endangered by fighting. A commercial plane was shot down over rebel territory in the Eastern Ukraine and 298 passenger died.

Why is the business community not opposed to war? Perhaps the negative impact of war upon businesses has not been sufficiently studied, researched, and publicized. Hopefully this will change in the near future.

Even foundations created by business leaders do not address the issue of war and peace effectively. For instance, the Bill and Melinda Gates Foundation does fabulous work eradicating diseases and preventing the death of millions of children. At this time the prevention of war and its threat to children is not addressed by the foundation. Many compassionate charitable organizations help victims of war. Still, to prevent a war in the first place would be far more beneficial.

Heads of state and elected representatives should and usually do work for the well-being of their countrymen. Considering the devastating impact World War II had on the populations of the warring nations, one may conclude that politicians would no longer propose war ever since. This has not happened. Why?

In his article: "Why We Fight War," Paul Krugman[4] points out that governments often gain politically from war, even if the war in question makes no sense in terms of national interest. For instance, President George W. Bush's approval rating soared when he invaded Iraq and so have Mr. Putin's when the Ukraine crisis began.

It is easy to believe that some dark forces or conspiracies lead to war, yet that may be far from the truth. Instead, we may have no one but ourselves to blame for the warmongering of our leaders.

It is true that our government has called our military to war under false pretenses. The second Iraq war is an example. But let us be fair. Our government has also worked hard for peace; perhaps more so than any other nation. Our presidents have worked for peace in Israel, negotiated an end of the war in Ireland, and ended the Balkan war. Our presidents established peaceful relations with China, Vietnam, and most recently with Cuba and Iran, to mention a few examples.

Like some of our presidents, many US citizens work tirelessly for peace. While in general everyone is for peace, many people see a need for war as well.

"Fighting wars will keep us safe at home," is a pro-war argument. This seems to be a far-fetched argument. People in other developed countries

4. Krugmann, "Why we Fight Wars."

do not seem to share that sentiment. They feel safer when their soldiers are at home for their protection, instead of fighting far away. If your son or daughter were serving in the military, would you feel safer if he or she was guarding our borders, rather than fighting a war somewhere in the world?

"We need to fight the terrorists abroad so they do not come here," is another pro-war argument that we used to hear from our government and in the news media. It is rarely mentioned now, because the facts on the ground are not supporting it. Instead of reducing terrorism, our military involvement in the Middle East appears to have increased it.

"People against war are 'peaceniks'. I don't like them. They undermine our military. We need a strong military to protect us in this dangerous world."

This reasoning sounds pro-war but it is mostly a call for safety. We all like to feel safe. It is a universally shared feeling. A large country like the US needs an army to protect our borders, an air force to protect our airspace and a navy to patrol our coastal waters. We all enjoy the safety our well-trained, well-equipped military provides. Even "peaceniks" want our Department of Defense to do the job its name implies—defend us against hostile armed foes.

If our military protects us without becoming entangled in far away places, it is too big for its mission. The goal would be to have a good military of the right size for the job on hand. You would not hire 500 carpenters to build you a three-bedroom house, but only as many as needed. Maybe five to ten construction workers would be required. More would not be better, because the workers would stand in each other's way. The same holds true in other situations including the military.

Why not find out what the military needs in order to do a good job here at home. The money saved could be allocated to other projects, such our crumbling infrastructure. For instance, wouldn't it be nice to have the money and workers to put all electric cables underground, and when the next bad storm hits, we would not lose electricity? I bet many more things could and should be done that would improve all of our lives.

To bring about such a change would require much time and effort. We live in a democracy. Each one of us has to decide what we want:

- Keep our large international fighting force, or

- Maintain a good home defense and put the taxes saved to good use right here.

It is up to us to decide and to make our voices heard. In our democracy every one counts. If you want change, it will not happen by itself, each of us needs to take part in the effort.

"Man can be as big as he wants."

Bibliography

Albright, Madeleine. *Prague Winter: A Personal Story of Remembrance and War.* 1937–1948. New York: Harper Collins, 2012.

Alliierten Museum Berlin. *The Berlin Airlift 1948/49: One city – two currencies.*

———. *The Berlin Airlift 1948/49, Supplies from the skies.*

Bessel, Richard. *Germany 1945: From War to Peace.* New York, NY: Harper Collins, 2009.

Broad, Williams J, and Sanger, David E. "Race for Latest Class of Nuclear Arms Threatens to Revive Cold War." International New York Times, April 16, 2016.

Daniel, Lisa: "New Office Aims to Reduce Military's Fuel Usage." U.S. Department of Defense News, July 22, 2010.

Daniell, Raymond. "'Revenge by Nazis', Industrial City Bombed All Night in ‚Reply' to R.A.F. Raid On Munich." New York Times, Nov. 16, 1940.

Duisburg "Bürger- und Ordnungsamt." Translated by Sieglinde Martin. http://www.duisburg.de/vv/32/index.php.

Dux, Holger A. *Cologne in the Early Post-War Years —Hooray, We're Still Alive!* Gudensberg-Gleichen, Germany: Wartberg, 2008.

Enzler, S. M. "Environmental Effects of warfare. The Impact of War on the Environment and Human Health." Lenntech, created September 2006. http://www.lenntech.com/environmental-effects-war.htm.

Exhibit of the City Museum of Cologne. "Das Neue Köln 1945–1995," April 22–August18, 1995.

Gaflig, Bernhard. In Grntzki, Nina et al. eds. *Feuersturm und Hungerwinter. Zeitzeugen erinnern sich an Krieg und Wiederaufbau.* Essen, Germany: Klartext, 2007.

Havel, Vaclav in Albright, *Madeleine. Prague Winter: A Personal Story of Remembrance and War. 1937-1948.* New York:Harper Collins, 2012

Johansen, Bruce E. "Remember the carbon footprint of war." In Bigelow, Bill, and Swinehart, Tim, eds. *A Peoples Curriculum for the Earth.* Milwaukee, WI: Rethinking Schools, 2014.

Kelley, Michael B., and Ingersoll, Geoffrey. "The Staggering Cost of the Last Decade's US War in Iraq—in Numbers." Business Insider, June 20, 2014. http://www.businessinsider.com/the-iraq-war-by-numbers-2014-6.

Kennedy, John F., Commencement Address at American University, June 10, 1963, John F. Kennedy Presidential Library, Boston, MA.

Krugman, Paul "Why We Fight Wars." INYT, Aug.17, 2014.

Lion, Siegfried G. *"Unsere Flucht aus Vollmarstein (Kreis Sensburg) in Ostpreußen."* Para. 16–18 translated by Sieglinde Martin. https://www.dhm.de/lemo/zeitzeugen/dr-

siegfried-g-lion-unsere-flucht-aus-vollmarstein-kreis-sensburg-in-ostpreussen.
    html.

Mathiesen, Karl. "What's the environmental impact of modern war?" The Guardian,
    Nov. 6, 2014. http://www.theguardian.com/environment/2014/nov/06/whats-the
    -environmental-impact-of-modern-war.

Medical News Today. "Wartime Rationing Helped the British get Healthier." June 21,
    2004. http://www.medicalnewstoday.com/releases/9728.php.

Mohrs, Willy. "Bombenkrieg über Duisburg." WAZ, December 2, 2014. http://www.
    derwesten.de/staedte/duisburg/bombenkrieg-ueber-duisburg-id9029375.
    html?onepage=true.

Möring, Niklas, *Cologne Cathedral in World War II*, Cologne: Verlag Kölner Dom, 2011.

Morris, Ian. "In the long run, war makes us safer and richer." The Washington Post,
    4-25-2014.

Pinker, Steven. The Better Angels of our Nature: Why Violence Has Declined. New
    York: Penguin Group 2011.

Reinecke, Christian, and Romeyk, Horst, eds. *Nordrhein-Westfalen. Ein Land und
    seine Geschichte. Aspekte und Konturen 1946-1996.* Münster: Aschendorffsche
    Verlagsbuchhandlung 1996.

Simon, Wolfgang. In Grontzki, Nina et al. eds. *Feuersturm und Hungerwinter. Zeitzeugen
    erinnern sich an Krieg und Wiederaufbau.* Essen: Klartext, 2007.

Schorn, Anita. *Anna—erwachsen vor der Zeit: Schicksal eines Kölner Mädchens 1941 bis
    1946.* Berlin: Friedling, 2000.

Sprey, Pierre. "Member of the Fighter Mafia Passes." In The Defense Monitor, April-
    June 2015.

Stadt Jülich. "2000 Jahre Jülich—ein historischer Überblick." http://www.juelich.de/
    geschichte

Stadt Langenfeld ed. *Forced Laborer in Langenfeld, 1939–1945.* Langenfeld, Germany:
    Stadtarchiv, 2000.

Thompson, Mark. "Costly Flight Hours." Time April 02, 2013 http://nation.time.
    com/2013/04/02/costly-flight-hours.

U.S. Department of Veterans Affairs. "Camp Lejeune: Past Water Contamination."
    www.publichealth.va.gov/exposures/camp-lejeune.

VHS Arbeitskreis Geschichte. *Langenfeld 1945–1949 Berichte und Erinnerungen.*
    Langenfeld, Rheinland, Germany: VHS 1998.

Zahra, Tara: *The Lost Children: Reconstructing Europe's Families after World War II.*
    Cambridge: Harvard University Press, 2011.

Żmijewska, Olga. "Kriegsende in Ostpreußen." Para. 7–8 translated by Sieglinde Martin.
    Spiegel, January 25, 2015. http://www.spiegel.de/einestages/2-weltkrieg-flucht-
    aus-ostpreussen-1945-a-1013898.html.